Discourse Analysis & The Study of Classroom Language & Literacy Events— A Microethnographic Perspective

Discourse Analysis & The Study of Classroom Language & Literacy Events— A Microethnographic Perspective

David Bloome
The Ohio State University

Stephanie Power Carter
Indiana University

Beth Morton Christian
Western Kentucky University

Sheila Otto
Middle Tennessee State University

Nora Shuart-Faris
Vanderbilt University

LAWRENCE ERLBAUM ASSOCIATES, PUBLISHERS
2005   Mahwah, New Jersey   London

Cover artist – Mindi Rhoades, Columbus, Ohio

Title – *masks and signs: a discourse*

Three interwoven masks each retain a sense of separateness and completeness while at the same time they flow fluidly into each other, creating a dynamic, pulsing tension and movement withing the work. The words surrounding the faces are text on many levels. The words are sections from the book taken in broken pieces and parts without capitals or much definitive punctuation, much like real dialogue. The words around the masks present themselves as near abstractions of real words – words manipulated into basic shapes of meaning, coded hints, suggestions. The text starts in the painting but there is no definite beginning to it in the traditional sense, it stops at the bottom border of the painting without any recognizable end, creating space for and welcoming the viewer into the interaction.

Permissions
"After Winter" from THE COLLECTED POEMS OF STERLING A. BROWN, EDITED by MICHAEL S. HARPER. Copyright © 1980 by Sterling A. Brown. Reprinted by permission of HarperCollins Publishers Inc.

Lawrence Erlbaum Associates, Inc., Publishers
10 Industrial Avenue
Mahwah, New Jersey 07430

Cover design by Kathryn Houghtaling Lacey

Library of Congress Cataloging-in-Publication Data

Discourse analysis and the study of classroom language and literacy
    events : a microethnographic perspective / David Bloome ... [et al.].
        p. cm.
    Includes bibliographical references and index.
ISBN 0-8058-4858-4 (cloth : alk. Paper)
ISBN 0-8058-5320-0 (pbk. : alk. Paper)
    1. Language arts—Social aspects. 2. Discourse anaylsis—Social as-
    pects 3. Communication in education—Social aspects. 4. Socio-
    linguistics.   I. Bloome, David.

LB1576.D4664 2004
371.102'3—dc22   2004040375
                                                       CIP

Books published by Lawrence Erlbaum Associates are printed on acid-free paper, and their bindings are chosen for strength and durability.

Printed in the United States of America
10 9 8 7 6 5 4 3 2 1

Contents

List of Figures, Tables, Transcripts

FIGURES

TABLES

TRANSCRIPTS

Foreword

O body swayed to music

O brightening glance

How can we know the dancer from the dance?

—W.B. Yeats, *Among School Children.* 1928, p. 215.

This excerpt, aptly quoted by Bloome, Carter, Christian, Otto, and Shuart-Faris from Yeats' own attempts as a school inspector in Ireland to understand classroom discourse, provides the leitmotif of this challenging and important book. In the context where it is cited, the authors use it to argue that "people are situated, they act in terms of the situation in which they find themselves whilst simultaneously creating that situation." More broadly, it signals what they mean by a microethnographic perspective and what they hope to accomplish by applying it to classroom events and practices. They are critical of approaches that start from too far "outside" of classroom "events": Rather, they want, to "hover low" over the immediate data, as Geertz would have it. As observers, researchers, and participants in such events we cannot just bring with us some prior definition—such as what constitutes a "dance"—before we actually see the people "dancing." The book is full of accounts of the dance of the classroom—teachers speaking and gesturing, students responding, students talking irrespective of the teacher, texts weaving through the talk, researchers commenting—how can we know the dance from these dancers?

The authors build upward and outward from the participants and the events in which they participate. They argue that we can only claim a "warrant" to draw larger inferences when research is "grounded in the setting itself." But this does not mean that they are focussed only on the "micro."

However critical they may be of approaches that impose outside ideas and concepts on the immediate and the local, their larger aim is to help us understand "macro level contexts"—or rather "to address the relationship between micro level contexts (specific events and situations) and macro level contexts." Their worry is that the interest in the latter, especially that in "grand narratives," fails to take account of the importance of specific events, an approach that denies participants' agency and even awareness of the constraints they operate within. In the authors' view, people continually construct relationships between events, including those that are not immediately present: "They are not unaware that there are broader contexts and dynamics that influence and are influenced by what they do in their daily lives.... Furthermore, people can and do take actions based on their understanding of broader contexts and dynamics."

The tools the authors provide, then, offer a distinctive contribution to the description of both these broader relationships in which people participate and their immediate enactments of meanings. For instance, in any event participants will refer to other components of the event and to other events outside of the immediate context, what the authors refer to as *intertextual* and *intercontextual* relationships. These terms, they argue, "provide insight into the relationship of micro-level contexts and macro-level context and provide a theoretical and methodological tool for describing micro–macro relationships." They invoke and adapt other terms, some taken from the surrounding disciplines of sociolinguistics, discourse analysis, ethnomethodology, New Literacy Studies, etc., such as *contextualisation cues, boundary making, message units, turn taking,* and *literacy events and practices* in order to probe closely the inner workings of these broader features of communication. The authors challenge powerfully some previous approaches to such "micro" analysis that have simply counted features like turn taking or cues in order to infer broader patterns—what they characterize, following Mitchell (1984), as enumerative induction. In the field of language and literacy as social practice such mechanical enumeration of the components of communication won't do—we need to know the interpretive frames that give meaning to such units and this involves what Mitchell termed *analytic induction.*

The authors, then, link close analysis of linguistic features of social interaction with what Gee (1999) termed the *social* turn in language study: They devote chapters to the social construction of identity; to power relations in classroom events and beyond; to the role of multiple literacies not just spoken language or a narrow "autonomous" model of literacy; and to the broader understanding of "people's everyday lives" of the kind acknowledged in the Oral History movement and the UK's Mass-Observation Project (which receives some original treatment in chap. 5). In doing so they complement other recent studies that have attempted to link issues of power and identity to literacy (Collins & Blot, 2003), to the ethnography of communication (Hornberger, 2003) and to Education (Street, in press).

Their approach, then, perhaps provides an answer to a debate that is currently raging in literacy studies, prompted by a paper by Brandt and Clinton (2002; see also Street, 2003), questioning "the limits of the local." Brandt and Clinton argue that there has been a tendency in the recent shift toward study of literacy as a social practice to over privilege the "local." On the contrary, they suggest, people in general, and in cases like those with which this book is concerned, children in classrooms usually experience literacy from "outside"—it is someone else's literacy to which they are exposed and the ethnographic account of literacy in situ fails to account for the larger constraints on their uses of such literacy. What the authors of this book show through their close microethnographic accounts is that we cannot know what uses people are making of such outside literacies—and of language more generally—without seeing it and understanding it in its immediate context. We cannot prejudge the meanings and uses of literacy on the basis of what they meant before and outside of their context of use. Although some studies might sometimes show that people simply imbibe what the outside discourse demands, we cannot presuppose this and indeed in many cases people do the contrary—they resist the dominant frame put on the language and literacy to which they are exposed, they "take hold" of the outsiders' literacies (as Kulick & Stroud, 1993, described New Guinea villagers' responses to missionary literacy). But this demonstrates that it is not a matter of posing the "local" against the "global," the "micro" against the "macro" but of understanding the relationships between them, as meanings are built in their encounter. To do this involves moving beyond traditional micro-linguistic approaches, such as Conversation Analysis or narrowly conceived Discourse Analysis, at the same time as rejecting this outside "determination": It involves developing theories and tools that take into account both the individual participant and of his or her social and cultural positionings and responses. It is these theories and tools that the authors of this book provide.

Such positionings are not just imposed on the subjects of inquiry, as if the researcher remained outside the frame. It is endemic to the kind of research the authors wish to introduce us to, that researchers themselves be reflexive and self conscious about their own theories and tools; such research has to challenge the assertions of "neutrality" that some of the more mechanical approaches to language in education have claimed. So, even while probing closely the micro events of classroom language and literacy, researchers are also self-consciously analyzing their own framing and interpreting of the events. They too are dancers in the dance, their glance and their bodies cannot be excluded from the question of choreography posed by Yeats, which runs throughout this elegant and well balanced book.

—Brian V. Street
Kings College, London

Acknowledgments

First and foremost, we are grateful to the teachers and students in whose classrooms we conducted the research reported in this book. Several of the teachers and students spent a great deal of time with us, discussing classroom events and our research, offering insights and perspectives.

We acknowledge our debt to JoBeth Allen, Donna Alvermann, and David Reinking, who have been generous with their feedback, time, and patience. We are especially appreciative of JoBeth Allen's commentary on an early version of this book. We also received comments from members of the National Reading Conference who attended a session where we presented an early version of the book. Similarly, we received helpful feedback from members of the National Conference on Research in Language and Literacy (NCRLL) at a session sponsored by NCRLL specifically for that purpose. We also acknowledge comments from anonymous reviewers for the publisher, Lawrence Erlbaum Associates, Inc. Naomi Silverman, of Lawrence Erlbaum Associates, Inc., was a joy to work with; we appreciated her professionalism, her feedback on the book, and her helpful directions.

We greatly benefited from feedback from the members of a writing workshop held during the summer of 2002 at Vanderbilt University. The members included Ayanna Brown, Jorie Henriksen, Chris Iddings, Evette Meliza, Christine Stenson, and Cynthia Williams. We also acknowledge the helpful feedback we received from Laurie Katz.

We express our thanks to Julie Justice, Suchie Bhattacharyya, Samara Madrid, Anna Mallett, and Nancy Middleton for editorial assistance.

Among the many scholars who influenced our thinking about the discourse analysis of classroom language and literacy events, we owe special debts to Brian Street and Dorothy Sheridan for helping us think through issues of power relations, culture, literacy, and schooling, and to Judith Green for helping us think through the dynamic nature of classroom conversations. Some of the research reported in this book builds on various collaborative research projects with Lynn Bercaw, Ayanna Brown, Laurie Katz, Jerome Morris, Ramona Muldrow, Dorothy Sheridan, and Brian Street. We thank them for their colleagueship and friendship.

Part of the research reported in chapters 3 and 4 was supported, in part, by grants from the U.S. Department of Education, Office of Educational Research and Improvement, for a research project entitled "Academic Achievement From a Whole Day Whole Year Perspective" (principal investigators: John Bransford; Susan Goldman; Ted Hasselbring; and David Bloome, then at the Learning Technology Center of Vanderbilt University). We appreciate the support that was provided by the U.S. Department of Education and the Learning Technology Center. We also appreciate the support that was given by The Ohio State University to David Bloome for writing parts of the book. The opinions and statements made in this book do not necessarily reflect those of the U.S. Department of Education, Vanderbilt University, or The Ohio State University.

Whatever shortcomings and inadequacies our thinking may have and whatever flaws remain in the book are our own responsibility.

David Bloome
Stephanie Power Carter
Beth Morton Christian
Sheila Otto
Nora Shuart-Faris

Introduction

The purpose of this book is to provide a description of an approach to the discourse analysis of classroom language and literacy events. The approach can be described as a *social linguistic* or *social interactional* approach. It combines attention to how people use language and other systems of communication in constructing language and literacy events in classrooms with attention to social, cultural, and political processes. For convenience, we label this approach a *microethnographic* approach.

The particular approach we take to discourse analysis builds on sociolinguistic ethnography (also known as the *ethnography of communication* (cf. Gumperz, 1986; Gumperz & Hymes, 1972; Hanks, 2000; Hymes, 1974); related discussions of language and culture, including humanistic linguistics (e.g., Becker, 1988), linguistic anthropology (e.g., Duranti, 1997; Duranti & Goodwin, 1992), anthropological studies of narrative and poetics (e.g., Bauman, 1986; Bauman & Briggs, 1990; Bauman & Sherzer, 1974; Hymes, 1996); the New Literacy Studies (cf. Barton & Hamilton, 1998; Barton, Hamilton, & Ivanic, 2000; Bloome, 1993; Gee, 1996, 2000; Heath, 1983; Street, 1995b, 1998); ethnomethodology (cf. Baker, 1993; Heap, 1980, 1985, 1988; Jefferson, 1978; MacBeth, 2003; Mehan, 1979; Sacks, Schegloff, & Jefferson, 1974); and those literary discussions of language that evolved from the work of Bakhtin (1935/1981, 1953/1986) and Volosinov (1929/1973) as well as those that evolved from the work of Benjamin (1969), Williams (1977), Dubois (1969), and de Certeau (1984, 1997). In addition, we build on the work of educational researchers who have been engaged in discourse analysis from similar perspectives and who have established their own histories. As Bloome (2003a), Green and Bloome (1998), and others have argued, educational researchers have created their own history of research on the use of language in classrooms that is distinct from but complements that in the disciplines of anthropology, linguistics, sociology, and social psychology. We discuss the intellectual and disciplinary foundations of our micro-ethnographic approach at length in chapter 1.

Microethnographic approaches foreground the daily life of classrooms. We take a strong view that the daily life of teachers and students in class-rooms is not to be taken for granted, homogenized under broad generalizations, or collapsed into deterministic processes of social and cultural reproduction. For us, classrooms are complex places where teachers and students create and re-create, adopt and adapt, and engage in a full range of human interactions. Teachers and students are viewed as active agents. Although teachers and students must act within the events, contexts, and settings in which they find themselves, and although they must react to the actions of others and the social institutions of which they are a part, they nonetheless act on the worlds in which they live.

At the center of what happens in classrooms is language: the language used by teachers and students, the language of texts and textbooks, the language of school and school district policies, the language of parents and children as they interact with each other and with educators, and myriad other uses of language. Language is both the object of classroom lessons (e.g., learning to read, write, and use academic discourse) as well as the means of learning (e.g., through classroom discussions and lectures, reading, and writing). Thus, language not only is the object of study in research on classroom language and literacy events but it is also the means through which the research occurs. It is through language that researchers conduct interviews and develop coding and other means of analyzing observations, videotapes, and other data, and it is through language that researchers conceptualize, write up, and report their research. Given the central role of language in people's lives, in the construction of classroom events, and in the conduct of research, understanding and attending to language as people and researchers use it is crucial to the microethnographic approach we describe here.

What people do in interaction with each other is complex, ambiguous, and indeterminate, and it often involves issues of social identity, power relations, and broad social and cultural processes. At the same time, every event provides opportunities for people to create new meanings, new social relationships, and new futures that eschew the reproductive tendencies of what is and what was. By focusing attention on actual people acting and reacting to each other, creating and re-creating the worlds in which they live, microethnographic approaches provide a contribution not otherwise found in research on classroom language and literacy events. If Raymond Williams (1977) is correct that a theory of language is always a definition of people in the world, then one underlying contribution of microethnographic approaches is their conception of people as complex, multidimensional actors who together use what is given by culture, language, and economic capital to create new meanings, social relationships, and possibilities and to re-create culture and language.

Our approach to the microethnographic analysis of classroom language and literacy events is informed by our continuously evolving understanding of language, literacy, and classrooms. For us, language is not a "transparent" vehicle for the communication of information. Any use of language (spoken, written, electronic, etc.) involves complex social, cultural, political, cognitive, and linguistic processes and contexts—all of which are part of the meaning and significance of reading, writing, and using language. As Robinson (1987) wrote:

It will no longer do, I think, to consider literacy as some abstract, absolute quality attainable through tutelage and the accumulation of knowledge and experience. It will no longer do to think of reading as a solitary act in which a mainly passive reader responds to cues in a text to find meaning. It will no longer do to think of writing as a mechanical manipulation of grammatical codes and formal structures leading to the production of perfect or perfectible texts. Reading and writing are not unitary skills nor are they reducible to sets of component skills falling neatly under discrete categories (linguistic, cognitive); rather, they are complex human activities taking place in complex human relationships. (p. 329)

Teaching students to be readers and writers is as much a matter of language socialization, enculturation, identity production, power relations, and situated interaction (i.e., knowing what to do and how to interact with others in a specific situation) as teaching how to manipulate symbol systems. It is also an intimate part of identity formation, both individual and social. How one engages in reading and writing, when, where, and with whom, as well as how one engages in learning to read and write, both reflects and constructs one's identity.

Such an understanding of the teaching of reading and writing provides a warrant for defining language and literacy learning as social processes. Bloome (1985) described such a view of literacy as follows:

In addition to being a communicative process, reading is also a social process (for, as Labov, 1972, points out all communication is social). That is, reading involves social relationships among people: among teachers and students, among students, among parents and children, and among authors and readers. The social relationships involved in reading include establishing social groups and ways of interacting with others; gaining or maintaining status and social positions; and acquiring culturally appropriate ways of thinking, problem solving, valuing and feeling. (p. 134)

In our description of our microethnographic approach we do not separate methodological issues and procedures from theoretical or epistemological issues. Indeed, we use the term *methodology* to refer to the integration of theoretical and methodological issues, reserving *method* for the techniques, tactics, and strategies of data collection, analysis, and reporting. The separation of theory from methods results in researchers engaging in unreflected action and holding magical beliefs; that is, they conduct research without questioning why they do what they do or how their actions are connected to understandings of knowledge, people, or language. Gee and Green (1998) argued similarly about the relationship of theory and method. They quoted Birdwhistell (1977) about the danger of separating theory and methodology and argued for the importance of articulating a logic-of-inquiry: "The interdependence of theory and methodology can be hidden by exclusive focus upon either philosophy or technique. Once separated, only the most sophisticated can reconstitute them into investigatory practice" (p. 120). Birdwhistell saw the separation of theory from methods as widespread over the previous 25 years, and Gee and Green argued that this was still the case. Although Birdwhistell and Gee and Green were specifically directing their comments at observational, ethnographic, and discourse analysis research, we believe their comments extend broadly.

We further take the stance that research methodologies are not distinct from the objects of their study; neither are they distinct from debates in the field about classrooms, language, and literacy. The conduct of research on classroom language and literacy events, when done well, creates a dialectical relationship among three sets of theories: (a) the extant set of theories in the field about the classroom language and literacy events being studied, (b) the set of theories that guide the specific approach to discourse analysis being used (what might be called the *methodological warrants*), and (c) the implicit theories embedded in the classroom event and jointly held by the people involved in the classroom event. Thus, throughout this book we integrate methodological discussions with theoretical ones, focusing on the insights that emerge from the productive tensions created through the juxtaposition of the three types of theoretical frames just noted.

We also take the view that research methodologies are situated. The specific situation of their use is part of their definition; that is, as a research approach is used within a specific event—for example, the capturing and analysis of a poetry lesson on Thursday morning in Ms. Wilson's 7th-grade classroom at City Middle School in an inner city in the southern United States—the research approach is defined by the classroom event, modified both with regard to procedures and theoretics. However, it is also the case that the research approach defines the event, shaping its representation, what is foregrounded and backgrounded. Thus, rather than merely presenting abstract methodological principles, we present cases of the use of microethnographic approaches in specific situations. By looking across the cases, one can better understand the situated nature of microethnographic research as well as the interpretive process that is at the heart of any research methodology.

ORGANIZATION OF THE BOOK

In chapter 1, we introduce key constructs for a microethnographic approach to the discourse analysis of language and literacy events in classrooms. The discussion is designed to provide a historical and intellectual context of microethnographic approaches, to provide some of the methodological warrants used in a microethnographic approach to discourse analysis, and to provide an explanation of key vocabulary.

Chapters 2, 3, and 4 are each organized around a particular research agenda. In brief, chapter 2 focuses on the use of microethnographic approaches to discourse analysis for describing classroom literacy events as cultural action, chapter 3 focuses on the social construction of identity in classroom literacy events, and chapter 4 focuses on power relations in and through classroom literacy events. We focus on specific issues because, as we noted earlier, the conduct of discourse analysis is intimately and inseparably connected with the research issue being pursued and the research site. Neither the researcher or the research perspective, nor the conduct of the research, stands outside of the research issue or the research site. No research methodology is autonomous but instead must be viewed as an ideological stance both toward what is being studied and toward how the research will be used. Each chapter begins with a discussion of theoretical principles that guide the microethnographic approach to discourse analysis; this is followed by a detailed illustration of the use of those principles in the analysis of a small number of classroom literacy events. The detailed microethnographic discourse analysis of classroom literacy events in each chapter illustrates how theoretical constructs, the research issue, the research site, methods, research techniques, and previous studies of discourse analysis come together to constitute a discourse analysis. It is important to note that we are not claiming to present *the* discourse analysis of a described classroom literacy event. First, depending on the research issue being pursued, the theoretical framing, the specific situation, and so on, there might be multiple discourse analyses, each highlighting a different aspect and perhaps each giving a different interpretation. More important, we reject the notion that the process of a microethnographic approach to discourse analysis should be conceived as an attempt to get at the "real" and "true" description of the classroom literacy event; rather, every attempt at discourse analysis is simultaneously an attempt to engage in the theorizing of the use of language (written, spoken, and of other modalities) and is also part of the event itself. That is, the conduct of a discourse analysis does not lie outside of the event, as if metaphorically the classroom events were put under a microscope. A better metaphor night be a semitransparent mirror, which at one and the same time provided a view of the event while also providing a view of the researcher and the field, each view clouding and bringing into focus the other.

Some readers will be more interested in the theoretical discussion in each chapter, others in the illustration of the microethnographic approach to discourse analysis of classroom literacy events. As we noted earlier, there is a dialectical relationship between a consideration of theoretical principles and their actual application; thus, it is not so much the case that the illustrations of discourse analysis in each chapter are simply illustrations of the application of theoretical principles—they are also a means of theoretical development and insight. The illustrations are detailed. Embedded in those details, however, is a series of decisions and deliberations, each of which challenges, adapts, reaffirms, or generates theoretical understandings about the nature of language use, face-to-face interaction, and classroom life. Thus, we recognize that the organization of each chapter—theoretical discussion followed by methodological illustration—partially obfuscates the recursive process of theory building.

Chapters 2, 3, and 4 address three often-discussed issues in research on classroom literacy events: (a) classroom literacy events as cultural action, (b) the social construction of identity, and (c) power relations in and through classroom literacy events. In chapter 2, we are concerned with how the theoretical constructs associated with a microethnographic approach define literacy (or, more accurately, literacies) and how such definitions connect with methodological constructs. We focus attention on cultural practices involving the use of written language (also labeled *literacy practices*). To do so, we must define and differentiate cultural practices from cultural events, not simply as theoretical constructs and heuristics but as the material actions people take with and toward each other. We illustrate the theoretical and methodological issues involved through the microethnographic analysis of a 7th-grade language arts lesson.

Chapter 3 examines how microethnographic approaches can be used to gain insight into the social construction of identity in classroom literacy events. By *identity* we mean the social positions that people take up or are maneuvered into by the actions of others. Such a definition of identity differs from definitions associated with social and developmental psychology that posit a more stable and less context-determined notion of identity. For example, in the data we use in Chapter 3 to illustrate how a microethnographic approach to discourse analysis can illuminate issues of identity in classroom literacy practices, a student is positioned as a nonreader. Although the student works to resist such an identity, he nonetheless collaborates in the construction of a situation that does not work to his social or educational benefit. Issues of identity require attention to both situational positioning and to positioning at broader social and cultural levels in terms of race, gender, class, ethnicity, and sexual orientation.

In chapter 4, we show how microethnographic approaches to discourse analysis can reveal the complexity of power relations in and through classroom literacy events. We provide three definitions of power: (a) power as product, (b) power as process, and (c) power as caring relations. We provide an analysis of several classroom situations to highlight how a microethnographic approach can reveal how people create power relations in classroom literacy events and how broad patterns of power relations in society are re-created, resisted, and transformed.

In the last chapter, 5, we discuss the complexity of "locating" microethnographic discourse analysis studies within the field of literacy studies and within broader intellectual movements. For us, *locating* refers to the processes involved in constructing a relationship between a particular line of inquiry or research study and other lines of inquiry or studies. The process of locating a study or line of inquiry is part of the process of giving and claiming meaningfulness; that is, in our view, research studies gain their meaning not solely from their own activities or solely from the words used to write up the study. It is never the case that a research study, including a microethnographic discourse study, is ever presented in isolation. The research study stands as part of some set or sets of studies and against other studies, and this is so whether acknowledged or not. In other words, research studies are inherently intertextual, and they are intertextual at many levels. Part of the meaningfulness of a research study or of a line of inquiry derives from its relationship to research efforts that have gone before and to those that will come after it.

But to which efforts, to which previous lines of inquiry, does a research study have a relationship? For us, such relationships are constructed and claimed. In chapter 5, we examine some of the processes involved in constructing and claiming a relationship among microethnographic discourse analysis studies of language and literacy in classrooms and other lines of inquiry, such as the New Literacy Studies. Gee (2000) defined the New Literacy Studies as one movement among others that are part of the "social turn" in academic disciplines away from a focus on individual behavior and individual minds "toward a focus on social and cultural internation" (p. 180). He continues, the New Literacy Studies "are based on the view that reading and writing only make sense when studied in the context of social and cultural [and we can add historical, political and economic] practices of which they are but a part." Reading and writing are not a thing in and of themselves (what Street [1984, 1995b] has labeled an *autonomous model* of literacy) but are bound up in and with the social, cultural, political, and economic practices and ideologies of which they are a part (what Street [1984, 1995b] has labeled an *ideological model* of literacy). It is clear that there is much in common with the approach to research described in this book and the New Literacy Studies; however, as we emphasize in chapter 5, no line of inquiry or research study is located in a single place. Rather, lines of inquiry and research studies have multiple and shifting locations. Relationships among lines of inquiry are not fixed but indeterminate, constantly in need of being constructed and reconstructed.

The process of locating a line of inquiry or research study is part of the process of constructing what we call the *research imagination*. We derive this term from Paul Atkinson's (1990) book, *The Ethnographic Imagination*, in which he examines how ethnographers use language to fashion a vision of the people, places, and activities studied. We are similarly concerned about how microethnographic discourse analysis studies imagine people, places, and activities, especially the vision of the classroom constructed. We note that recognizing that microethnographic discourse analysis studies both reflect and create an image of the classroom does not invalidate the study or its usefulness. It merely recognizes that research is a human process caught up in the complexity of human relationships while also recognizing the importance of being reflective about those complex human relationships.

We argue in chapter 5 for locating the microethnographic discourse analysis of language and literacy events in classrooms within a broader, intellectual movement concerned with people's everyday lives. As we discuss in that chapter, an intellectual focus on people's everyday lives directs attention to how people act on the worlds in which they live and foregrounds both their individual and collective agency in constructing their everyday lives. Such an emphasis contrasts with those intellectual movements that emphasize broad social, cultural, and political processes that encapsulate people and their everyday lives, as if they were playing out a script already written—as if the particularities of their lives did not really matter. Our effort in chapter 5 is not to argue for one vision of people's everyday lives versus another. Indeed, we do not view the research imagination as monolithic. Rather, our effort in chapter 5 to highlight the fact that part of what is accomplished through research—part of its meaning—is the construction of a vision (or visions) of people, places, and activities, and reflection on that vision should be an integral part of any research effort.

A Microethnographic Approach to the Discourse Analysis of Classroom Language and Literacy Events

We take it as given that any definition of *discourse* and any approach to discourse analysis are historically located (and similarly so with other concepts and approaches to research). By this we do not mean that there is an authorized history that provides the definition of discourse analysis. Similarly, there is no given set of traditions that define the boundaries of what counts as discourse and discourse analysis. This is not to suggest that the prior experiences, endeavors, and arguments of researchers are not useful to people seeking to define discourse analysis but rather that a history or a set of traditions must be claimed, argued, and labored for by the present;[1] that is, the task of locating discourse analysis (or any approach to research) historically is one not predetermined by the past but is acted on by the present as it looks to the future.[2]

As we noted in the Introduction, the particular approach we take to discourse analysis builds on sociolinguistic ethnography (also called the

---

[1]West (2000), citing T. S. Eliot (1919), wrote that "tradition is not something you inherit. If you want it, you must obtain it with great labor. I [West] would add toil and engagement and service" (pp. 39–40).

[2]We are not advocating revisionist or fanciful histories. The task of historically locating an approach to discourse analysis depends, in part, on the influences claimed (both by those engaged in conducting the discourse analysis and those attributed to them by others); by the actions taken by researchers in the past to provide opportunities for others to claim historical connections; by the actions of researchers in the present taking up those opportunities as well as creating new warrants; and, in part, on the intellectual and social, cultural, and political agendas to which the efforts contribute.

ethnography of communication), related discussions of language and culture, including humanistic linguistics; anthropological studies of narrative and poetics; the New Literacy Studies; ethnomethodology; critical discourse analysis; the literary discussions of language that evolved from the work of Mikhail Bakhtin, V. I. Volosinov, Walter Benjamin, and Raymond Williams; and the cultural critiques and social theories that evolved from the work of W.E.B. Dubois and Michel de Certeau, as well as the work of educational researchers who have been engaged in discourse analysis from similar perspectives. Although this list of disciplinary fields may seem large, it may be more accurately viewed as an ongoing attempt within the social sciences and humanities to understand and describe the ways in which people engage in and construct their everyday lives (Gee, 2000; Gergen, 1999). Special attention is given to the role of language as a prime tool in creating and negotiating everyday life. Thus, rather than view the fields above as distinct, we view them as variations on a theme, an ongoing conversation that continues to raise questions. The conduct of microethnographic discourse analysis is another variation on the theme, another way to continue the conversation.

Next, we discuss two key issues that we believe define and distinguish approaches to the analysis of language and literacy events in classrooms: (a) implied personhood and (b) the foregrounding of events. We then discuss some theoretical tools for conducting a microethnographic analysis and locate our approach to discourse analysis within a historical movement often referred to as the linguistic turn in the social sciences.[3]

Although classrooms are part of a broader social institution and set of social, cultural, and political processes, we do not view classrooms as merely playing out a predetermined process of cultural and social reproduction; neither do we view teachers and students as cultural dupes unable to act except in ways predetermined by the social structure or by unconscious psychoanalytic drives. Together, teachers and students address the circumstances in which they find themselves, and together they construct their classroom worlds. They often do so with creativity, adapting the cultural practices and social structures thrust on them in ways that may undercut or eschew the ideological agenda of the broader social institutions within which classrooms are embedded.

---

[3]An alternative set of constructs was provided by Gee and Green (1998), who argued for an examination of the aspects of situation. The four aspects are (a) the material aspect (actors, place, time, objects present, values, language, institutions, and cultural models), (b) the activity aspect (the specific social activity or chain/sequence of activities), (c) the semiotic aspect (situated meanings and cultural models connected to various "sign systems"), and (d) the sociocultural aspect (personal, social, and cultural knowledge, feelings, and identities). Gee and Green argued that, in addition to these four aspects of situation, attention must also be paid to what people are attempting to accomplish within a situation. They identified four "building tasks": (a) world building, (b) activity building, (c) identity building, and (d) connection building.

IMPLIED PERSONHOOD

The concept of the "person" is often taken for granted, yet definitions of what is constituted by the category "person" vary. According to Egan-Robertson (1998a), "Personhood is a dynamic, cultural construct about who is and what is considered to be a person, what attributes and rights are constructed as inherent to being a person, and what social positions are available within the construct of being a person" (p. 453).

Personhood includes shared assumptions about the characteristics and attributes that are assumed to be inherent in a person. Thus, how a cultural group defines *person* has broad implications and is intimately connected to issues of morality, cognition, social structure and social interaction, rationality, sanity/insanity, and so on. The shared concept of personhood held by a group is part of the process of producing models of action and self-awareness, for assigning meaning and significance, and for structuring the social order (Geertz, 1973).

Personhood is socially constructed (Gergen & Davis, 1985) through symbolic action (Shweder & Miller, 1985); it is not given or predetermined. Whenever people interact with each other, they are always negotiating personhood, which is merely to say that people in interaction with each other need to establish a working consensus for how they define each other and what characteristics they assign to each other merely through the recognition of being a "person." Among these characteristics may be the categories of *person* that are assumed: what is assumed to be inherent to a *person* versus what is learned, what rights and courtesies are obliged to a person, and how a *person* is connected to or separate from others. Williams (1977) connected language and personhood: "A definition of language is always, implicitly or explicitly, a definition of human beings in the world" (p. 21).

Williams's (1977) insight has implications for research on classroom language and literacy events. First, within a classroom, part of what the teacher and students are doing is defining language and thus also personhood. They define language and literacy as a part of language through numeration of its constituent parts, through the association or nonassociation of language with culture, social structure, and action; through a hierarchy of language varieties (e.g., dialects, registers); through standardization; and by locating language in the mind, in social interaction, in a textbook, and so on. But it is not just in the classroom that language is being defined; it is also being defined in the research itself. Researchers must decide what it is they are studying when they claim to study classroom language and literacy events. The boundaries they impose on what they are studying, what they connect their bit of research to, what frames of reference they use, are all part of a definition of language, whether explicit or implicit, as is their use of language both in the conduct of the research (e.g., how they talk to people, how they use language to create coding categories and analytic frames) and in the writing of the research. Whether they write up the research as a journal article, book, or conference presentation, how they write, and what they assume about the writing, are part of how they are defining *language*. In brief, a definition of *language* and a definition of *personhood* are implicit in any theoretical framing and research endeavor, including ours.[4]

Although it is perhaps impossible to fully explicate the "definition of human beings in the world" held within a theoretical framing, it is nonetheless important to examine the key underlying constructs that provide the warrants for the generation of research questions, definitions of data, and the interpretation of data. In the approach we take to discourse analysis, we foreground three aspects of personhood as conceptualized in our approach to the study of classroom language and literacy events.

First, people are active agents in and on the worlds in which they live. They are strategic. Such a view of personhood does not deny that people are often influenced by factors beyond their control or by historical circumstances; neither does it deny that there may be occasions when people lack "conscientização" (cf. Freire, 1970/1995), the ability to analyze the social and economic situation in which they live and to view themselves as efficacious. People, however, are not dependent variables:[5] they create and re-create the worlds in which they live; purposefully struggle with each other over meaning, action, material, and social relationships; resist the imposition of unwanted control; and fashion alternative ways of living their lives that eschew given structures and strictures. They retain the potential of agency even in situations in which agency is unlikely or typically absent.

Second, people locate themselves both locally and globally, both in the present and historically. That is, although people engage in face-to-face encounters with others, and although their lives necessarily consist of such encounters, they are not unaware that there are broader contexts and dynamics that influence and are influenced by what they do in their daily lives. They talk about these broader contexts and dynamics, care about them, struggle and argue with others about them, and use them in part to give meaning and value to what they do. Furthermore, people can and do take actions based on their understanding of broader contexts and dynamics.

Third, there is no separation of people from what they do, from the events of which they are a part. As Yeats (1928/1996, p. 215) wrote:[6]

---

[4]See Egan-Robertson (1994, 1998a, 1998b) for an extended discussion of personhood within literacy practices and literacy research.

[5]There are, of course, numerous research studies in which people are defined by researchers as dependent variables and their behavior correlated with some independent variable, such as an instructional program. By contesting such a definition of people, we are arguing that such studies too narrowly define people and thus lack construct validity and, furthermore, that such studies both reflect and constitute a political and policy view of teachers and students that justifies a set of hierarchical power relationships.

[6]This is an excerpt from the poem "Among School Children" (1928), which can be found in *The Collected Poems of W. B. Yeats* (1996). We are indebted to Denny Taylor for bringing Yeats's poem to our attention.

O body swayed to music

O brightening glance

How can we know the dancer from the dance?

It is in this sense that we argue that people are situated, that they act in terms of the situation in which they find themselves while simultaneously creating that situation. There are at least two implications to denying a separation of people from what they do. The first is that people are always doing something, always involved in some event that is defining them and that they are defining. There is no possibility of conducting research involving the analysis of a person or people outside of some event, only the possibility of denying that one is doing so. The second implication is that, in addition to examining the concept of personhood implied in an approach to research, one must also examine the concept of "event" implied, which is what we address in the following section.

FOCUSING ON EVENTS

The title of this book, and the immediately preceding discussion, emphasize a focus on events (more accurately labeled *social events*). This requires some explanation, because our use of the term may differ from others and because "events" are not necessarily the focal unit of analyses in discourse analysis studies of language and literacy in classrooms. For us, "event" is a theoretical construct. It is a heuristic for making an inquiry into how people create meaning through how they act and react to each other. "Event" is also a way to place emphasis on the dynamic and creative aspect of what people do and accomplish in interaction with each other. A *literacy event*, then, is any event in which written language plays a nontrivial role.

There is some controversy over how *event* should be defined, especially in relation to the concept of *social practice*. Street (2003) defined a *literacy practice* as referring to the "broader cultural conception of particular ways of thinking about and doing reading and writing in cultural contexts" (p. 2). For Street and those building on his conception of social practice (e.g., Barton & Hamilton, 1998; Baynham, 1995), an event is an empirical manifestation, the bit observed from which social and cultural practices are inferred and conceptualized. The definitions of *event* and *practice* provided by Street are useful for an agenda emphasizing the articulation of literacy practices; however, they are less useful in focusing attention on what and how people in interaction with each other create, accomplish, adapt, adopt, reproduce, transform, etc., the social and cultural practices extant within a particular social scene. The theoretical relationship given to the concepts of event and practice also has implications for the conceptions of personhood embedded in the research. To the extent that literacy events (and events in general) are conceptualized as the empirical space in which literacy practices (and practices in general) come into play with each other, the people within those events are by definition similarly conceptualized as agents of those literacy practices. By definition, people are captured by those literacy practices and by the discourses within which those practices are embedded. Alternatively, if literacy events are theorized as spaces in which people concertedly act on their circumstances and act on and with the literacy practices that are given and available, and that the conception of literacy exists not in some background abstraction or shared cognitively held cultural model but in its doing, then people are conceptualized as creators and actors (in the sense of people acting on ...), even if the creation is a reproduction of what has been.[7] From this point of view, literacy practices are conceptualized less as shared cognitively held cultural models and more as semiotic resources (e.g., webs of significance; cf. Geertz, 1973, 1983) conceptualized from within the event by participants through their individual and collective histories interacting with each other, with others in related and pertinent situations, and including and within the material environments in which they live.

Despite the differences in definitions and theorizing of events and practices just discussed, the differences are best viewed as different heuristics for varying emphases in research. If a research agenda is focused on articulating the literacy practices of a particular institution, such as schools, then conceptualizing events as empirical spaces for inferring practices is both appropriate and useful. If the research agenda focuses on how people use extant literacy practices to create new histories, new social relationships, or new social identities, or even how they use extant literacy practices to reproduce histories, social relationships, and social identities, then conceptualizing events as spaces where people concertedly create meaning and significance is both appropriate and useful. Our focus in this book is on the latter.

We define an *event* as a bounded series of actions and reactions that people make in response to each other at the level of face-to-face interaction.[8] Stated simply, people act and react to each other. Although seemingly a simple notion, its unpacking shows it to be complex and, taken in the context of academic scholarship, controversial.[9]

---

[7]The distinction between definitions of events and practices is discussed more fully in Bloome (in press) and Bloome and Bailey (1992).

[8]This does not mean that there have to be two or more people copresent in order for there to be an event. People are sometimes by themselves. However, whether with others or alone, a person is acting and reacting in response to other people, what they have done and what they will do. The task, in part, for the researcher interested in understanding the meaning of a person's social behavior (whether that person is alone or in a group) is to identify the people context and the action context within which that person is acting and reacting (cf. Erickson & Shultz, 1977).

[9]Contrasting theories include action as a consequence of setting, unconscious drives, learned behavioral response, genetic makeup, and cultural and economic determinism, among others.

First, it is *people* who are acting and reacting to each other; that is, the basic analytic unit, as we noted earlier, is not the individual but a group of people. People are the context for each other (cf. Erickson & Shultz, 1977).

Second, people *act* and *react*.[10] People react to actions immediately previous; to actions that occurred sometime earlier; and to sets, groups, and patterns of action. People also react to future actions. Any action, including a reaction, inherently includes a concept of consequence. Consequences presume future actions either by others or by oneself. As such, a "nonaction" can be a reaction.

Third, the actions and reactions people take to each other are not necessarily linear. People may act together, and actions and reactions may occur simultaneously.

Fourth, people may act and react to each other through sequences of actions and not just through individual actions. As an aside, we note that the use of language is an action (cf. Austin, 1962; Volosinov, 1929), it is something people do to each other, and to themselves, and it is part of the way that they act on the situations in which they find themselves.

Fifth, meaning and significance are located in the actions and reactions people take to each other, not in abstracted or isolated psychological states. Inasmuch as there is no separation of people from events, there can be no separation among meaning, significance, and action. This is not to say that people do not think about and reflect on the meaning and significance of actions and events; rather, such thinking and reflection are part of an event and are constituted by social relationships, language, and history.

We view the actions and reactions people make to each other as primarily linguistic in nature (and especially so in classrooms). By *linguistic* we mean that they involve language (verbal and nonverbal, human or other) and related semiotic systems (e.g., architecture), inclusive of words, prosodics, gestures, grouping configurations (e.g., proximics and relationships of postural configurations), utterances, and across media systems (e.g., oral, written, electronic). By characterizing people's actions and reactions as linguistic processes we are emphasizing that their actions and reactions derive from language *systems*, systems for making meaning and taking social action through the use of language.[11] These language systems are not static; neither are they singular. As Bakhtin (1935/1981) wrote:

> The living utterance, having taken meaning and shape at a particular historical moment in a socially specific environment, cannot fail to brush up

---

[10]Our use of *react* is similar to and based in part on Bakhtin's (1935/1981) and Volosinov's (1929/1973) discussion of *response*.

[11]Although the discussion here about social interaction as linguistic is not framed by systemic linguistics or functional grammar, there clearly are many concepts here that owe an intellectual debt to Halliday's (1978) and Halliday and Hasan's (1985) theoretical work on language.

against thousands of living dialogic threads woven by socio-ideological consciousness around the given object of an utterance; it cannot fail to become
an active participant in social dialogue. After all, the utterance arises out of
dialogue as a continuation of it and as a rejoinder to it—it does not approach
the object from the sidelines. (pp. 276–277)

Utterances then, among other linguistic behaviors, are acts that are
part of a series of actions and reactions. The meaning of an utterance or
other language act derives not from the content of its words but rather from
its interplay with what went before and what will come later. Its meaning, or
even the kind of act it is, cannot be determined outside of the ongoing
event. Furthermore, because any utterance is not only a response but also a
refraction of preceding language acts (a revision of the meaning of other actions), the meaning of an utterance varies with the point in the ongoing conversation at which it is considered. Meaning is not stable, even when an
utterance is considered in context. There are limits on the certainty that
people in an event can have about what things mean, what the event is
about, and about who they are (Bloome, 1993); never mind limits on the
certainty that researchers can have (cf. Heap, 1980).

THEORETICAL TOOLS FOR THE MICROETHNOGRAPHIC ANALYSIS OF CLASSROOM LANGUAGE AND LITERACY EVENTS

In this section we discuss five theoretical tools for the microethnographic analysis of classroom language and literacy events: (a) contextualization cues, (b)
boundary making, (c) turn-taking, (d) negotiating thematic coherence, and (e)
intertextuality. These tools often result in research products such as transcripts,
maps, descriptive analyses, and various graphic representations of events and
discourse processes. As DuBois (1991), Edwards (2001), Edwards and Lampert
(1993), Mishler (1991), and Ochs (1979) have pointed out, these products are
theoretical and rhetorical statements. Even more so, however, each of these research products is, for us, part of an ongoing process of theorizing what is happening in an event and of problematizing assumptions about the nature of
discourse processes and events. Thus, this discussion of tools for the
microethnographic analysis of classroom language and literacy events is fundamentally a theoretical one that continuously turns on itself.

Contextualization Cues

As people interact with each other, they must do so in ways that their "intentions" can be understood by others in the event.[12] To make their intentions
known, people use what Gumperz (1986) called *contextualization cues*:

---

[12]The concept of "intention" is perhaps misleading, as it suggests that communication is a
process of a person encoding a thought into language and sending it to another person who attempts to decode the thought as accurately as possible. For us, intention lies closer to agency
and the sense that people act on the situations in   (continued on next page)

Roughly speaking, a contextualization cue is any feature of linguistic form that contributes to the signaling of contextual presuppositions. Such cues may have a number of such linguistic realizations depending on the historically given linguistic repertoire of the participants.... Although such cues carry information, meanings are conveyed as part of the interactive process. Unlike words which can be discussed out of context, the meanings of contextualization cues are implicit. They are not usually talked about out of context. (p. 131)

Contextualization cues include verbal, nonverbal, and prosodic signals as well as the manipulation of artifacts. A partial list of contextualization cues is provided in Table 1.1.

An illustration of the identification of contextualization cues in a short conversational segment is presented in Table 1.2. Identifying a contextualization cue does not provide an understanding of what the cue means or of the speaker's intention or the listeners' interpretation. The meaning and function of a contextualization cue (or a set of contextualization cues) depends on many factors, including participants' shared understanding of the social context (of what they are doing and the purpose of the event), and what has already happened and what is being anticipated to happen, as well as explicitly and tacitly held linguistic conventions for interpretation *in that situation*. However, because contextualization cues are part of the acts that people make toward each other, those actions and reactions provide a material basis for generating *a* description (not *the* description) for what is going on and what it means *in situ* and to the people involved. That is, in order to react, a person or a group must have something to react to. What they react to is, in part, previous acts that involve contextualization cues[13] and their understanding of what those contextualization cues mean and what the act does. It is because contextualization cues must be "visible" and understood (even if understood differently) within the framework of actions and reactions by the people involved that there is a material basis for understanding what is happening in an event.[14]

---

[12](*continued*) which they participate. Thus, it is not so much that a person formulates a thought that they then attempt to transmit as that people build on what has occurred in the event and collaboratively create the event and the series of meanings that constitute the event. Meaning therefore lies not in the encoding and decoding of each individual's thoughts but in the jointly constructed actions that people take in the event.

[13]Distinction can be made between an *act* and a *contextualization* cue, although in practice the two are inseparable (you cannot have an act without a contextualization cue, and vice versa). Contextualization cues signal meanings and intentions; acts are something done by people to each other. *Meaning* and *action* can be synonymous (as in "I now pronounce you married"), but they do not have to be.

[14]Bloome and Bailey (1992), building on Volosinov's (1929/1973) theoretical discussions of language, defined *materially realized* as "all those aspects of an event which can be experienced by the participants." This includes not only the physical setting (i.e., room, desks, chairs, etc.) where the event takes place, the artifacts (e.g., textbooks, handouts, pencils) manipulated by the participants during an event, the participants (i.e., adults and children) who construct the events, and the behavior of the participants (e.g., how they act and react to each other, the utterances they make).

TABLE 1.1

Partial List of Contextualization Cues

Paralinguistic/prosodic

Volume shifts

Tone shifts

Rhythmic shifts

Stress

Stress patterns and stress pattern shifts

Velocity shifts

Pausing

Intonation patterns and intonation pattern shifts

Stylizing patterns of intonation and stress (e.g., using an intonation and stress pattern from a different type of situation and overdoing an intonation and stress pattern)

Kinesics

Gesture

Facial expression

Eye movement

Eye gaze

Eye contact, lack of eye contact or shifts in contact

Posture

Body movement

Facial direction

Parakinesic shifts (style of body movement)

Proxemics

Postural configurations

Distancing

Verbal

Register shifts

Syntactical shifts

Note. This partial list of contextualization cues is derived in part from Green and Wallat (1981) and Bloome (1989).

TABLE 1.2

Sample of a Description of Contextualization Cues to a Transcript

Speaker	Message Unit	Description of Contextualization Cues
Ms. Wilson	Who can explain to the concept of sounding white ↑	Stress on "who"; Rising intonation pattern peaking at end of message unit.
Maria	OK I have an example	Stress on "OK"; "OK" acts as a placeholder; Flat intonation pattern after "OK."
Maria	When I be at lunch and I say li+ke	Stress on "When"; Stress on first "I"; Stress on second "I"; Elongated vowel in "li+ke."
Andre	When I be *laughs*	Different speaker; "When" overlaps part of "li+ke"; Repetition of "I be" intonation and style pattern; Speaker stops verbal message at end.
Ms. Wilson	*Wait a minute*	Greatly increased volume; Nonverbal hand gesture; Highly stylized voice and intonation pattern; Stress on "Wait."
Ms. Wilson	I'm sorry |	Lower volume; Cessation of highly stylized voice and intonation pattern; Mock intonation pattern; Pause after "sorry."

Note. A key to transcription symbols can be found in the Appendix.

As Yolosinov (1929/1973) wrote:

> Every ideological sign is not only a reflection, a shadow of reality, but is also itself a material segment of that very reality. Every phenomena [sic] functioning as an ideological sign has some kind of material embodiment, whether in sound, physical mass, color, movements of the body, or the like. In this sense, the reality of the sign is fully objective and lends itself to a unitary, monistic, objective method of study. A sign is a phenomenon of the external world. Both the sign itself and all the effects it produces (all those actions, reactions, and new signs it elicits in the surrounding milieu) occur in outer experience. (p.11)

Of particular interest to Bloome and Bailey was the notion that language is fundamentally a material response, not only to what has been said or done before but also to what will be said or done in the future. The traditional view of reading and writing as isolated reader/writer and text diminishes or dis-

misses the material realization of reading and writing events, locating reading and writing only in the mind and in abstract, unrealized semiotic systems.

Green and Smith (1983) described the importance of contextualization
cues to the study of classroom events (see also Dorr-Bremme, 1990):

> Since ... students, teachers and observers alike must actively interpret mean-
> ing from sequences of behaviors, contextualization cues become an important
> source of information. Description of these cues provides: (a) a level of objec-
> tivity, (b) a means of specifying the range of behaviors that appear to contrib-
> ute to decision making, and (c) identification of variables so that others can
> validate the findings. Contextualization cues, therefore, are central to under-
> standing the transmission and construction of meaning. Observations of con-
> text-specific behaviors as used and interpreted by students and teachers, then,
> has led to the exploration of the effects of these communicative behaviors on
> participation and evaluation. (Green & Smith, 1983, p. 380)

One of Gumperz's (1986) insights about contextualization cues was that
their use was often just below the level of consciousness; that is, people were
usually unaware of the subtle intonation patterns they used or the way in
which their postural configurations signaled meaning. In many cases, there
is no need for explicit awareness of contextualization cues, because their use
is shared among the people interacting with each other. Thus, although
none of the participants are explicitly aware of it, the use of a particular intonation pattern might signal and be understood as courtesy and politeness; a
particular pattern and rhythm of stresses might signal and be understood as
"We understand each other" or "We can work together"—or, stated collo-
quially, "We are on the same wavelength." But because our awareness of the
use and nature of contextualization cues lies just below the surface of awareness, when there is a breakdown in the use of a contextualization cue people
may be at a loss to understand how it is that the mutual cooperation needed
to make an event work has broken down. For example, overlapping the end
of another person's utterance can be a contextualization cue signaling understanding and engagement, but if the other people in the event do not
share that sense of overlapping, they may interpret the overlapping as
rudeness or arrogance.

It was also Gumperz's (1986) insight that our understanding of how
contextualization cues work depends a great deal on our cultural background; that is, part of what is shared within a culture are the use and
meaningfulness of contextualization cues. As long as we are interacting
with people from the same culture, the chances are good that they will be
using and interpreting contextualization cues in a similar way. However,
when we interact with someone from another culture, our uses of
contextualization cues may differ. For example, a rising intonation pattern

accompanying the words "thank you" may be seen by some as appropri ately signaling sincerity but others, based on their cultural background, may view a rising intonation pattern as signaling insincerity. Furthermore, if none of the interlocutors are aware of how the contextualization cue operates—that is, if it remains below their level of consciousness—then there is likely to be a misinterpretation, and people may errantly ascribe negative attributes to each other.

In classrooms, the use and interpretation of contextualization cues can be important cross-cultural issues. Studies conducted by Michaels (1981, 1986), Scollon and Scollon (1981), Gee (1999), and Champion (1998, 2002), for example, have shown that there are cross-cultural differences in how people signal coherence within a narrative. Teachers who do not detect how a student is using which contextualization cues to signal coherence may view the student as telling an incoherent story and therefore misevaluate his or her readiness for further educational opportunities. Similarly, teachers may misinterpret student silence (Carter, 2001; Phillips, 1972) or students' responses to disciplinary measures (Gilmore, 1987) or to the organization of instruction (Au, 1980; Christian & Bloome, in press), among other aspects of teacher–student interaction.

The use of contextualization cues is not fixed; that is, people often code-switch, using contextualization cues in a manner appropriate to the situation even if it requires them to engage in cross-cultural behavior. For example, inside a classroom a student may produce a narrative using the contextualization cues for signaling coherence that are expected by the teacher. Outside of school, when interacting with friends in an informal setting, the same student may tell a story signaling coherence using a very different set of contextualization cues. And although in some cases code-switching is merely a matter of using contextualization cues in a manner appropriate to the situation, it can also be a matter of complex and pervasive power relations.

Boundary-Making

One problem that researchers face in analysis of any event[15] or any interactional behavior is determining the boundaries of an event, a behavior, or a sequence of behavior. There are similar problems in the analysis of text: Where does one text end and another begin? The problems researchers have in determining the boundaries of events, interactional behavior,

---

[15]We recognize that we are using the term *event* at multiple levels. It can refer to the event of an interaction between a teacher and a student, to a storytelling event in a classroom, or to the classroom period as a whole (from the beginning bell to the ending bell). Our use is intended to point to a bounded set of interactional behaviors that may occur at different levels. Whenever context cues do not make clear the level of our use of event, we use other terms (e.g., *interactional unit*, *phase*, etc.).

texts, and so on, are similar to the problems that people in an event have. They need to know what the boundaries are so that they can understand what is happening and how to construct meaning. In other words, boundaries are part of the way that people have of signaling to each other what is going on, the social relationships of people to each other, and what meanings are being jointly constructed.

Boundaries are socially constructed. They are not given *a priori* or as a natural consequence of some setting or activity. For example, consider the boundaries for telling a story during a classroom lesson. Imagine that the teacher and students are having an academic question-and-answer discussion and one of the students wants to tell a personal story related to the topic of discussion. How do the teacher and the other students know that a story has begun and that they have shifted from a short-question-and-answer mode to a storytelling-and-listening mode? How do they know that the storytelling is continuing? How do they know what is "in" the story and what is not? How do they know when the story has ended? Consider Transcript 1.1, of a 7th-grade language arts classroom in which the teacher and students are discussing dialects and whether there is a "white" language and a "Black" language.

TRANSCRIPT 1.1
Seventh-Grade Language Arts Lesson, Lines 140–206

140	Ms. Wilson:	OK
141		John
142		Could you *possibly* explain this concept to me maybe ↑
143		What is "sounding white" …
144	Students:	XXXXXXXXXXXXXX Many students talk at once and yell out responses
145	Ms. Wilson:	I'm asking John
146		No ↑
147		You have no idea
148		Who can explain to me the concept of sounding white ↑
149	Maria:	OK I have an example
151	Andre:	When I be laughs
152	Ms. Wilson:	*Wait a minute*
153		I'm sorry
154		When you said | when I be | Andre said *when I be ha ha ha* how is that funny ↑
155	Students:	Many students laugh and make comments
156	Drake:	That don't make no sense. [Drake's head is on his desk]
157	Ms. Wilson:	Hold on
158		I heard you say I be [Ms. Wilson is looking at Drake]

159		What does I be mean ↑
160		What is that
161	Students	XXXXXXXXXX students yelling out
162	Ray	Stupid
163	Student	It's like figure of speech
164	Drake:	When I am [Drake's head is on his desk]
165	Ms. Wilson:	I really wanna hear this because your intellectualism is dazzling me *Ms. Wilson is looking at the whole class and not at Drake.*
166		I mean *I'm dancing now* *Ms. Wilson does a little dance.*
167	Drake:	Like when I'm at lunch
168		She says when I be
169	Theresa:	Why are you correcting someone when you say it yourself
170	Ms. Wilson:	Do I ever say that ↑
171		Have I ever said *I be you be he be she be we be * ↑
172	Theresa:	You don't make mistakes
173	Ms. Wilson:	Is it a mistake ↑
174	Theresa:	It's not mistake
175		It's how we talk
176	Ms. Wilson:	OK
177		Finish your story
178		I feel like I'm on Oprah
179		A talk show
180		Finish your story
181	Students:	⎡ Students laugh
182	Student:	⎢ Oprah
183	Ms. Wilson:	⎢ Work it girl
184		⎢ When I be …
185	Student:	⎣ Oprah Wilson.
186	Maria:	When I like say somethin' and uuh ||
187		Sheila says | *Girl* | you sound white*.
188		And I say I don't sound white || That's the way I was brought up
189		And she said that || something different

(continued on next page)

TRANSCRIPT 1.1   *(continued)*

190		Like you know
191		*You sound white*
192	Students:	Students yell out comments
193	Ms. Wilson:	Jeanetta | girl | talk it out
194	Janet:	I think when people say you sound white
195		I think it's when you talkin' proper.
196	Ms. Wilson::	What is proper ↑
197	Students:	Students yell out responses
198	Maria:	When I was talkin' …
199		I wasn't sayin' *I be like *
200		And then my friend came over to me she said
201		I sound white because I wasn't talkin' I be or talking slang or *Whassup with that
202		Most people are confused
203		That's why some people say if you don't talk a certain way then you talk white or white people gonna sound Black or somethin' like that …
204	Ms. Wilson:	Camika
205	Camika:	It's like if you talkin' about if you talk white
206		Or you talk proper
150		When I be at lunch and I say like

Note. A key to transcription symbols can be found in the Appendix.

Maria responds to Ms. Wilson's question with the utterance, "OK I have an example" (line 149). By stating that she has an example, she is announcing that an example is coming, reserving the next turn at talk for herself. Her example is a story indicated in part by the way she begins the next utterance, "When I be at lunch …" (line 150). By using "When I …" she is signaling that her example is a personal story that occurred over time and that there is a character in the example, herself, who is acting over time. Thus, Maria has signaled the beginning of a story, a boundary with the question–answer discussion just previous. The beginning boundary of the storytelling is ratified implicitly as Maria is allowed the floor by Ms. Wilson and the other students. Andre's comment, "When I be" and his laughter (line 151) is not a challenge to the storytelling boundary established; it is an aside, although loud enough to be heard by the whole class. Its intonation pattern suggests that he did not mean for it to bring a halt to the story (that is, he was not trying to abrogate the storytelling and establish a boundary for some other type of interaction). But Ms. Wilson picks up on Andre's aside and interrupts the storytelling (line 152). "Wait a minute" (line 152) could be directed at Andre, but it also could have been directed at Maria, telling her to put the storytelling on hold. What Ms. Wilson actually intended is less important here than the interpretation given to her comment, which can be inferred from the subsequent action; namely, the storytelling stops and Andre has to defend his comment and laughter (line 151). One way to interpret Ms. Wilson's utterance in line 152 is that she has violated the boundary of the storytelling, and the serious nature of doing so is reflected in her apology: "I'm sorry" (line 153).

It may be that there are two simultaneous and incompatible definitions of how a storytelling event happens. For Ms. Wilson, *storytelling* may be defined as one person doing the telling and others listening; for Andre, storytelling may include side comments and verbal audience participation. Given just Transcript 1.1, it is impossible to determine whether there are two different definitions of storytelling at play or whether either of those definitions derives from definitions of storytelling from other settings or cultural backgrounds. Such questions become important in investigations of the classroom as a cultural setting and investigations of cross-cultural communication in the classroom. However, even in studies where cultural and cross-cultural questions are not foregrounded, care needs to be taken not to assume that there is a single definition of storytelling at play or that cross-cultural dimensions are absent.

Ms. Wilson holds a discussion with the students on "I be" and "I am" through line 175 and then signals the completion of her interruption in line 176 with "OK" and reinstates the boundary for Maria's storytelling on line 177: "Finish your story." The phrase "finish your story" suggests that the teacher viewed lines 151 through 175 as an interruption in the storytelling, but lines 178 to 179 leave open an alternative interpretation. In line 178, Ms. Wilson compares herself to Oprah Winfrey and being on a talk show. One reason why lines 178 and 179 might be significant from a theoretical perspective is that they give an alternative view of the boundaries of the storytelling. On a talk show like the Oprah Winfrey Show, the telling of a story involves interaction with the host and includes reflections on aspects of the story (similar to those in lines 151–175). Maria then continues retelling what occurred to her (lines 186–191). Ms. Wilson designates Janet to have the next turn at talk although many students are yelling out comments in response to Maria's story. Janet's comment is "I think when people say you sound white, I think it's when you talkin' proper" (lines 194 and 195). One way to view Janet's comment is as a reaction to Maria's story, but another way to view Janet's comment is as the addition of a coda to Maria's story. Ms. Wilson responds to Janet's comment by asking a question based on Janet's comment: "What is proper" (line 196). In so doing, Ms. Wilson has signaled the end of Maria's story (the classroom conversation is no longer building on or responding to Maria's story), and the conversation returns to the question–answer type of discussion they had earlier. However, Maria responds by referring back to her story (lines 198–203). She adds additional detail to the story (lines 200–201) and then adds what might be considered a coda: "Most people are confused, that's why some people say if you don't talk a certain way then you talk white or white people gonna sound Black or somethin' like that" (lines 202 and 203). One way to interpret Maria's action at this point is that she is contesting where Ms. Wilson placed the ending boundary of the storytelling, extending the boundary further. Ms. Wilson then calls on Camika to talk, and the class continues the question–answer type of discussion.

The preceding analysis of the boundaries of telling a story in a classroom conversation shows that (a) boundaries have to be socially constructed—proposed and ratified, (b) boundaries must be actively maintained, and (c) boundaries are contestable. (As an aside, the analysis also shows that different genres can be embedded within each other, for example, a story within a classroom conversation, a question–answer discussion within a storytelling. Signaling and acknowledging what is being embedded into what unit is part of the way that people create meaning.) Accepting such a view of boundaries has serious theoretical and methodological implications. For example, if the boundaries of a story are socially constructed by the participants of an event, then what counts as a story depends not on an *a priori* definition but on what is inside of the boundaries of the storytelling as constructed by the participants. Furthermore, what counts as a story in one classroom event may be dissimilar to what counts as a story in another classroom event and from nonclassroom events. The challenge for researchers is to identify and interpret the boundaries of stories based on the same "data" that people in the event use, with the same sense of indeterminacy and openness to reinterpretation based on what happens later in the event. Such theoretical and methodological implications apply not just to stories and the boundaries of stories but to other linguistic and social units as well, including utterances (which, following Green & Wallat, 1981, we call *message units*), interactional units, phases of a lesson, lessons, and so on. Indeed, a key theoretical and methodological question that researchers must address is "What are the units of analysis that people in an event are using to construct the event and make meaning?" (see also Edwards, 2001).

In our approach to the discourse analysis of classroom events we assume that boundaries are constructed at many different levels. Although we give labels to the levels, what is key for us is not the label or the number of levels suggested by the labels but the concept of multiple and embedded levels that are socially constructed by participants in an event. Thus, in any analysis of a classroom event we take the theoretical warrant to create additional levels and types of units as indicated by the interactional behavior of the participants, as opposed to an *a priori* definition of an event.

With this caveat in mind, and following the work of Green and Wallat (1981), we take the message unit to be the smallest unit of conversational meaning. We identify message units through participants' use of contextualization cues, including the use of pausing, stress patterns, intonation patterns, changes in volume and speed of delivery, stylistic changes (e.g., a shift to another voice, such as often occurs during mocking or quoting someone else). As Green and Wallat (1981) noted:

> a message can be defined only after it has occurred. That is, the end of a message can only be determined on a *post hoc* basis by observing the verbal, coverbal (prosodic), and nonverbal cues, and cues to contextualization (Gumperz & Herasimchuk, 1973) and the onset of a new message. Lack of predictability also occurs at the level of contextualization cues. Just which nonverbal and prosodic cues will be used by a speaker to help transmit the meaning of a given message cannot be predicted in advance. (p. 164)

For example, consider the conversational segment in Table 1.3. As the table shows, the boundaries of message units cannot be determined by examining the words alone. Message units are not sentences; their boundaries do not follow the prescriptive rules for forming written sentences, phrases, or clauses. Rather, the theoretical warrant for determining the boundaries of message units is that participants in interaction with each other need to construct shared unit boundaries in order to communicate and construct meaning, and the means they use for doing so are the same means that researchers must use for identifying unit boundaries. Participants must signal to each other what is in a unit so that others will know how to assign meaning to their behavior (linguistic, prosodic, and nonverbal).

Message units also differ from *utterances* and *turns*, two units often used in analyses of classroom conversation. Utterances are often defined in terms of breath or in terms of prosodic features that signal boundaries via pauses or breathlike markers. One critical question to ask is whether the utterance or other basic conversational unit is being defined from an *illocutionary* perspective (from the perspective of what the speaker wants to accomplish) or a *perlocutionary* perspective (from the perspective of the behavior's impact on listeners). Utterances tend to be defined, in our view, from an illocutionary perspective; message units are defined from a perlocutionary perspective. Turns of talk as basic conversational units are very different from either message units or utterances. Turns of talk are defined by changes in who is speaking. As Table 1.3 shows, a single turn may include several message units, and thus, although turns at talk are important to note, they do not

TABLE 1.3

Illustration of Message Unit Boundaries Via Contextualization Cues

Speaker	Message Unit	Contextualization Cues Used to Determine Message Unit Boundaries	Interpretation of Contextualization Cues in Identifying Message Unit Boundaries
Ms. Wilson	Who can explain to the concept of sounding white ↑	Stress on "who"; rising intonation pattern peaking at end of message unit; Ms. Wilson gives up floor.	Stress on "who" indicates beginning of the message unit; rising intonation pattern signals question, and lack of speaker designation allows students to compete for the next turn.
Maria	OK I have an example	Stress on "OK"; "OK" acts as a place-holder; flat intonation pattern after "OK"; no pause after end.	Stress on "OK" signals both a beginning to the message unit and a claim on speaking rights; flat intonation pattern and lack of pause at end signal maintains turn-at-talk.
Maria	When I be at lunch and I say li+ke	Stress on "when"; stress on first "I"; stress on second "I"; elongated vowel in "li+ke."	Stress on "when" signals shift to a new message unit; elongated vowel in "li+ke" suggests that either more is coming in this message unit or speaker is holding the floor for the next turn at talk.
Andre	When I be *laughs*	Different speaker; "when" overlaps part of "li+ke"; repetition of "I be"; speaker stops verbal message at end.	Message unit is part of a side conversation; timing of "when" to overlap "li+ke" in previous message unit suggests that either "li+ke" was interpreted as end of a message unit and that the floor was open or that Maria has violated rules for maintaining the floor or Andre has violated rules for getting the floor; laughter is not a signal of maintaining the floor or of a continuing message unit.

Ms. Wilson	*Wait a minute*	Greatly increased volume; nonverbal hand questions; highly stylized voice and intonation pattern; stress on "wait."	New speaker; style and intonation pattern signal beginning and end to the message unit; volume (coupled with Ms. Wilson's authority to designate turns at talk) signals that the next turn at talk belongs to Ms. Wilson.
Ms. Wilson	I'm sorry		Lower volume; cessation of highly stylized voice and intonation pattern; pause after "sorry."	Shift in volume and style signal another message unit; intonation pattern indicates beginning and end of message unit; pause indicates end of message unit.

Note. A key to transcription symbols can be found in the Appendix.

provide a sufficiently integral unit of conversation to use as a basic unit of analysis for the purpose of understanding the social construction of conversational meaning and action.

People in interaction with each other also indicate the boundaries of larger units of conversation. Following Green and Wallat (1981), one level up from a message unit can be called an *interactional unit*. Green and Wallat define an interactional unit as "a series of conversationally tied message units. Which message units tie to form an interaction unit depends on consideration of verbal aspects of the message and cues to contextualization (p. 200)." Interactional units cannot be determined *a priori;* neither can they be assumed because a particular type of event is occurring. For example, consider the classroom discussion in Transcript 1.2. The transcript is already divided into message units determined through the analysis of contextualization cues, as described earlier. The teacher, Ms. Wilson, begins with "okay," (line 201), stressing "okay" and elongating the second vowel. In so doing she marks the beginning of an interactional unit that consists of lines 201 through 204. Her gestures with her arms and the steady rhythm of delivering lines 202, 203, and 204 form a contour of a single intonation pattern unit (even though it is made up of four message units that each have their own boundaries). Starting on line 205, the intonation pattern changes into a rising tone (what many people would recognize as a question intonation pattern). The change in intonation pattern, accompanied by the change in arm movement, suggests that a new interactional unit has begun. This is important as the participatory demands have changed. During the first interactional unit, Ms. Wilson did the talking, and the students listened. But line 205 creates a space that demands a response, which is given by Camika in line 206: "uh huh." Lines 205 and 206 form an interactional unit because in those lines Ms. Wilson and Camika begin and complete an interaction of a question–answer. In identifying an interactional unit one must be careful not to examine just the syntax of the message units, because an interactional unit is signaled by prosodic and nonverbal means more so than by the syntax of a message unit. Thus, just because there is a question and answer does not mean that an interactional unit has begun and ended. In lines 207 and 208 Ms. Wilson asks another question and receives a response. It could be that the interactional unit ends with line 209; the question has been answered, and the teacher is moving on to ask another question. But the intonation pattern; the exact repetition of the student's response by the teacher, who uses the response and a consistent rhythm to link "slang" to "versus" (line 211) to extend to another question; plus the lack of any pause or stress; and an intonation pattern that suggests no closure (neither a rising nor falling intonation), suggest that the interactional unit is extended to line 213, when Ms. Wilson provides closure and confirmation with "okay."

TRANSCRIPT 1.2

**Parsing of Lines 201–251 Into Interactional Units
With Contextualization Cues**

Speaker	Message Unit	*Partial Description of Contextualization Cues*
INTERACTIONAL UNIT 1		
201 Ms. Wilson	okay+	Stressed and elongated vowel
202	Based on Camika's explanation	Pointing to Camika
203	There is this high level of talking	Waving arms high in air
204	Which most often is associated with talking white	
INTERACTIONAL UNIT 2		
205	Is that what you're saying↑	Pointing to Camika question intonation
INTERACTIONAL UNIT 3		
206 Camika	uh-huh	
207 Ms. Wilson	And then this low way of talking	Holding hands
208	Is associated with talking what	low question intonation
209 Student	slang	
210 Ms. Wilson	slang	
211	versus	Question intonation
212 Students	proper	
213 Ms. Wilson	okay	
INTERACTIONAL UNIT 4		
214	Drake what was your comment	Question intonation
INTERACTIONAL UNIT 4 SUSPENDED		
INTERACTIONAL UNIT 5		
215	Someone said something in reference to talking white	
216	Versus talking Black etcetera etcetera	
217	But Drake made a comment	

(continued on next page)

	Speaker	Message Unit	*Partial Description of Contextualization Cues*
218		Where he completely disagrees with the whole thing	

INTERACTIONAL UNIT 4 REINSTATED

	Speaker	Message Unit	Cues
219		Drew	Looking at Drew
220		So everyone can hear you	
221		What is	
222		What is your opinion	Question intonation
223		*Break break it*	
224		* put put it up*	Ms. Wilson holding up right hand and getting a "high five" from Drew
225		*I mean *	
226		*Break it down for em *	
227		talk	Pointing to Drew and then walking away
228	Drake	Y'all talkin about white people	Looking at classmates
229		Talkin a different way and stuff	
230		There ain't no certain	
231		Language called white	
232	Students	[indecipherable]	
233	Student	Oh my God	
234	Ms. Wilson	whoa	

INTERACTIONAL UNIT 6

	Speaker	Message Unit	Cues
235		now	stressed
236		Roger's retort to Drake was	Question intonation
237	Roger	There ain't no certain language	Looking at Ms. Wilson
238		There's no language as Black	
239	Ms. Wilson	There is no language called Black	
		Begin Side Conversation	
240	Camika	Yes it is	

241		Yes it is	
		End Side Conversation	
242	Ms. Wilson	And there's no language called white	

INTERACTIONAL UNIT 7

243		But all the time	Stress on first word
244		We are accused of talking	Motioning with hands and using question intonation
245	Students	white	
246	Ms. Wilson	Or talking	Motioning with hands and using question intonation
247	Students	Black	
248	Ms. Wilson	Or talking	

INTERACTIONAL UNIT 8 INITIATED

| 249 | Camika | But y'all | Off camera |
| 250 | | But y'all | |

INTERACTIONAL UNIT 8 ABANDONED

| 251 | Ms. Wilson | Black | |

END INTERACTIONAL UNIT 7

Note. A key to transcription symbols can be found in the Appendix.

Ms. Wilson uses a new question in line 214 to begin Interactional Unit 4. The question creates a space and demand for a response. But before Drake or anyone else can respond, Ms. Wilson fills the space with the beginning of a new interaction unit. The rhythm of her talk changes in line 215. What she has done is suspend Interactional Unit 4, returning to it in line 219. In lines 219 through 227 she provides many connections back to Interactional Unit 4 and to giving Drake the right and obligation to respond. Lines 223 through 226 are a stylized embellishment that can be a signal of emphasis, a way to provide Drake with time to get his response ready, a way to shift the register of the conversation, or other functions. Ms. Wilson explicitly tells Drake when to give his response and fulfill his obligation to respond in line 227 when she tells him to talk, which he does in lines 228 through 231. However, the interactional unit is not yet finished as students and the teacher respond to his answer (lines 232, 233, and 234). Their responses are tied to Drake's responses just as Drake's response is tied to the teacher's question. Thus, unlike Interaction Unit 2, which was constituted by a question and answer, Unit 4 is constituted by a question, answer, and response, embellished by elaborations. The boundaries of the interactional unit signaled by prosody, body movement, and the contingent relation among responses (lines 232, 233, and 234 are linked closely with lines 230 and 231).

Interactional Unit 6 is similar to Interactional Unit 4, consisting primarily of a beginning boundary marker ("now"; line 235), a question (line 236), a response (lines 237–238), and a response to the response (line 239), which is extended in line 242 ("and there's no language called white"). The teacher's near repetition of Roger's answer ("there is no language called Black"; line 239) can be viewed as a positive evaluation of Roger's response to her question. However, one must be careful in making such inferences, examining the interaction for subsequent evidence that the teacher's response (line 239) was taken to be a positive evaluation by the people involved in the event.

The side conversation, which was loud enough to be overheard but spoken in a tone that identified it as a side conversation, gives at least some evidence that Ms. Wilson's response to Roger was viewed by at least some of the students as a positive evaluation. In the side conversation, Camika contests Ms. Wilson's remark, presumably because Camika interpreted Ms. Wilson's response (line 239) as authorizing Roger's comment as a fact. Ms. Wilson either chooses to ignore Camika (which is a response) or does not hear Camika's side comments. Interactional Unit 7 consists of a boundary marker (line 243) with a heavy stress on the first word and then a series of questions and responses that some might view as similar to a call-and-response routine that might be found in some churches. The particular call-and-response intonation pattern found in Interactional Unit 7 is consistent across the unit, even though Camika attempts to disrupt the interactional unit by contesting the premise. However, because no one is responding to her initiatives, Interactional Unit 8 is abandoned.

As is made clear in the analysis of interactional units in Transcript 1.2, interactional units can be suspended, reinstated, overlapped, and abandoned. Within each interaction unit a series of demands are made of participants, either to behave as listeners, as responders to questions, and so on. People in interaction with each other are required to determine what is being demanded of them and to address those demands in some manner. The demands can and do change from interactional unit to interactional unit. Interactional units can be viewed as the smallest units of joint social activity; that is, by definition an interactional unit involves both the actions and reactions of people toward each other.

At a broader level, sets of interactional units constitute phases of an event and then the event itself. The boundaries of phases and events are also signaled and sometimes named. For example, in the lesson from which Transcripts 1.1 and 1.2 were taken, there were six phases: (a) the introduction to the lesson, (b) silent reading, (c) cooperative oral reading, (d) comprehension questions, (e) discussion, and (f) coda. With the exception of the introduction and the coda, each phase of the lesson was explicitly labeled and told to the students by the teacher. The shift to a new phase was explicitly marked by the teacher, who announced the shift. Although two phases were not explicitly named, they were marked by the teacher, who noted that it was getting near the end of the class period, and the shift to the topic of homework and what was going to happen the next day. The shift was noted and ratified by the students as they responded by gathering their papers, packing their backpacks, and shifting their bodies into a "getting ready to leave" posture. The labels that we have used for these phases may give the false impression that the phases of an event are defined by the planned instructional phases of a lesson. It would perhaps be more accurate to label the phases 1, 2, 3, 4, and so on, rather than naming them. In classrooms, teachers often have the authority and obligation to define the phases of the event that occur in their classrooms, which they call *lesson* or *class*. Thus, the boundaries of a phase of an event are often coterminus with the boundaries of a component of the lesson. However, there is nothing inherent in a classroom event that requires that the boundaries are coterminus. If they are coterminus, it is because of the way the teacher and students have interactionally constructed it.

At issue here is not whether the terms *phases* and *events* need to be used but that part of the resources available to people in interaction with each other is the creation of multiple levels of units of interaction. They signal these levels and their boundaries to each other and use them as a resource to guide their interactions with each other and the creation of shared meaning.

Turn-Taking

Although earlier we discounted the use of turns at talk as a basic unit of conversational analysis, they are nonetheless important features of social interaction. At the simplest level, an analysis of turn-taking involves counting the number of turns at talk each participant has in a conversation. Such analyses might also include number of words or message units per turn at talk, the content of those turns, and types of utterances in each turn (e.g., question, statement), among similar countables. The difficulty with such analyses is that they exist separate from a definition of the event being analyzed and thus are not interpretable. For example, consider a turn-taking analysis of a lecture. The lecturer would have nearly all of the turns at talk, with a few turns at talk distributed among other participants.

How does a researcher interpret such data? It would seem ludicrous to interpret such an imbalance of turns at talk as a "silencing" of the audience and similarly ludicrous to interpret the data as defining a hierarchical power relation between the lecturer and the audience (e.g., what if the lecturer were a doctoral student defending her dissertation research to an audience of examining professors?).

Thus, analyses of turn-taking need to involve a definition of the event, but even that is not sufficient. Consider a classroom conversation in a reading group. Each student is given a turn at talk to read aloud the words in his or her book. Although we know the type of event it is, and its explicit purpose, as researchers we are still unable to interpret what is happening or the contribution of the turn-taking procedures to what is happening. Each student is given the same amount of turns at talk and approximately the same number of words to read aloud; what are we to make of that? Would it be reasonable to correlate such a turn-taking protocol with reading achievement? In doing so one would be making the assumption that there was something in the turn-taking protocol (e.g., saying a set of printed words aloud) related to learning to read and that other factors did not matter. But assuming there was a significant correlation, how could it be interpreted? On what basis would the turn-taking protocol itself (as opposed to the saying aloud of printed words) be theoretically linked with learning to read? One could as easily argue that what mattered was the not-having-to-read-aloud component of the turn-taking protocol as the reading-aloud component or the predictability of turn-taking or the comfort of a familiar routine. Neither could an argument for equity be made, although each student received an equal number of turns and words said aloud. In order to interpret what is happening with turn-taking as contributing to a sense of equity, we would have to first locate equity (e.g., from whose perspective: students, a particular student, the teacher, the researcher?), define it, and make a convincing argument that equity was a foregrounded concern.

In brief, simple counts related to turn-taking do not provide access to interpretation. A more nuanced approach to turn-taking has focused on *participation structures* (e.g., Au, 1980; Phillips, 1972; Shultz, Florio, & Erickson, 1982), which can be defined as shared expectations among participants regarding the patterns of turn-taking protocols for a particular type of situation or event. For example, in an event explicitly labeled a lecture, participants would expect the event to begin with a call to order, after which either the lecturer would begin or someone else would introduce the lecturer. During the lecture, the participants (including both the lecturer and the audience) would expect the lecturer to talk at length, and turns at talk by members of the audience would be considered inappropriate unless explicitly called for by the lecturer. After the lecturer had finished, there might be a question-and-answer phase during which the participation structure would change in a manner that would make it appropriate for members of the audience to ask questions, resulting in a repeating pattern of audience question followed by lecturer answer until that phase of the event concluded.

As this brief example suggests, participation structures may vary from event to event and even from one phase of an event to another phase of the same event. Furthermore, the nature of the event defines in part the participation structure, and the participation structure defines in part the event (and perhaps even the social institution in which the event occurs). For example, consider Transcript 1.3.

The teacher and students are having a classroom conversation about the poem they have read and are enacting a turn-taking pattern familiar to them and found frequently in classrooms. The underlying structure of the pattern is: (a) Teacher Question or *In*itiation, (b) Student *R*esponse, and (c) Teacher *E*valuation or *F*eedback.

This pattern is often abbreviated as *I-R-E* or *I-R-F* sequences or referred to as the asking of known information questions. In Transcript 1.3, the underlying pattern is repeated four times (see Table 1.4).

Each component of the pattern can occur in many different ways. The teacher does not necessarily have to initiate the pattern with a question. A statement in that slot in the pattern will likely be interpreted as calling for a student response. Teacher evaluation or feedback can occur explicitly or can be implied by repeating the answer (as in line 22: "They did not have the same opportunity") or by ellipsis (by moving on to the next question, as occurs after line 05).

As Transcript 1.3 makes clear, there is a series of shared assumptions about who has the right to the floor during that conversation, based in large part on shared expectations about rights and responsibilities in an I-R-E type conversation. For example, when a student takes the floor at a point where it should have reverted back to the teacher (line 08), the teacher holds up her hand and there is a split second of silence (line 10) that has the effect of enforcing the distribution of rights to the floor associated with their enactment of the I-R-E sequence.

It is also interesting to note that the I-R-E sequence is not a "clean" pattern, at least not in the conversation in Transcript 1.3 and in many other classroom conversations. There is other talk that occurs, multiple student responses, people talking over each other, errant attempts to gain the floor, repairs being made, and so on. Yet the nature of the conversation, its participation structure, is clear to both the teacher and the students. This suggests that the participation structure is an abstraction jointly held by the teacher and the students, an interpretive frame for them to guide their participation and to interpret what is happening.

The I-R-E pattern of turn-taking is closely associated with schooling. In most conversations, a question is interpreted as a sincere request for new in-

Seventh-Grade Language Arts Lesson, Lines 01–21

01	Ms. Wilson:	We're talkin' about 1865.
02		And we're talkin' about a period of time when slavery was still instituted _
03	Students:	Yes.
04	Ms. Wilson:	Was slavery still instituted? _
05	Students:	Yes.
06	Ms. Wilson:	Were Blacks allowed the same type of education as whites? _
07	Students:	No
08	Theresa:	XXXXXXXX no
09		That's why. _.
10	Ms. Wilson:	_ [Holds up hand] I'm still making my point
11	Theresa:	OK, go ahead.
12		Just go ahead.
13	Ms. Wilson:	OK,
14		So if we know that slavery was still instituted
15		If we know that African Americans were not afforded the same education as other people
16		Is it a matter that they don't *quote unquote* know any better
17		Or they never had the opportunity to get an education _
18	Camika:	They never had an opportunity
19	Ms. Wilson:	I'm not asking you Directed to students calling out responses
20		I'm asking the person who made comment Theresa (T) had earlier made the comment Ms. Wilson was referring to, that Black people talked "that way" in 1865 "because they did not know any better"
21	Theresa:	They didn't have the opportunity
22	Ms Wilson:	They did not have the same opportunity

Note. A key to transcription symbols can be found in the Appendix.

TABLE 1.4
IRE Sequences*

Teacher Question or Initiation	01	Ms. Wilson: we're talking about 1865.
	02	Ms. Wilson: And we're talking about a period was slavery was still instituted?
Student Response	03	Students: Yes.
Teacher Evaluation or Feedback		[Approval of answer in 03 inferred by moving on to next question]
Teacher Question or Initiation	04	Ms. Wilson: Was slavery still instituted?
Student Response	05	Students: Yes.
Teacher Evaluation or Feedback		[Approval of answer in 05 inferred by moving on to next question]
Teacher Question or Initiation	06	Ms. Wilson: Were blacks allowed the same type of education as whites
Student Response	07	Students: No
	08	Theresa: No
	09	Theresa: that's why
Teacher Evaluation or Feedback	13	Ms. Wilson: OK
Teacher Question or Initiation	14	Ms. Wilson: So if we know that slavery was still instituted
	15	Ms. Wilson: If we if we know that African-Americans were not afforded the same education as other people
	16	Ms. Wilson: Is it a matter of they don't quote unquote know any better or
	17	Ms. Wilson: they never had the opportunity to get an education
Student Response	21	Theresa: They didn't have the opportunity-
Teacher Evaluation or Feedback	22	Ms. Wilson: They did not have the opportunity (muted, as if to herself).

*A key to transcription symbols can be found in the Appendix.

formation, not as an opportunity to evaluate whether the other person knows the right answer. Thus, invoking an I-R-E sequence indexes a social institution as well as constituting roles for people to adopt.

There has been a great deal written about the I-R-E pattern of turn-taking (for in depth discussions see Cazden, 1988; Mehan, 1979, 1980; Watson & Young, 2003; and Wells, 1993). Questions have been raised about the consequences of I-R-E sequences for academic learning, power relations, cross-cultural communication, and language learning (e.g., learning the language of an academic discipline, the learning of English by students who may not be fluent in English). Investigation of such questions is not straightforward, as there can be no assumption that form equals function or meaning or that form equals cognitive processing or learning. For example, although it may appear that authorized knowledge is being indicated through an I-R-E sequence (by the teacher giving positive evaluations and feedback to particular student responses), it may be that the teacher and students are merely enacting a lesson (engaging in procedural display; cf. Bloome, Puro, & Theodorou, 1989) and the designation of authorized knowledge is irrelevant in that event. With regard to cross-cultural communication and miscommunication, researchers have shown that there can be similarities in participation structures across settings and events between the classroom and the students' homes (e.g., Au, 1980; Phillips, 1972). When there are cross-cultural differences between the teacher and the students (or among the students), expectations may not be fully shared for how to participate in an event or within a particular phase of an event. As a result, people may act in ways that are unexpected by others. How teachers interpret the unexpected behaviors of students may be crucial to a student's educational opportunities (for additional discussion, see Cazden, 1988; Cazden, John, & Hymes, 1972; Heath, 1982, 1983; Michaels, 1981, 1986; Miller, Nemoinani, & Dejong, 1986). From a research perspective, questions must be asked about the evidence needed for a valid argument of cross-cultural miscommunication. Differences in participation structures in what may be considered analogous events (e.g., a dinner table conversation and a reading group conversation) are not by themselves sufficient evidence of cross-cultural miscommunication; they are only evidence of a difference in participation structures. Additional evidence must be brought to bear that the differences influence both how people participate and how they negotiate the participation structure. That is, inasmuch as people constantly adjust and readjust their behavior toward others on the basis of what the others are doing (or not doing), to claim cross-cultural miscommunication (as opposed to just miscommunication or the communication of hierarchy), there must be evidence that not only are there differences but also that (a) the differences are derived from cultural domains and (b) the differences manifest themselves in ways that prevent teacher and students from negotiating ways of interacting with each other that are effective for communication of intentions and for the purposes of the instructional events.

The social function and meaning of an I-R-E sequence, or any participation structure, depend on what people in interaction construct the function and meaning to be. As we discussed earlier, people must signal to each other what is happening and what conversational behavior and patterns mean. Researchers, therefore, must make an argument about the function and meaningfulness of a participation structure using evidence from the conversation itself, from how people act and react to each other.

Although the focus here has been on I-R-E sequences, participation structures vary greatly and are generative. The issues we have raised about I-R-E sequences are issues about participation structures in general. Most important, attention must be paid to the pattern of turn-taking rather than to simple counts of turns and similar items. Participation structures may be invoked by the type of event occurring (e.g., a lecture) and may constitute and define that event. Caution must be exercised in assuming that the form of a participation structure equals its function or meaning. Arguments about the social function and meaning of a participation structure(s) must be built on how the people within a particular event act and react to each other.

Negotiating Thematic Coherence

We define *thematic coherence* as the organization of a set of meanings in and through an event. These meanings may be ideational, interpersonal, or textual. An event is considered to have thematic coherence when the meanings generated in and through the event have a relationship to each other that the people in the event define as coherent. Roughly speaking, thematic coherence is the answer to the questions "What is this event about?" and "What is it that they are all talking about?" Thematic coherence can exist within an event and across events, and there can be multiple themes at multiple levels.

Thematic coherence cannot be assumed; that is, not all events have thematic coherence. One indication that an event lacks thematic coherence is when people in an event begin to question what the event is about. Similarly, an event can appear to have thematic coherence, but it may exist only superficially.

Identifying thematic coherence can be difficult, both for participants and researchers. On the one hand, thematic coherence may be assumed given a type of event. For example, during a classroom lesson one can reasonably assume that a foregrounded theme is instruction and the research question might also foreground instruction. But what if the research question is simply "What is happening in this classroom now?" How can thematic coherence be identified and analyzed when it is not derived from a given research question?

This task is similarly difficult for participants and researchers. A participant in an event might assume, given the nature of the event, what the foregrounded themes might be. An event defined as a classroom lesson in a language arts class can be assumed to foreground themes on instruction in language, composition, reading, or literature. To do otherwise would require the teacher, or some other participant with appropriate authority, to declare and mark the event as being about something else (e.g., fundraising, an upcoming sports event, student behavior in the cafeteria, etc.). Similarly, if the teacher declares at the beginning of the instructional event that they will be reading and discussing a poem, students and the teacher can assume that the classroom conversation will be about poetry and, more specifically, about the poem indicated. If the classroom conversation shifts—that is, if somebody introduces a new theme—the new theme will need to be made overt and ratified. Thus, if a classroom conversation that begins thematically about a poem and its meaning shifts to a discussion about language variation, then that thematic shift has to be made clear to all of the participants, and they have to ratify the shift either explicitly or by following the shift through their subsequent responses. For example, consider Transcript 1.4.

Just previous to the interaction in Transcript 1.4, the students had been working in small groups, discussing among themselves who the subject of the poem was. They had offered a range of ideas and when prompted by the teacher had offered evidence from the poem to support their idea. Except for a brief and seemingly tangential comment at the beginning of the lesson approximately 23 min earlier, neither the teacher nor any student had made a comment about the language of the poem or about language variation. In lines 401, 402, and 403 the teacher is continuing their discussion of the subject of the poem by providing a last opportunity for a person or group to take the floor. None does. Then, in line 405, the teacher initiates a new phase of the lesson (they are no longer working in or reporting out of groups but have changed to a whole-class discussion) and a new theme. The new theme is language variation and the various assumptions and associations that people have with regard to African American Language (labeled in Transcript 1.4 as *Ebonics*; line 419). However, the teacher does not explicitly state the new theme that she is initiating at the beginning of the new phase of the lesson. Instead, she prompts the thematic change by asking the students to reconsider the meaning of the poem in light of a new fact, that it was taking place in 1865. Camika (lines 415 and 418–422) provides the first explicit reference to language, and Ms. Wilson builds on Camika's comments by focusing on "Ebonics." In so doing Ms. Wilson has indirectly initiated a new topic and has ratified it (line 424). The students have also ratified the shift in conversational theme as they respond to the new topic and theme on the floor (lines 426, 427, and 429).

TRANSCRIPT 1.4
A Mapping of Lines 201–231

Line No.	Speaker	Message Unit	Theme Poem	Lang	Other
401	Ms. Wilson	Anything else from this group that was not said anywhere else |	↓		
402	Ms. Wilson	Is there a point you have that no one else has mentioned ↑	↓		
403	All	[2 second silence]	↓		
404	Ms. Wilson	No ↑	↓		
405	Ms. Wilson	OK	↓		
406	Ms. Wilson	What if I told you |	↓	↓	
407	Ms. Wilson	That the year this poem was written was	↓	↓	
408	Ms. Wilson	The year that the year this poem was taking place	↓	↓	
409	Ms. Wilson	The time in this poem |	↓	↓	
410	Ms. Wilson	Was 1865 |	↓	↓	
411	Ms. Wilson	OK |	↓	↓	
412	Ms. Wilson	1865 |	↓	↓	
413	Ms. Wilson	Does that change the meaning of this poem just a little bit ↑	↓	↓	
414	Students	Yes Yeah Yes	↓	↓	
415	Camika	Yes because they speakin'	↓	↓	
416	Ms. Wilson	OK somebody explain it to me	↓	↓	
417	Ms. Wilson	Camika	↓	↓	
418	Camika	Because of the writin	↓	↓	
419	Camika	It's like they speakin Ebonics	↓	↓	
420	Camika	They not talkin on a regular level	↓	↓	
421	Camika	They talkin about *And fo the little feller*	↓	↓	
422	Camika	They not speakin our term in English there	↓	↓	
423	Ms. Wilson	What		↓	

(continued on next page)

TRANSCRIPT 1.4   *(continued)*

Line No.	Speaker	Message Unit	Poem	Lang	Other
				Theme	
424	Ms. Wilson	What's Ebonics ↑		↓	
425	Ms. Wilson	I mean you used this word what is it ↑		↓	
426	Student	Street slang		↓	
427	Camika	Ebonics is like a language		↓	
428	Camika	A language like that we used when we wasn't taught anything		↓	
429	Student	Street slang		↓	
430	Ms. Wilson	Who is we ↑		↓	
431	Camika	Black people		↓	

Note. A key to transcription symbols can be found in the Appendix.

A variety of questions can be asked about thematic coherence and thematic shift in Transcript 1.4. For example, in what ways did the students and teacher signal thematic coherence? In what ways did they signal thematic shift? Such questions help identify the linguistic resources (both verbal and nonverbal) that are available for teachers and students to use with regard to negotiating thematic coherence, as well as what resources they actually use. For example, in Transcript 1.4 thematic coherence is created in part through the use of specific lexical items. A series of lexical chains are created, as shown in Table 1.5.

A close analysis of Table 1.5 reveals a structure that is more like a chain of associations than one of a main idea and supporting comments; that is, rather than stating the topic and purpose of the discussion and then relating all subsequent comments to that topic and purpose, the teacher and students build on what each other brings to the conversation. For example, in response to Ms. Wilson's question about whether the meaning of the poem changes if it is located in 1865, Camika focuses on the way the characters ("they") speak (line 415). Camika's response is not a direct response to the teacher, and it is not clear what argument Camika is making with regard to a change in meaning based on the time of the poem. But Ms. Wilson builds on what Camika has offered, engaging Camika and the class in conversation about what inferences can be made about people from the way they talk. By line 424 the poem itself has dropped out of the conversation, and Ms. Wil-

TABLE 1.5
A Lexical Chain Map of Lines 401–431

Line No.	Chain 1	Chain 2	Chain 3
407	Poem (poem) ← →	Time (year)	
	↓	↓	
408	Poem (poem) ← →	Time (year)	
	↓	↓	
409	Poem (poem) ← →	Time (time)	
	↓	↓	
410	Poem (ellipsis) ← →	Time (1865)	
	↓	↓	
412	Poem (ellipsis) ← →	Time (1865)	
	↓	↓	
413	Poem (meaning of this poem) ← →	Time (that)	
	←		
415	Poem (they)	←————→	Language (speakin')
	↓		↓
416	Poem (it)	←————→	Language (it)
	↓		↓
418	↓	←————→	Language (writin')
			↓
419	Poem (they)	←————→	Language (speakin' ebonics)
	↓		↓
420	Poem (they)	←————→	Language (regular level)
	↓		↓
421	Poem (they) ("and fo the little feller")	←————→	Language ("and fo the little feller")
	↓		↓

37

TABLE 1.5 (continued)

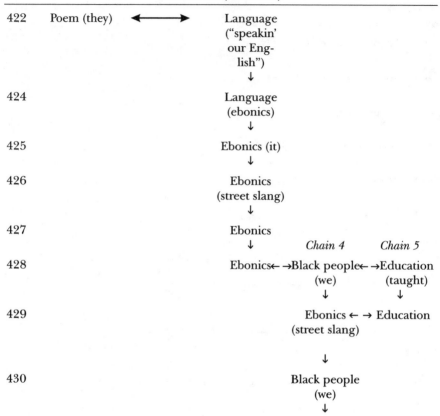

son is responding to and building on Camika's comments and those of other students about Ebonics.

We note that the direction and structure of the conversation is neither weakly structured nor accidental. On the basis of our interviews with Ms. Wilson after the lesson and on observations of many other instructional conversations in this classroom, we concluded that the thematic structure reflects an instructional style and a literary philosophy. By carefully selecting literary works for classroom discussion, Ms. Wilson encourages particular topics to be foregrounded. She selected "After Winter" for reading and discussion because, given her knowledge of her students, previous classroom discussions, and how she anticipates orchestrating the discussion, there is a high probability that the topic of language variation will be raised. Using literary texts in such a manner is consistent with her view of literature, which is that literature provides a way to examine the world. It acts as a prompt and a tool to help one better understand oneself, others, and the world in general. As such, in Ms. Wilson's view, literary analysis is important as a way to gain insight into the world; it is not an enterprise conducted for its own sake. Whatever meaning or insight is derived from a literary work comes from what the reader brings to the literary work and what is gained through interaction with others around the literary work, not just from the literary work itself. Thus, the thematic shift from the meaning of the poem itself to language variation is consistent with the teacher's literary and pedagogical philosophy. (We provide additional analysis of this lesson in chapter 2.)

Analysis of thematic coherence can also be useful in examining "hidden" social processes, such as constructing gendered identities, establishing social hierarchies, promoting "individualism," and so on—what is often referred to as the *hidden curriculum* of schools. Before pursuing an analysis of thematic coherence with regard to a dimension of the hidden curriculum, one must have a warrant for doing so. In our view, reference to scholarship on broad trends, what Ellen (1984) called *enumerative inferencing*, is not a sufficient warrant for making a claim about thematic dimensions or thematic coherence within a particular event. For example, statistical reports showing a national trend that boys perform better in math and science than girls do is not a sufficient warrant to analyze thematic coherence around gender bias in the teaching of math and science in a specific classroom. Rather, there has to be something in the setting itself to warrant such an analysis (perhaps the teacher has mentioned that the boys in the class do better in science and math than the girls do). Even so, one would need to worry whether the teacher's comment, although perhaps accurate, reflects his or her awareness of national trends applied to his or her classroom—the teacher's use of enumerative inferencing. Furthermore, one would need to worry that the way the research question was formulated reflected not popular press or the formulations of other research but was grounded in the setting itself. Beyond concern with the research question, one would also need a clear conception of the data to be used in constructing a representation of thematic coherence related to the hidden curriculum.

For example, consider *individualism*, an ideology that a number of social theorists have suggest permeates Western, Anglo education, curricula, and instruction (e.g., Eagleton, 1983/1996; Patterson, 1992). Assuming that one had a valid warrant for asking about the promotion of individualism in a classroom being studied, what would count as valid data in constructing a representation of thematic coherence? Would participation in a reading group be evidence of individualism? Would a student working quietly alone at his or her desk constitute evidence of individualism? Would the meaning of the data change if what the student was working on was a collective project? We argue that what should count as data and the framing of data for researchers is what counts as data and the framing of data for participants—that is, if the events being analyzed in the classroom are promoting individualism (or any other aspect of the hidden curriculum), then at some level the material circumstances of the classroom events (including verbal behavior and interactional behavior) need to reflect that. The material circumstances involved may be revealed only when there is a disruption or violation. For example, if a student openly copies another student's paper, and there is no disruption or public notice of violation, then it would be hard to claim based on that data alone that writing a paper constitutes the promotion of individualism in that classroom. However, if there were an outcry, and a complaint were made and a rebuke or punishment involved, especially if the participants state a rationale for the rebuke, then it is reasonable to claim that copying violates a social rule and that the social rule was potentially related to an ideology of individualism. The outcry and complaint make visible the implicit and hidden social rule, and researchers are provided the opportunity to investigate the meaningfulness of the social rule to the participants.

In brief, what count as data and what data mean cannot be taken for granted. What count as data and what data mean must be grounded in how people act and react to each other. However, once one has valid data, one can create representations of thematic coherence, and in so doing one can examine how teacher and students contribute to and resist the construction of various "hidden" social and cultural processes.

Intertextuality

Intertextuality refers to the juxtaposition of texts. A word, phrase, stylistic device, or other textual feature in one text refers to another text; two or more texts share a common referent or are related because they are of the same genre or belong to the same setting, or one text leads to another (as occurs when the writing of one letter leads to the writing of another, or when the buying of a theater ticket provides admission to a play). It is commonplace to view any text as indexing many others, imbued with the voices of many people and many past texts. Scholarship on intertextuality has tended to focus on written texts, but in our view questions about intertextuality can include conversational texts, electronic texts, and nonverbal texts (e.g., pictures, graphs, architecture), among others. In a classroom the students may simultaneously have their textbooks open on their desks, be engaged in a conversation with the teacher, and have maps hanging on the wall, while the teacher is writing on the whiteboard. Intertextuality is something that teachers and students take for granted, so much that they may not even realize that they are doing so.

From the perspective we take here, rather than ask what are the potential intertextual links of a text or set of texts, the question to ask is "What intertextual connections do people in interaction with each other jointly construct?" That is, intertextuality is socially constructed rather than given in a text. To claim that an intertextual connection has been constructed, it must have been proposed, acknowledged, recognized, and have social consequence. For example, consider a kindergarten teacher who passes out a worksheet to students on letter–sound relationships. The teacher tells the students to complete the worksheet using what they learned in reading group that morning when they reviewed letters and sounds in their basal reader. Merely because the teacher has proposed an intertextual connection does not necessarily mean that the students have taken it up. They may acknowledge that the teacher was making an intertextual connection but not recognize the connection itself (perhaps they do not remember the earlier reading group, were absent, or are unable to locate the reference because they use a different label for the event or text). Also, even if they recognize the specific intertextual connection, they may not understand the social significance it has for the current event (what knowledge from the previous text they are to use with the current text).

Consider another example: In Transcript 1.4, line 407, Ms. Wilson makes an explicit reference to the poem that the 7th-grade students have been talking about during the lesson. Table 1.6 shows one way in which the social construction of intertextuality can be described. Notice that in the table explicit attention is given to identifying how the teacher and students propose an intertextual connection, acknowledge it, recognize it, and give it social consequence.

In lines 406 through 412 Ms. Wilson proposes an intertextual link between the poem and the end of the Civil War (she is assuming that the students have a shared narrative about the Civil War and the end of slavery). In line 413, she asks whether such a connection has social significance. It is social significance in the sense of changing the discussion they are having and changing the interpretation of the poem that the class is constructing. Implicit in her request for providing social significance is a request for acknowledgment and recognition of the intertextual link, because no social significance of the intertextual link could be constructed without giving it acknowledgment and recognition. In line 414, the students confirm that there is an intertextual link, but their comments do not give any evidence of the nature of that intertextual link. Also, as shown later in the transcript, the intertextual link that the students make is not to the Civil War narrative but to a general sense of the language of the poem being old. In line 416, Ms. Wilson asks the students to clarify their response in line 414 by indicating their recognition of the intertextual link and by articulating its social significance. She calls on Camika to do so. Camika provides a recognition of the intertextual link, but it is not (at least, it does not appear to be) the intertextual link to the Civil War narrative; it is a connection to the language style, the dialect, Ebonics. In line 420, Camika begins to explain the social significance of the intertextual link, as she has defined it. In the next line she supports the intertextual link she has "recognized," and she adds to the

TABLE 1.6

Intertextuality: Lines 406–428

Line No.	Speaker	Message Unit	Intertextuality Proposed	Intertextuality Acknowledged	Intertextuality Recognized	Social Consequence
406	Ms. Wilson	What if I told you /	X →			
407	Ms. Wilson	That the year this poem was written was	X →			
408	Ms. Wilson	The year that the year this poem was taking place	X →			
409	Ms. Wilson	The time in this poem /	X →			
410	Ms. Wilson	Was 1865		X →			
411	Ms. Wilson	OK		X →			
412	Ms. Wilson	1865		X →			
413	Ms. Wilson	Does that change the meaning of this poem just a little bit —		Request	Request	Request
414	Students	Yes Yeah Yes		Confirmation		
415	Camika	Yes because they speakin'				
416	Ms. Wilson	OK somebody explain it to me			Request for explanation →	
417	Ms. Wilson	Camika	New Topic →			
418	Camika	Because of the writin			New Topic →	
419	Camika	It's like they speakin ebonics	New Topic →		New Topic →	

42

#	Speaker	Utterance			Evidence for the intertextual link proposed	
420	Camika	They not talkin on a regular level	X→			Defines the language and the people
421	Camika	They talkin about *And fo the little feller*	X→			Models how to provide evidence in support of the social construction of an intertextual link
422	Camika	They not speakin our term in English there		X→		Defines the language and the people
423	Ms. Wilson	What		X→		
424	Ms. Wilson	What's ebonics↑		X→	X→	
425	Ms. Wilson	I mean you used this word what is it↑		X→	X→	
426	Student	Street slang				
427	Camika	Ebonics is like a language				Defines the language and the people
428	Camika	A language like that we used when we wasn't taught anything		X	X	Connects language, people, and education

Note. A key to transcription symbols can be found in the Appendix.

social significance of the link by modeling how to support the social construction of an intertextual link. Although not shown in Table 1.6, line 421 is also an intertextual link to previous conversations in this lesson and other lessons in which the teacher asks the students for textual evidence to support their claims. Ms. Wilson, in lines 424 through 425, asks Camika for additional clarification of the social significance of the intertextual link that Camika has proposed. In so doing, Ms. Wilson has acknowledged and recognized the intertextuality proposal Camika made in lines 418 through 421. The result is that the "footing" (cf. Goffman, 1981) of the instructional conversation has shifted. Another student answers, in line 426, providing evidence that the intertextual link made by Camika has been picked up by other members of the class (or at least, the new footing has been taken up). In line 428, Camika connects the new topic, Ebonics, with a topic of discussion from earlier in the lesson, the education of African Americans in the past. It is not a proposal for a new intertextual link but a delayed acknowledgment, recognition, and articulation of social consequence.

Closely related to intertextuality is the construct of *intercontextuality* (cf. Heras, 1993). Part of the creation of any event involves the construction of relationships between the event and other events. Sometimes such relationships are created overtly; for example, a teacher might say "Today's lesson builds on what we did in reading group yesterday." Of course, merely proposing a relationship between one event and another does not in and of itself create a connection. For example, the students might not have heard what the teacher said, a fire drill might occur immediately after the utterance, or there might be no ongoing creation of connections (i.e., the connection is dropped). A connection among events has to be ratified by others; the participants have to acknowledge and recognize the connection, and the connection has to have some social consequence.

Of course, it may be that only those students who participated in the interaction and the teacher share in the intertextuality or intercontextuality that has been socially constructed. The other students could be sitting passively and unaware. Such a situation raises an important question for researchers and for participants. When can participants (and researchers) claim that intertextuality or intercontextuality has been socially established—or, more broadly, that any aspect of a shared understanding of what is happening has been socially established? Does the answer to "What is happening here and now?" require that everyone have the same answer? If not, how many of the participants must share the same sense of intertextuality and of what is happening? And to what degree must they share that understanding? 100%? 90%? 50%? We take a different approach than that of quantifying sharedness. We ask whether a "working consensus" (cf. McDermott, Gospodinoff, & Aron, 1978) has been established and what interactional behavior is available to participants to signal that a working consensus has been established. That is, in order for people to create an event, interact with each other, and communicate meanings and emotions, they need to invoke a working consensus of what is happening and what meanings are being established. If they mistake the working consensus, then their efforts at interacting and communicating will break down or fail, and they and others will need to engage in a process of repair. In repairing an interaction, participants must make clear to each other what the working consensus is.

One of the reasons for discussing intertextuality and intercontextuality is to address the relationship between micro level contexts (specific events and situations) and macro level contexts (broad social and cultural structures). This relationship between micro level and macro level contexts has been more asserted than documented, more enumerated than theorized (see Macbeth, 2003, for a detailed discussion). In much social theory, specific events are dismissed as unimportant and relegated to the status of examples of macro level social theory in play, as if people's lives and events were merely the playing out of grand narratives in which they have little authorship or efficacy, and any sense of efficacy they might have is merely a false consciousness and self-deception. In contrast, the view we take here is that the relationship between and among events is one constructed by people in the event, inasmuch as people construct relationships among events, not only among events in which they are physically present but also among those in which they are not (e.g., an instructional lesson on letter–sound relationships may be constructed by teachers and students as related to a school board meeting on the reading curriculum). The analysis of intertextual and intercontextual relationships provides insight into the relationship of micro level contexts and macro level contexts and provides a theoretical and methodological tool for describing such relationships.

MICROETHNOGRAPHIC DISCOURSE ANALYSIS OF CLASSROOM LANGUAGE AND LITERACY EVENTS AND THE LINGUISTIC TURN IN THE SOCIAL SCIENCES

Now that we have described some of the theoretical and methodological constructs we use in our particular microethnographic approach to discourse analysis, we share how we locate our approach in evolving intellectual directions. We locate our approach to discourse analysis of language and literacy events in classrooms in the intellectual movements that have grown out of the "Linguistic Turn" in the social sciences. We view the "Linguistic Turn" as part of a historical and ongoing movement within the social sciences and humanities to explicate how uses and forms of language create and re-create knowledge, power relations, identities (for individuals, peoples, institutions, etc.), and what counts as research (both as a way of acting on the world and as a social institution), as well as language itself.

We can only briefly discuss the "Linguistic Turn" here. Readers interested in more in-depth discussions of the "Linguistic Turn" in the social sciences are referred to Allen (2000), Clifford and Marcus (1986), Atkinson (1990), Said (1979, 1985), Rorty (1992), and Tyler (1987), among others. We anticipate that there will be scholars who would want to locate microethnographic approaches to discourse analysis elsewhere, in other intellectual histories. There will also be scholars who would describe the "Linguistic Turn" differently from us.

The linguistic turn in the social sciences builds on the recognition that language is not a "transparent" vehicle of communication. Although language may communicate information from one person to another, it also is always an act of constructing social relationships among people and of bringing a cultural ideology to bear on an event, group, or other phenomenon. That is, rather than examining a sign and asking questions about its meaning and use, one examines a sign (including its use) in relationship to other signs and their uses, focusing on the linguistic or semiotic system rather than the meaning of a sign in isolation. Meaningfulness, therefore, is located not in the sign itself but in the relationships of signs; their uses; and in the relationships of linguistic, social, cultural, economic, and political systems. On the basis of this recognition questions can be asked about how uses of language contribute to the social, cultural, political, and economic processes within which and through which people live their lives. No use or instance of language is neutral or autonomous, regardless of how innocent or transparent it seems, and this is the case with research no less than with any other social institution.

Part of the intellectual agenda associated with the linguistic turn in the social sciences is understanding the degree to which interpretive frameworks can travel across cultures and languages.[16] Understanding an unfamiliar phenomenon, culture, or way of life in a valid manner requires an interpretative framework situated in the original research site and the lives of the people there. It is not just the phenomenon or way of life that needs to be translated but the interpretive framework. There may be limits to the degree of understanding that may be possible across cultures and languages. The language of description and interpretation, both as a framing device and as a device of representation to others, is neutral neither with regard to its ideology nor with regard to the structuring of social and power relations among all of the people involved (researchers, researched, funders, audiences, the state, other economic and political stakeholders, etc.). And yet, because the language of research itself is rarely examined, it is "invisible" and its consequences taken as natural. The result can be more than simple misunderstanding—it can

---

[16]Although not usually associated with the linguistic turn in the social sciences, Benjamin's (1969) work is informative on this issue.

result in a subtle but powerful form of colonialism not only among countries but also within a country, among social institutions and among different groups within a society.

For many researchers, the "Linguistic Turn" is synonymous with a heightened emphasis on reflection on the language of research and its consequences. Although reflection on and even interrogation of the language of research is certainly important and necessary (after all, it is through "scientific"[17] research that contemporary society makes claims of truth), for us the "Linguistic Turn" is closely related to intellectual and political concerns with how people and institutions use language within everyday life to exert power and control on the one hand and to engage in resistance, creativity, agency, and caring relations on the other hand. Attention has been focused on how language is used to create categories of "us," "them," and "the other"; to marginalize some and foreground others; to create differential conceptions of personhood (i.e., who, what, and how is a person); to authorize knowledge; to deceive; and to limit and to provide access to economic, cultural, and symbolic capital—all of which, metaphorically speaking, can be viewed as a sort of domestic colonialism sometimes manifest along racial, gender, and class lines and sometimes along other lines that are more subtle but just as ubiquitous. However, attention has focused as well on how language has been used to resist and undercut the uses of language just noted; to create loving and mutually respectful and caring relationships among individuals and among groups; to find agency even in the midst of subordinating institutions; to adapt and transform oppressive linguistic and cultural forms; and to create new ones, for liberating uses, to engage in what Morrison (1994) called the "midwifery" properties of language.

Attention to the social, cultural, and political nature of the language of research was made popular, in part, by the 1979 publication of Edward Said's *Orientalism* and the 1986 publication of Clifford and Marcus's edited volume *Writing Culture*. In these two volumes, among others, researchers examined the language of research and found that beneath a veneer of "scientific objectivity" was a series of linguistic constructions and processes that promoted hierarchical power relationships between Western cultures, countries, and institutions and those that were or had formerly been colonized and subordinated. What is especially powerful about the insights of Said and Clifford and Marcus, and others, is that the issue is not the failure of the language of research to be neutral but rather the impossibility of a

---

[17]Our use of *scientific* is intended both as ironic and to contest current definitions. It is ironic in the sense that the adjective *scientific* is often used to distinguish between authoritative claims to the truth and wistful claims to the truth (*unscientific*), and our discussion calls for interrogation of that dichotomy, of the assignment of authority, and of "truth" itself as a monolithic phenomenon. Yet, at the same time, we do not want to relinquish use of the term to those who define science as experimental and quantifiable research.

neutral language and of neutral research. This is the case whether one is researching cultural groups in other countries or groups within one's own lo-
cality. The concern with the language of research is not an isolated curiosity
or a technocratic issue of the efficiency and accuracy of research but part of a
larger concern with how relations of power, dominance, and control are
manifested and, more broadly, with the processes of the production of social, cultural, political, and economic life at both the levels of broader soci-
ety(ies) and daily life.

Because the research process requires one to write up experiences and
translate them from one social and cultural setting to another, researchers
are required to redefine the research experience (e.g., descriptions, findings) within the frameworks of the audiences for whom the writing is intended (even if the audience is only the researcher him- or herself). Rarely is
the audience of research primarily the individuals who are studied; instead,
the experience captured as part of a research endeavor becomes framed by
the language, purposes, history, institutions, and ideologies of the audience
for whom the research is intended.

Recognizing the subtle but powerful ways that language can constitute
social, cultural, political, and economic relations, social events, and
knowledge, scholars have investigated issues and mechanisms involved in
the conduct of research and in the writing up of research, often under the
rubrics of scientific language or academic language (e.g., Atkinson, 1990;
Halliday & Martin, 1993; Lemke, 1990, 1995; Marcus & Clifford, 1986).
Examining research reports, scientific articles, and other documents, researchers have focused attention on such linguistic processes as metaphors (e.g., Atkinson, 1990; Bloome, Cassidy, Chapman, & Schaafsma,
1988), organization structures and argument structures (e.g., Bloome &
Carter, 2001; Fahnestock, 1997), nominalization (e.g., Halliday & Martin,
1993), uses of time and space (Bloome & Katz, 2003), ways of structuring
cohesion and coherence (e.g., Halliday & Martin, 1993), narrative structures and frameworks (e.g., Bazerman, 1997; Beaugrande, 1997; Bloome
& Katz, 2003), and author and audience relationships (e.g., Scollon &
Scollon, 1981; Waddell, 1997), among others. Such investigations have
led to an increased emphasis on investigation of the social, cultural, political, and linguistic nature of academic discourses and to an increased reflexivity in the conduct and reading of research (e.g., Atkinson, 1990;
Street, 1995a, 1995b). By *academic discourse* we are referring to the ways of
using language—the genres, the social and cultural practices, the
epistemologies, and the ideologies of an academic or professional field.
By *increased reflexivity* we mean conducting research with an awareness of
translation issues and of how the discourse of research and related academic discourses may influence or perhaps impose an interpretation on
the experiences captured through research. Attention to academic discourse is warranted in part because of the role academic discourses play in

the creation and promulgation of the ideologies of the state and of dominant social institutions (Said, 1979, 1985). Some researchers have called for a stronger reaction to the recognition of translation issues and problems, noting that research and academic discourses play a role in power relations between researchers (and those who sponsor and use their research) and the subjects being researched. For example, Tyler (1987) called for collaborative efforts between researchers and the researched framed by goals that eschew exploitation and that are of mutual benefit.

The "Linguistic Turn" in the social sciences and humanities is important for research on classrooms. Research on classrooms, teachers, and students (and their homes and communities) is rarely intended for them as audience[18]—it is usually intended for other academic researchers or policymakers at an administrative or legislative level, those charged with promulgating, articulating, and implementing state and corporate ideologies. For such an audience, classrooms, teachers, students, families, and communities other than their own are unfamiliar cultures (their previous experience as students or visits to schools notwithstanding) and at times dissident cultures to be perhaps controlled or "colonized." As such, the issues involved in the use of language in researching and writing about classrooms are similar to those involved in research on other countries and cultures.

However, merely shifting the audience of classroom research explicitly to teachers, students, and local communities does not inherently make the research antihegemonic or resistant to state or corporate control of classrooms or communities. Rather, questions need to be asked about the uses of language underlying the research endeavor, including what is being studied, for what purposes, by whom, for whom, and with which assumptions about the nature of language. In sum, given the linguistic turn in the social sciences and humanities, our approach to discourse analysis of classroom language and literacy events focuses attention on language: both the language used by teachers and students and the language used in the conduct of and the writing of the research. Similarly, our approach to framing the various extant definitions of discourse and approaches to discourse analysis is grounded in the linguistic turn in the social sciences and humanities. We ask who is doing what, to whom, where, and how through the use of language in classrooms, and we ask that of ourselves as well as of teachers and students.

---

[18]When research on classrooms is intended for teachers and students, it is primarily used as a warrant for generating rules, guidelines, frameworks, or mandates for teachers and students to follow and not as an overture to further explication of the topic by teachers and students.

A Microethnographic Approach to the Discourse Analysis of Cultural Practices in Classroom Language and Literacy Events

The purpose of this chapter is to highlight methodological issues involved in the microethnographic analysis of cultural practices within classroom language and literacy events. A *cultural practice* can be defined as a shared abstraction (a cultural model) that is enacted in a particular set of events. We define a *literacy practice* as a cultural practice involving the use of written language (cf. Street, 1984, 1995b) and a *classroom literacy practice* as a cultural practice involving the use of written language associated with "doing classroom life."

For example, teachers and students may share a cultural model for how to do reading group or how to enact reading aloud during a recitation lesson. In any specific event the particular way in which the reading practice is enacted may vary from the abstract, cultural model (although nonetheless being recognizable to all as an enactment of that abstract cultural model of reading). Cultural practices (and, correspondingly, literacy practices) are not just held in the minds of a group of people but are also "held" in the material structure and organization of a setting. For example, in the United States, elementary school classrooms are often designed with an alcove that fits a table and a set of six to eight chairs. Reading programs and textbooks that the school purchases often present lessons for use in a reading group, and teacher evaluations are often set up to examine how teachers use reading groups. In brief, the classroom literacy practice of "reading group" is held by the classroom architecture, the bureaucracy, and others both inside and outside the classroom as well as being a shared, cultural model held cognitively by the teacher and the students.

One of the reasons for wanting to examine the cultural practices of classroom language and literacy events is that these practices define who does what with written language, with whom, when, where, how, and with what significance and meaning. More simply stated, what students learn when they learn to read and write is how to engage in a specific set of situated literacy practices. Therefore, describing and understanding these literacy practices—including who is engaging in them; how; and how the engagement in literacy practices varies across students, events, classrooms, and school and nonschool settings—is critical to understanding what literacy learning is within a classroom or school.

In this chapter, we discuss the microethnographic analysis of literacy practices in a 7th-grade classroom lesson. At one level, our purpose is to illustrate how various theoretical constructs might be used in conducting a microethnographic discourse analysis and how such an analysis can yield an interpretation of what is happening in the lesson. At another level, we are also making an argument about the nature of classroom language and literacy events. As we suggested in the Introduction, methodological discussions do not stand distinct from theoretical discussions about the nature of the phenomenon being analyzed and described. Any research endeavor always involves a dialectical relationship among three sets of theories: (a) the extant set of theories in the field about the classroom language and literacy events being studied, (b) the set of theories that guide the specific approach to discourse analysis being used (what might be called the *methodological warrants*), and (c) the implicit theories embedded in the classroom event and jointly held by the people involved in the classroom event. Thus, the discussion that follows is as much about the nature of classroom language and literacy practices and events as it is about the practice of microethnographic discourse analysis. We begin by considering what it might mean to view classrooms and classroom language and literacy events as sites of cultural practice.

CLASSROOMS LANGUAGE AND LITERACY EVENTS AS SITES OF CULTURAL PRACTICE

Classrooms are more than open spaces with furniture—they are cultural sites where children and adults enact a series of cultural practices, including "doing school," "doing lesson," "doing classroom reading and writing," and "doing learning." "Doing school," "doing lesson," "doing learning," and "doing classroom reading and writing" are not the same as what is commonly meant by *learning* or "learning to read and write." That is, reading and writing are not a set of autonomous psychological processes for acquiring new academic knowledge and skills, just as the performance of a play such as Shakespeare's *The Tempest* is not the same as the actors' learning about weather, human relationships, poetry, or the cultural politics of colonialism. Although the actors may learn about such things, their focus is on the performance, on enacting the play, and the knowledge and skills they use and acquire are geared toward creating a performance (how to enact the role; how to feign romance, fear, and wisdom; how to project suspense and catharsis). In the case of teachers and students, the "play" is the concerted performance of "doing school," "doing lesson," "doing learning," and "doing classroom reading and writing." Such a view of classrooms does not deny that learning may also occur in classrooms, but it does problematize the construct of classroom learning. Indeed, one could argue that the "learning"[1] that occurs in classrooms is mostly about how to "do school," "do lesson," "do learning," and "do classroom reading and writing."

Yet teachers and students are not simply cultural dupes enacting the predetermined scripts of the cultural practices of "doing classroom reading and writing." They may modify, adapt, and transform those cultural practices, or they may import cultural practices from other social institutions and from other domains of cultural life—more like semi-improvisational theater than a rigidly scripted drama.

At any particular moment in a classroom, there are tensions and conflicts between the tendency for continuity (reproduction of extant classroom cultural practices and social structures) and change and, put more grandly, between maintaining a cultural ideology or challenging and transforming it. This tension exists both at the level of performance and at the level of the meaning and significance of the performance. Therefore, it is not sufficient to merely list and describe the classroom literacy practices one finds in a particular set of classrooms; one must also describe those classroom literacy practices within the dialectics of continuity and change. As such, classroom literacy practices are perhaps better viewed as fluid and dynamic than as fixed and static—more like a verb (cf. Bloome & Solsken, 1988; Lewis, 2001; Street, 1993a) than a noun.[2] Methodologically speaking, what we are after is more than thick description (cf. Geertz, 1973, 1983); we are after thick description in motion.

Before presenting the microethnographic analysis of a specific classroom lesson, we need to discuss two constructs that have influenced our approach: (a) school literacy practices and (b) the dilemma of structure and substance. The former emerged out of early ethnographic studies of literacy in community and school settings. The latter derives not from a particu-

---

[1]For discussions on the problematizing of the concept of learning in classrooms, see Bloome, Puro, and Theodorou (1989) and Marshall (1992).

[2]There is a limit to the certainty that can be had in describing a *process* (verb); in order to describe the process or action it must be fixed, and held stable, but as soon as one does so, one loses part of what that process or action is, because the movement and change are part of what defines it.

lar set of studies per se but from discussions in linguistics and literary theory over the past several decades that have been concerned with the meaning of structure—or, perhaps more accurately stated, with how structure means.

MICROETHNOGRAPHIC CULTURAL DESCRIPTION AND SCHOOL LITERACY PRACTICES

The classroom is more than a physical context for the enactment of literacy practices. It is a defining context that dictates how written language is used, to do what, by whom, when, and what it means. School literacy practices are an integral part of "doing classroom life." They are part of what defines classroom life as much as being defined by classroom life. One way to heuristically frame the relationship of classrooms and literacy is by conceptualizing the classroom as containing two types of discourse. There is the discourse of schooling, and there is the discourse of disciplinary fields (also referred to as *academic discourse* or *disciplinary discourse*). The first of these (the discourse of schooling) consists of ways of using language, ways of interacting with others, values, goals, and resources that promulgate the culture of schooling. Raising one's hand to get a turn at talk; sitting at one's desk quietly; responding to the teacher's questions, as opposed to asking questions; taking tests; getting grades; responding to written texts in ways that display appropriate participation (as opposed to using texts to acquire knowledge or for entertainment), and so on, are related to the discourse of schooling. *Academic discourse* refers to the organization, selection, and display of knowledge consistent with the practices of a disciplinary community (e.g., writing up the results of a biology experiment as a biologist would). In classrooms, the discourse of schooling and academic discourses bump up against each other, forcing each to change. A student does not merely write up the results of a biology experiment and submit them in a way similar to biologists; rather, the student must consider and respond to the schooling context, including how to display learning, achievement, and adherence to the implicit norms of the classroom and school.

Street and Street (1991) suggested that, in classrooms, language is objectified, procedures (as opposed to content) are emphasized, and uses of written language are homogenized. In brief, in classrooms "teachers appeared to treat language as though it were something outside both the students and themselves, as though it had autonomous, nonsocial qualities that imposed themselves upon its users" (Street & Street, 1991, p. 152). Teachers have emphasized literacy as consisting of "procedural skills in moving around texts, assert[ing] who has authority over the text, and reinforc[ing] the pressure on students to see written language as something separate and detached" (Street & Street, 1991, p. 159). One consequence of what Street and Street called the *pedagogization of literacy* is to [associate] literacy acquisition with the child's development of specific social identities and positions, the privileging of written over oral language, the interpretation of "metalinguistic" awareness in terms of specific literacy practices and grammatical terminology; and the neutralizing and objectification of language that disguises its social and ideological character ... [these processes] contribute to the construction of a particular kind of citizen, a particular kind of identity, and a particular concept of the nation. (p. 163)

Thus, the stakes for understanding and describing classroom literacy practices go beyond the classroom itself and open up key dimensions of cultural ideology, social identity, and nationalism (see also Gee, 1996; Gee, Hull, & Lankshear, 1996; Lewis, 2001; Street, 1992, 1995b) and how literacy practices get played out, adapted, resisted, or transformed in classroom events.

A classroom literacy practice does not have to occur in a classroom *per se;* neither are all events that occur in classrooms, classroom literacy practices. For example, at home, parents and children can enact classroom literacy practices, turning their kitchens and dining rooms into classrooms (see Cairney, 2002; Cairney & Ashton, 2002; Twymon, 1990; White, 2002). In classrooms, students can engage in a series of *subrosa* literacy activities (e.g., writing notes or trading baseball cards) that are distinct from the activities associated with the classroom lesson or with doing other formal classroom activities (Gilmore, 1987). Literacy practices, and cultural practices in general, may travel across different types of situations and across different social institutions, sometimes maintaining their character[3] and sometimes becoming mockery, satire, or assuming other similar aesthetics.[4] Such traveling is a critical dynamic in the constitution of power relations among different cultural groups and different social institutions, for example, between schooling and business.

What constitutes the classroom literacy practices within any particular classroom cannot be assumed or given *a priori;* neither can classrooms or classroom literacy practices be viewed as monolithic. In brief, two questions must be asked. First, how do the use and meaningfulness of written language in a particular classroom index the continuity of classroom literacy practices (across and within classrooms)? Second, how does it constitute change? Although Street and Street (1991) provided useful insights about the social and cultural nature of classroom literacy practices and about the connection of classroom literacy practices to the broader dynamics of nationalism and cultural ideology—and thus alerted all researchers to the need to consider and investigate such dynamics—what

---

[3]Hymes (1974) used the term *key* to refer to what we mean by *character* in this instance.

[4]We use *aesthetics* similarly to the way Tannen (1989) did. In brief, the aesthetic of a communicative practice is part of the process (a means) of defining a social relationship between the speaker/writer/sender and the listener/reader/receiver and giving it meaning.

actually happens in any particular classroom with regard to literacy practices cannot be predetermined.

MICROETHNOGRAPHIC CULTURAL DESCRIPTION
AND THE DILEMMAS OF STRUCTURE AND SUBSTANCE

Another of our goals in this chapter is to show the difficulties and dangers involved in the discourse analysis of classroom literacy events when *structure* is confused with *substance*. For example, discourse analyses of classroom literacy events have often focused on the structure of turn-taking during teacher–student interaction. A widespread finding has been the prevalence of the Initiation–Response–Evaluation (I-R-E) conversational structure (e.g., Mehan, 1979). A teacher may ask a question or *i*nitiate a topic of discussion, nominate a student to *r*espond, and then *e*valuates the correctness of the student's response or otherwise offers feedback. For example, after students have read a passage in a book, Ms. Wilson may ask a comprehension question, a student may respond, and Ms. Wilson then evaluates the correctness of the answer. One interpretation of the I-R-E structure is that it limits student participation to short answers bounded by what the teacher already knows and that it may be detrimental to more sophisticated types of learning (e.g., formulating complex responses, addressing ambiguous texts, and generating alternative interpretations). Analysis of I-R-E structures have also addressed issues of power, locating power with the teacher, creating an unhealthy situation for many students, and potentially marginalizing some students. However, close analyses of teacher–student conversations in diverse situations have shown that although a conversation may be characterizable as having an I-R-E structure, the meaningfulness of that conversation may be underestimated when the analysis does not go beyond the I-R-E structure itself (cf. Wells, 1993). Through the ways that teachers engage in the evaluation phase they may be providing students with important verbal models for engaging in an academic register (O'Connor & Michaels, 1993), or providing feedback that raises the level of thinking (Wells, 1993); through the ways teachers initiate a topic or a question they may provoke students to engage ideas in a different and perhaps more critical manner; and through how teachers link one I-R-E structure to another or to other instructional conversations they may be encouraging students to pull together many different topics or perspectives. Of course, it could also be the case, as critics contend, that the I-R-E structure is being used to locate control and power in the teacher and to limit what counts as legitimate knowledge.

   The point here is that a convincing argument about what is happening and the meaning it has in and through a classroom event cannot be made through analysis of structure alone. Although we argue that it is important to analyze the structure of instructional conversations, and although it is important to consider the implications those structures might have, we also argue that microethnographic analysis of classroom literacy events requires that one examine how written language is being used, by whom, when, where, and for what purposes, along with *what* is being said and written, by *whom*, and *how*, and what *import* the uses of spoken and written language have to the people in the event and to the conduct and interpretation of other events. Such an analysis requires consideration of how the event is located in time and place (both geographically and socially), what is brought into the event (e.g., its history, what previous events are invoked, what common knowledge is assumed, cultural practices, and literacy practices), what happens in the event (how people act toward and react to each other), the particularities of the event (what makes the event distinct from other events of its type in similar situations), and what social significance and consequence the people in the event assign to the event as a whole and to what happens in the event. In brief, analysis of the structure of discourse alone (whether at a face-to-face level or a broader level) is unlikely to yield the kind of insight into what is happening in a classroom that has either emic validity or the potential to reveal systems of power and control (and resistance to them) that are grounded in the realities of people's everyday lives, the ways or possibilities through which people create meaningful lives and caring relationships for themselves and others.

The transcript that we discuss later in this chapter, Transcript 2.1, comes from a 7th-grade language arts classroom. On the surface, the lesson looks much like a traditional lesson (e.g., reading aloud, asking/answering questions about comprehension, characters, cycles of I-R-E structures, etc.) and, as such, represents continuity of classroom practices, including classroom literacy practices. However, through their use of language, the teacher and students transform the "doing of classroom"—more specifically, they transform traditional classroom literacy practices. They do so in part by shifting the focus away from the content and structure of the written text they were studying (a poem) to an interrogation of language variation and race and by shifting the location of knowledge from the text and traditional sources of valorized knowledge in classrooms (e.g., the teacher) to students' prior knowledge and experiences as members of a shared community. In so doing, they shift the import of learning from the accumulation of bits of literary knowledge and literacy skills to literacy learning defined as the problematization of taken-for-granted understandings of the world in which they live through the use of written language.

In the transcript, Ms. Wilson questions her students in a manner that bridges politics, the students' experiences with language and race, and the poem. Through the use of questions, she opens a space where students can bring to bear their experiences as racialized people. It is also important to note how the students ratify and validate what Ms. Wilson is doing through their responses. They follow her lead. The students' ratification of the teacher's conversational engagement is one important indication that the classroom practices in which they are engaged and transforming are jointly constructed. Regardless of whether one is looking at transformative processes or stabilizing ones, one should not only look at what teachers do but also how teachers and students interact with each other and how they jointly construct and reconstruct classroom literacy practices.

A MICROETHNOGRAPHIC DISCOURSE ANALYSIS OF CULTURAL PRACTICES IN A 7TH-GRADE LANGUAGE ARTS CLASS

Throughout chapters 2, 3, and 4 we use excerpts from various classroom literacy events to illustrate theoretical and methodological issues. In each case, the excerpts come from broader research studies that are either ethnographic in nature or that otherwise involve the collection of data in natural settings over lengthy periods of time. One classroom lesson that we discuss in depth in this chapter and in chapter 4 comes from a 7th-grade language arts classroom that was part of a long-term ethnographic study. Therefore, we provide here a background description of the classroom, students, and teacher.

Background Description of the 7th-Grade Language Arts Classroom

The teacher, Ms. Wilson,[5] was a collaborative member of the research team. She shared with the other members of the research team concern with the educational issues that prompted the research; she was involved in the data collection and data analysis process;[6] she was involved in the interpretation of the videotapes and other data from the study; she was involved in presenting the research at professional conferences; she was a coauthor on a subset of research articles regarding the research study; and she incorporated the data collected within her own, separate (although related) research study. Ms. Wilson was in her 2nd, 3rd, and 4th years of teaching during the research study (the particular lesson we examine here took place during her 2nd year of teaching). She had a master's degree in language and literacy education and had written a thesis on culturally responsive pedagogy. Ms. Wilson is an African American woman who is deeply involved in the African American community and who has a special commitment to the education of children from working-class and low-income African American communities.

---

[5]All of the names of the teachers, students, schools, and so on, are pseudonyms; this was a condition of the school district's permission to conduct the research and of conditions set by the institutional review board.

[6]Ms. Wilson was a paid member of the research team and spent part of several summers working full time with the rest of the research team analyzing and interpreting data.

There were 25 students in the room. The academic skills of the students covered a wide range, from students who were reading and writing above their grade level to those who had difficulty reading simple books.

The school included only Grades 7 and 8. The school was predominately African American, and most students came from working-class or low-income communities. The school had a reputation as low achieving. Some students who otherwise would have attended the school went instead to one of the "magnet" schools in the school district based on interests and academic achievement. Figure 2.1 shows the layout of the room. With perhaps the exception of the location of Ms. Wilson's desk and the inclusion of a couch, the classroom layout appears traditional. Students sat at individual desks, in rows, facing forward. However, the student's desks were movable. Ms. Wilson often had the students move their desks to form groups.

Not depicted in Fig. 2.1 are the heating and cooling problems. During the Summer, Fall, and late Spring, the classroom could get very hot, especially without air conditioning. The air conditioner was a large window unit that made a great deal of noise. When it was turned on, it was difficult to hear Ms. Wilson or the students unless they talked loudly.

Although Ms. Wilson often gave directions to the class from her desk, she also used a lectern located at the opposite side of the room. The lectern and the desk, metaphorically speaking, were anchors for Ms. Wilson's movements in the classroom. As she would lead a discussion or give directions, she would

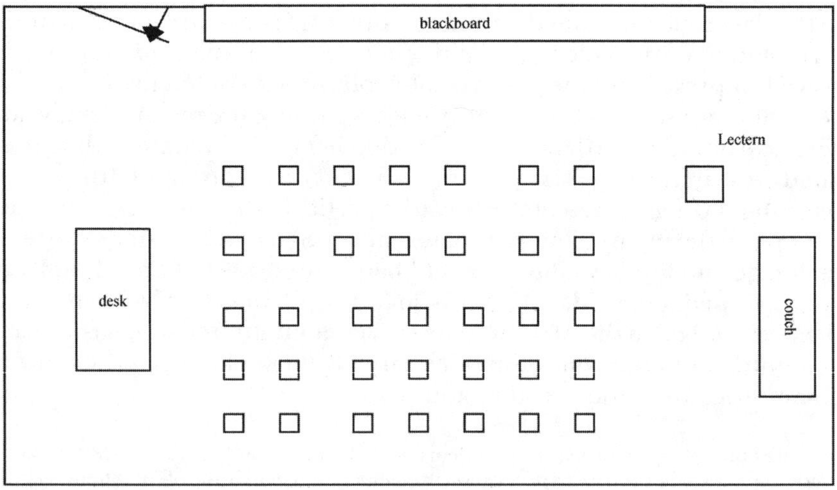

FIG 2.1   Classroom Layout.

walk to the front of the classroom or through the student desks toward one anchor and then migrate back to the other anchor. In brief, although Ms. Wilson was frequently in movement during classroom lessons, the desk and the lectern served as two focal points for directing classroom lessons.

Ms. Wilson began the language arts lesson by stating the task for the class period: to read and analyze the poem *After Winter*. She passed out copies of the poem and directed the class to read it in groups (their desks were already organized in groups of three or four). Each group appointed a designated reader, and that person was to read the poem aloud to the group. Ms. Wilson appointed a reader to those groups who appeared to be having difficulty choosing a reader. After each reader finished the poem, Ms. Wilson directed the class to read the poem silently. Then she read the poem aloud to the class.

After Winter
Sterling Brown

He snuggles his fingers
In the blacker loam
The lean months are done with
The fat to come

His eyes are set
On a bushwood fire
But his heart is soaring
High and higher

Though he stands ragged
An old scarecrow
This is the way
His swift thoughts go,

"Butter beans fo' Clara
Sugar corn fo' Grace
An' fo' de little feller
Runnin' space.

"Radishes and lettuce
Eggplants and beets
Turnips fo' de winter
An' candied sweets.

"Homespun tobacco
Apples in de bin

> *Fo' smokin' an' fo' cider*
> *When de folks drop in."*

He thinks with the winter
His troubles are gone;
Ten acres unplanted
To raise dreams on.

> The lean months are done with,
> The fat to come.
> His hopes, winter wanderers,
> Hasten home.

"Butter beans fo' Clara
Sugar corn fo' Grace
An' fo' de little feller
Runnin' space ..."

After reading the poem aloud, Ms. Wilson asked each group to appoint a designated writer to take notes during their group's discussion. She asked students to discuss in their groups the subject (the main character/narrator) of the poem. Students discussed who the person might be and gave the reasons behind their speculations. Ms. Wilson invited students to share their speculations in a whole-class discussion. The discussion continued until the end of the class period. A graphic representation of the lesson as described in this overview is shown in Table 2.1.

The transcript we discuss, Transcript 2.1, begins about 48 minutes into the 60-minute class period. The class is in the midst of discussing the people in the poem. The transcript was taken from a videotape of the classroom lesson.

TABLE 2.1
Overview of the 7th-Grade Language Arts Lesson

I. Teacher introduces task.

II. Students read the poem in groups.

    Iia. Read poem aloud.

    Iib. Read poem silently.

III. Teacher reads the poem aloud to the class.

IV. Students in groups discuss the main character of the poem.

V. Whole-class discussion of the poem.

Event 2.1 : "We're Talkin' About 1865"

Transcript 2.1 shows some contextualization cues in addition to the words spoken by the teacher and students, but it does not provide a detailed description of the contextualization cues. Each line is a message unit determined by the procedures described in chapter 1. Although we indicate some overlaps in turns, the conversation was not as clean and orderly as might be inferred from the transcript. There were side conversations among students, and shufflings of chairs and feet, among other noises. What we provide in Transcript 2.1 is intended to give an impression of what occurred while also focusing attention on one dimension of what was occurring: the interaction between the teacher and the students.

TRANSCRIPT 2.1

Lines 1–175 of the 7th-Grade Language Arts Lesson

01	Ms. Wilson:	We're talkin' about 1865.
02		And we're talkin' about a period of time when slavery was still instituted ↑
03	Students:	Yes.
04	Ms. Wilson:	Was slavery still instituted? ↑
05	Students:	Yes.
06	Ms. Wilson:	Were Blacks allowed the same type of education as whites ↑
07	Students:	No
08	Theresa:	XXXXXXXX no
09		That's why … ⌐
10	Ms. Wilson:	⌐ [Holds up hand] I'm still making my point
11	Theresa:	OK, go ahead.
12		Just go ahead.
13	Ms. Wilson:	OK,
14		So if we know that slavery was still instituted
15		If we know that African Americans were not afforded the same education as other people
16		Is it a matter that they don't *quote unquote* know any better
17		Or they never had the opportunity to get an education ↑

(continued on next page)

18	Camika:	They never had an opportunity
19	Ms. Wilson:	I'm not asking you *Directed to students calling out responses*
20		I'm asking the person who made comment *Theresa had earlier made the comment Ms. Wilson was referring to, that Black people talked "that way" in 1865 "because they did not know any better"*
21	Theresa:	They didn't have the opportunity
22	Ms. Wilson:	Now.
23		Over a period of time
24		1865 all the way to 1997
25		There are still people who use terms and phrases
26		*De, fo', folks*
27		That are similar to what we read in the poem
28	Theresa:	⌈ Yea but …
29	Ms. Wilson:	⌊ Is that by choice ↑
30	Theresa:	Choice
31	Ms. Wilson:	Or is that because *quote unquote* a lack of knowledge
32		We're not saying they don't know any better because it's very clear that many people speak this way
33		Outside of African Americans
34		[*Janet raises her hand*]
35	Theresa:	XXXXXXX because you have a chance choice
36	Ms. Wilson:	Janet
37	Janet:	I don't think it's choice.
38		I think like they used to it
39		Cuz' like they ancestors it prob'ly runs down
40		⌈ Cuz' I think.
41	Theresa:	⌊ XXXXXXXXXXXXXXXXXXXXXX *Theresa's talking overlaps lines 36–39.*
42	Ms. Wilson:	Theresa I can't hear Janet when you're talking
43	Janet:	They prob'ly talking that way cuz they grandmama prob'ly talked that way and they prob'ly heard it so much
44		I don't think there's a choice.

45	Ms. Wilson:	So you think
46		Over time *Slowly rendered*
47		There is not any choice in how you talk
48		So after awhile you hear your grandmother and your mom and your dad and your cousin and your aunt and you hear it like this all the time
49		You're gonna talk that way ↑
50	Students:	XXXXXXXXXXXXXXXXXX *Many students start to answer at the same time*
51	Ms. Wilson:	Oh Oh
52	*Students stop talking*	
53	Ms. Wilson:	*Points at a student, signaling a turn at talk.* Is it true Camika ↑
54	Camika:	Even though a lot of
55		Even though a lot of people like Africans or whatever talked that way
56		That meant that the white people thought they were better than everyone else
57		If we're talkin' about this point in time when there were slaves and the white people talked all proper
58		Then they probably thought they were better than everyone else
59	Ms. Wilson:	OK
60		So you think it's still an issue of race and still an issue of time
61		Roger you had a comment that I was interested in hearin'
62		But XXXXXX I can hear you over here
63	Roger:	I said I said ummm I said that people the reason why Black people talk like that is because they probably XXXXXXXX
64	Ms. Wilson:	OK
65		How many of you say
66		You can put your hands down because I'm gonna go on my little soapbox now
67		How many of you say that you talk one way when you're in the classroom and when you go home you talk another

(continued on next page)

68		It doesn't matter what that way is
69		I'm not askin' you if whether speak other languages
70		I'm not askin' you whether or not you don't curse when you get home
71		I'm not askin' you the differences
72		But I am askin' you
73		When you come to school
74		When you walk into this classroom particularly
75		You choose to speak one way
76		When you go home | you speak another.
77		How many of you say yes ↑
78	Students:	*Several students raise their hands*
79	Ms. Wilson:	Mandrel *who did not raise his hand*
80		You mean the way you speak in class is the same way you speak at home
81		The same way you speak at church
82		The same way you speak at the club
83		All day long
84	Mandrel:	Yes XXXXXXXXXXXXX
85	Ms. Wilson:	Um ||
86		Alright |
87		Um ||
88		How many of you feel that when you do switch
89		We're gonna call this code-switching *Ms. Wilson makes quote marks with her fingers*
90		When you do switch
91		You do it by choice
92		Or do you actually think *Ding*
93		*I'm in the classroom
94		I will now say this*
95		Or how many of you say that automatically soon as you * fly+* into the classroom your words just change
96		You just know*click*

97	Students:	XXXXXXXXXXXXXX *Many students raise their hands and yell out responses*
98	Ms. Wilson:	OK
99		So this is the clicking group *Ms. Wilson is looking at a group of students*
100		You just go bam *Teacher claps her hands*
101		*I'm in class* Woooo
102		Chad so you mean you actually switch in and out of language yes ↑
103		Give me an example
104	Chad:	XXXXXX switching XXXXXXX
105	Ms. Wilson:	You switch ||
106		You say one thing at school
107		At home you say another
108	Theresa:	You do cause you get in trouble
109	Ms. Wilson:	Does have anything to do with the color of your skin ↑
110	Students:	Nooo
111	Camika:	He wanna be like Black people *under her breath*
112	Ms. Wilson:	But why the recognition Denise ↑
113	Denise:	It all depends how you carry yourself because
114		I mean
115		There some Black people that talk proper and slang and there some white people who talk proper and slang
116		So it all depends if you wanna talk that way
117		You gonna talk that way
118	Ms. Wilson:	OK
119		*What* is proper and what is slang ↑
120		*Help me out*
121		Let me give you a small story
122		You guys
123		Where was I born ↑
124		You guys know this.
125	Camika:	California ↑

(continued on next page)

126	Ms. Wilson:	no
127	Janet:	⌈ New York
128	Student:	⌊ Chicago.
129	Student:	I dunno.
120	Ms. Wilson:	I was born in New York and moved to California.
131	Theresa:	Yea that's where you grew up.
132	Ms. Wilson:	When I moved to California I was teased when I was little because people told me I talked white
133		How many of your ever heard that phrase *you sound white* ↑
134	Students:	XXXXXXXXXX *Many students talk at once and raise hands*
135	Ms. Wilson:	Now
136		How come white people never hear that phrase *you sound white* ↑
137	Camika:	Cause we tell them they sound they wanna be Black
138	Ray:	Cause they do XXXXXXXXXXXXX
139	Theresa:	I've heard *you sound country* but not white
140	Ms. Wilson:	OK
141		John
142		Could you *possibly* explain this concept to me maybe ↑
143		What is "sounding white" …
144	Students:	XXXXXXXXXXXXXX *Many students talk and once and yell out responses*
145	Ms. Wilson:	I'm asking John
146		No ↑
147		You have no idea
148		Who can explain to the concept of sounding white ↑
149	Maria:	OK I have an example
150		When I be at lunch and I say like ⌉
151	Andre:	⌊ When I be *laughs*
152	Ms. Wilson:	*Wait a minute*
153		I'm sorry

154		When you said | when I be | Andre said *when I be ha ha ha* how is that funny ↑
155	Students:	*Many students laugh and make comments*
156	Drake:	That don't make no sense. *Drake's head is on his desk*
157	Ms. Wilson:	Hold on
158		I heard you say I be *Ms. Wilson is looking at Drake*
159		What does I be mean ↑
160		What is that
161	Students	XXXXXXXXXX *Students yelling out*
162	Ray:	Stupid
163	Student:	It's like figure of speech
164	Drake:	When I am *Drake's head is on his desk*
165	Ms. Wilson:	I really wanna hear this because your intellectualism is dazzling me *Ms. Wilson is looking at the whole class and not at Drake.*
166		I mean *I'm dancing now* *Ms. Wilson does a little dance*
167	Drake:	Like when I'm at lunch
168		She says when I be
169	Theresa:	Why are you correcting someone when you say it yourself
170	Ms. Wilson:	Do I ever say that ↑
171		Have I ever said *I be you be he be she be we be * ↑
172	Theresa:	You don't make mistakes
173	Ms. Wilson:	Is it a mistake ↑
174	Theresa:	It's not mistake
175		It's how we talk

Note. A key to transcription symbols can be found in the Appendix.

The line-by-line discourse analysis that follows emphasizes continuity and change in classroom literacy practices. To highlight continuity and change, we need to establish which school literacy practices are being maintained or changed. Doing so is not easy, because what constitutes an "established" classroom literacy practice has more to do with abstractions of the uses of written language than with empirical studies of what actually occurs in classrooms—that is, the established school literacy practices are those shared ways (expectations and standards) for doing reading and writing in classroom lessons held by participants (including stakeholders who may not be present)[7] and, as such, they exist not by the force of their frequency but by the force of their valorization by people (teachers, students, administrators, others) as a framework for evaluating whether classroom reading and writing is occurring. In brief, does what occurs sufficiently match the cultural model of classroom literacy practices that the participants jointly hold? We argue that any instance of a classroom literacy event may sufficiently match the shared cultural model of classroom literacy practices at one level while at other levels it may diverge from the shared cultural model. Thus, in Table 2.2 we provide a graphic representation of continuity and change in the classroom literacy practices enacted in the events captured in Transcript 2.1.

Table 2.2 presents a two-level description of what is occurring in the teacher–student conversation on a message-unit-by-message-unit basis. Each message unit is described at the surface level and at an underlying "argument" level. The conversational function of each message unit at each level is described. The list of conversational functions we use are informed by those listed by Green and Wallat (1981) and Bloome (1989), but we are not limited to those conversational functions. We do not view conversational functions as a set of discrete and mutually exclusive categories; rather, the labels are merely intended to provide a description of how people—teacher and students—are responding to each other. Thus, at the beginning of Table 2.2 at the surface level, the teacher is described as informing the students, they acknowledge the information, the teacher requests additional acknowledgment and acceptance of the information she is providing, and the students provide the desired response. In line 9, a student attempts to initiate a topic and claim the floor, but the teacher responds by holding the floor, asserting her right to determine who has the floor at any point in the conversation. It is not the case that the underlying level is the "real" event or interaction and that the surface level is merely a wrapping, not to be taken seriously. All levels constitute the event, all levels are important to analyze, and the levels interact with each other.

Table 2.2 also displays where knowledge is located. Locating knowledge is a problematic endeavor. Knowledge may have originated in the experi-

---

[7]Parents, school board members, administrators, and members of the general public, among others, also have shared cultural models of classroom reading and writing practices. To various degrees they can also be considered participants in classroom reading and writing events, especially with regard to what counts as doing reading and writing. In brief, although a person might not be immediately present, if what occurs does not sufficiently match the cultural models he or she holds for doing reading and writing, he or she may not view what is occurring as reading and writing and may take action. One way to view the imposition of specific reading and writing programs is as an attempt by individuals outside the classroom to ensure (impose) that their cultural model of reading and writing is enacted in the classroom even if they are not physically present.

TABLE 2.2

Two-Level Line-By-Line Description of Lines 01–167 of Transcript 2.1

Line No.	Speaker(s)	Message Unit	Surface Level		Underlying Level		
			Conversational Function	Location of Knowledge	Conversational Function	Location of Knowledge	Argument Elements
01	Ms. Wilson	We're talkin' about 1865.	Informing	Teacher	Challenging	Teacher	Grounding
02		And we're talkin' about a period of time when slavery was still instituted ↑	Informing	Teacher	Clarifying	Jointly held	Grounding
03	Students	Yes	Acknowledgment	Teacher	Acknowledgment	Jointly held	
04	Ms. Wilson	Was slavery still instituted ↑	Requesting Acknowledgment	Teacher	Establishing a common referent	Jointly held	Grounding
05	Students	Yes	Evaluating/Response	Teacher	Response/Acknowledgment	Jointly held	
06	Ms. Wilson	Were Blacks allowed the same type of education as whites? ↑	Evaluating/Informing/Requesting Acknowledgment	Teacher	Establishing a common premise	Jointly held	Claim
07	Students	No	Acknowledgment	Teacher	Acknowledgment	Jointly held	
08	Theresa	XXXXXXXX no	Acknowledgment	Teacher	Acknowledgment	Jointly held	

(continued on next page)

TABLE 2.2 (continued)

Line No.	Speaker(s)	Message Unit	Surface Level		Underlying Level		
			Conversational Function	*Location of Knowledge*	*Conversational Function*	*Location of Knowledge*	*Argument Elements*
09		That's why	Student initiation of topic/claiming floor	Student	Connecting the supposition to the text and to previous response	Student	Attempting to make a claim
10	Ms. Wilson	*Holds up hand* I'm still making my point	Maintaining floor	Teacher	Maintaining floor/establishing a norm for turns at talk as bounded by the boundaries of an argument of "making my point"		
11	Theresa	OK go ahead	Yielding floor		Providing turn space		
12		Just go ahead					
13	Ms. Wilson	OK	Marking return to previous interaction of line 06		Connecting parts of an argument—as in "therefore"		

#	Speaker	Utterance					
14		So if we know that slavery was still instituted	Repetition of fact	Teacher	Repetition of inference	Jointly held	Backing
15		If we know that African Americans were not afforded the same education as other people	Repetition of fact	Teacher	Repetition of inference	Jointly held	Backing
16		Is it a matter that they don't *quote unquote* know any better	Requesting conclusion	Teacher	Statement in the form of a rhetorical question	Open	Contrastive claims
17		Or they never had the opportunity to get an education ↑	Requesting conclusion	Teacher	Statement in the form of a rhetorical question	Open	Contrastive claims
18	Camika	They never had an opportunity					
19	Ms. Wilson	I'm not asking you	Directing turn-taking	Teacher			
20		I'm asking the person who made comment	Directing turn-taking	Teacher			
21	Theresa	They didn't have the opportunity	Response	Teacher	Acknowledgment	Student	Claim
22	Ms. Wilson	Now	Confirmation/Marking of new interaction	Teacher	Connecting parts of an argument—as in "therefore"		

(continued on next page)

TABLE 2.2 (continued)

Line No.	Speaker(s)	Message Unit	Surface Level		Underlying Level		
			Conversational Function	Location of Knowledge	Conversational Function	Location of Knowledge	Argument Elements
23		Over a period of time	Providing information	Teacher	Stating a premise	Teacher	Grounding
24		1865 all the way to 1997	Providing information	Teacher	Stating a premise	Teacher	Grounding
25		There are still people who use terms and phrases	Providing information	Teacher	Stating a premise	Teacher	Grounding
26		*De, fo', folks*	Providing information	Teacher	Stating a premise	Teacher	Grounding
27		That are similar to what we read in the poem	Providing information	Teacher	Stating a premise	Jointly held	Grounding
28	Theresa	Yea but …	Interruption	Student	Disagreeing with the premise	Student	Challenging assumption implicit in the warrant
29	Ms. Wilson	Is that by choice ↑	Question	Teacher	Statement in the form of a rhetorical question	Open	Contrastive claim
30	Theresa	Choice	Response	Teacher		Student	Claim

	Speaker	Utterance	Move	Source	Function	Participant	Element
31	Ms. Wilson	Or is that because *quote unquote* a lack of knowledge	Ignoring/Question	Teacher	Statement in the form of a rhetorical question	Open	Contrastive claim
32		We're not saying they don't know any better because it's very clear that many people speak this way	Elaborating question	Teacher	Elaboration of claim	Teacher	Rejection of a particular backing, refuting a potential rebuttal, establishing a warrant
33		Outside of African Americans	Elaborating question	Teacher	Elaboration of claim	Teacher	Qualifier
34	Janet	[Janet raises her hand]	Bidding for turn				
35	Theresa	XXXXXXX because you have a chance choice	Response/statement of a moral imperative	School/Assumed shared morality		Student	Warrant
36	Ms. Wilson	Jeannetta	Allocating turn				
37	Janet	I don't think it's choice.	Response	Teacher	Statement	Student	Claim
38		I think like they used to it	Elaboration/justification of response	Teacher	Statement	Student	Warrant
39		Cuz' like they ancestors it prob'ly runs down	Elaboration/justification of response	Teacher	Elaboration	Student	Backing

(continued on next page)

TABLE 2.2 (continued)

Line No.	Speaker(s)	Message Unit	Surface Level		Underlying Level		
			Conversational Function	Location of Knowledge	Conversational Function	Location of Knowledge	Argument Elements
40		Cuz' I think.				Student	Backing
41	Theresa	XXXXXXXXXXXXXX XXXXXXXX					
42	Ms. Wilson	Theresa I can't hear Janet when you're talk-ing	Managing turn-taking		Managing turn-taking		
43	Janet	They prob'ly talking that way cuz they grandmama prob'ly talked that way and they prob'ly heard it so much	Restating justification	Teacher	Restating	Student	Backing
44		I don't think there's a choice.	Restating response	Teacher	Restating	Student	Claim
45	Ms. Wilson	So you think	Initiating a new interaction		Restating argument	Student	
46		Over time	Restating response	Teacher	Restating argument	Student	Backing
47		There is not any choice in how you talk	Restating response	Teacher	Restating argument	Student	Claim

	Speaker	Utterance					Warrant
48		So after awhile you hear your grand-mother and your mom and your dad and your cousin and your aunt and you hear it like this all the time	Restating response	Teacher	Restating argument	Student	Warrant
49		You're gonna talk that way ↑	Restating response	Teacher	Restating argument	Student	Claim
50	Students	XXXXXXXXXXXXXX XXXX					
51	Ms. Wilson	Oh Oh					
52		*Students stop talking*					
53	Ms. Wilson	*Points at a student, signaling a turn at talk.* Is it true Camika ↑	Negating Janet's response/assigning a turn	Teacher	Assigning turn and setting up a response	Student	Challenging claim and backing
54	Camika	Even though a lot of	Partial start				
55		Even though a lot of people like Africans or whatever talked that way	Response	Teacher	Explaining	Jointly held/assumed common knowledge	Backing
56		That meant that the white people thought they were better than everyone else	Response	Teacher	Elaboration	Jointly held/assumed common knowledge	Backing

(continued on next page)

TABLE 2.2 (continued)

Line No.	Speaker(s)	Message Unit	Surface Level		Underlying Level		
			Conversational Function	Location of Knowledge	Conversational Function	Location of Knowledge	Argument Elements
57		If we're talkin' about this point in time when there were slaves and the white people talked all proper	Response	Teacher	Elaboration	Student	Warrant
58		Then they probably thought they were better than everyone else	Response	Teacher	Elaboration	Student	Claim
59	Ms. Wilson	OK	Evaluating/Validating	Teacher	Acknowledging argument		
60		So you think it's still an issue of race and still an issue of time	Validating	Teacher	Rephrasing argument	Student	Warrant
61		Roger you had a comment that I was interested in hearin'	Allocating turn/initiating interaction		Allocating turn/testing an argument		
62		But XXXXXX I can hear you over here					
63	Roger	I said that XXXXXXXXXX					

			Evaluating/ Initiating a new interaction	Teacher	Ending a previous interaction/Initiating a new interaction	Shared experience	
64	Ms. Wilson	OK					
65		How many of you say	Naming interlocutors		Naming interlocutors		
66		You can put your hands down because I'm gonna go on my little soapbox now	Shifting to a new interactional structure		Shifting to a new interactional structure		
67		How many of you say that you talk one way when you're in the classroom and when you go home you talk another	Question	Teacher	Stating an argument	Shared experience	Claim
68		It doesn't matter what that way is	Elaborating question	Teacher	Clarifying the argument	Shared experience	Defining terms
69		I'm not askin' you if whether speak other languages	Elaborating question	Teacher	Clarifying the argument	Shared experience	Defining terms
70		I'm not askin' you whether or not you don't curse when you get home	Elaborating question	Teacher	Clarifying the argument	Shared experience	Defining terms

(continued on next page)

TABLE 2.2 (continued)

Line No.	Speaker(s)	Message Unit	Surface Level			Underlying Level		
			Conversational Function	Location of Knowledge	Conversational Function	Location of Knowledge	Argument Elements
71		I'm not askin' you the differences	Elaborating question	Teacher	Clarifying the argument	Shared experience	Defining terms
72		But I am askin' you	Elaborating question	Teacher	Clarifying the argument	Shared experience	Defining terms
73		When you come to school	Elaborating question	Teacher	Clarifying the argument	Shared experience	Defining terms
74		When you walk into this classroom particularly	Elaborating question	Teacher	Clarifying the argument	Shared experience	Defining terms
75		You choose to speak one way	Elaborating question	Teacher	Clarifying the argument	Shared experience	Defining terms
76		When you go home | you speak another	Elaborating question	Teacher	Clarifying the argument	Shared experience	Defining terms
77		How many of you say yes ↑	Elaborating question	Teacher	Requesting validation of the argument	Shared experience	grounding
78	Students:	*Several students raise their hands*	Response		Confirming the argument	Shared experience	grounding

79	Ms. Wilson	Mandrel *who did not raise his hand*	Allocating a turn	Teacher	Allocating a turn / Student	grounding
80		You mean the way you speak in class is the same way you speak at home	Correcting a wrong answer	Teacher	Challenging a statement of fact / Student	Contrastive grounding
81		The same way you speak at church	Correcting a wrong answer	Teacher	Challenging a statement of fact / Student	Defining terms
82		The same way you speak at the club	Correcting a wrong answer	Teacher	Challenging a statement of fact / Student	Defining terms
83		All day long	Correcting a wrong answer	Teacher	Challenging a statement of fact / Student	Defining terms
84	Mandrel	Yes XXXXXXXXXXXXXXX	Response	Teacher	Asserting a statement of fact, contesting a challenge / Student	Claim
85	Ms. Wilson	Um ||	Turn holder	Teacher	Turn holder	
86		Alright |	Evaluation	Teacher	Acknowledging an argument / Student	
87		Um ||	Turn holder	Teacher	Turn holder	
88		How many of you feel that when you do switch	Correcting student response	Teacher	Beginning a new argument / Student	Warrant
89		We're gonna call this code-switching	Defining	Teacher	Defining / Teacher	Defining

(continued on next page)

TABLE 2.2 (continued)

Line No.	Speaker(s)	Message Unit	Surface Level		Underlying Level		
			Conversational Function	Location of Knowledge	Conversational Function	Location of Knowledge	Argument Elements
90		When you do switch	Restating fact	Teacher	Defining	Student	Warrant
91		You do it by choice	Requesting information	Teacher	Elaborating argument	Open	Contrastive claims
92		Or do you actually think *Ding*	Elaboration of question	Teacher	Elaborating argument	Open	Contrastive claims
93		*I'm in the classroom	Elaboration of question	Teacher	Elaborating argument	Student	Defining claim
94		I will now say this*	Elaboration of question	Teacher	Elaborating argument	Student	Defining claim
95		Or how many of you say that automatically soon as you * fly+* into the classroom your words just change	Elaboration of question	Teacher	Elaborating argument	Student	Defining claim
96		You just know*click*	Elaboration of question	Teacher	Elaborating argument	Student	Defining claim
97	Students	XXXXXXXXXXXXXXX	Response	Teacher	Acknowledging an argument	Student	Claim

#	Speaker	Utterance		Teacher		Student	
98	Ms. Wilson	OK	Evaluating/ initiating a new interaction	Teacher	Connecting one part of an argument to another		
99		So this is the clicking group	Defining students who made correct response	Teacher	Defining		
100		You go bang	Elaborating a question	Teacher	Restating an argument	Student	Warrant
101		*I'm in class*	Elaborating a question	Teacher	Restating an argument	Student	Warrant
102		So you mean you actually switch in and out of language ↑	Elaborating a question	Teacher	Rephrasing an argument	Student	Claim
103		Give me an example	Requesting information	Teacher	Request for grounding of argument	Student	Request for grounding
104	Chad	XXXXXXXXXX switching XXXXXXXX					
105	Ms. Wilson	You switch ||	Stating a fact	Teacher	Restating argument	Student	Claim
106		You say one thing at school	Stating a fact	Teacher	Restating argument	Student	Warrant
107		At home you say another	Stating a fact	Teacher	Restating argument	Student	Warrant

(continued on next page)

TABLE 2.2 (continued)

Line No.	Speaker(s)	Message Unit	Surface Level		Underlying Level		
			Conversational Function	Location of Knowledge	Conversational Function	Location of Knowledge	Argument Elements
108	Theresa	You do cause you get in trouble	Response	Shared folk morality	Side comment	Student	Warrant and rationale
109	Ms. Wilson	Does have anything to do with the color of your skin—	Requesting conclusion	Teacher	Contesting extension of argument to a new premise	Student	Claim
110	Students	Nooo	Response	Teacher	Agreeing	Student	Validating a claim
111	Camika	He wanna be like Black people under her breath	Response	Student	Side comment	Student	Warrant and rationale
112	Ms. Wilson	But, why the XXXXXXX Denise ↑	Elaboration of question	Teacher	Contesting extension of argument to a new premise	Student	Rebuttal
113	Denise	It all depends how you carry yourself because	Response	Shared folk morality	Initiating a topic	Student	Warrant for rebuttal
114		I mean	Response	Shared folk morality	Clarification	Student	

115		There some Black people that talk proper and slang and there some white people who talk proper and slang	Response	Shared folk morality	Elaboration	Student	Warrant
116		So it all depends if you wanna talk that way	Response	Shared folk morality	Repeating a topic	Student	Claim
117		You gonna talk that way	Response	Shared folk morality	Elaboration	Student	Claim
118	Ms. Wilson	OK	Evaluation/Initiation of new interaction	Teacher	Acknowledgment		
119		What is proper and what is slang ↑	Requesting definition	Teacher	Initiating a topic	Student	Defining and backing for a rebuttal
120		*Help me out*	Requesting definition	Teacher	Allocating turns		
121		Let me give you a small story	Shift to a new interactional structure	Teacher	Initiating a narrative		Grounding
122		You guys	Designating potential turn takers	Teacher	Illustrating a counterargument		
123		Where was I born ↑	Requesting information	Teacher	Illustrating a counterargument	Jointly held	Grounding

(continued on next page)

TABLE 2.2 (*continued*)

Line No.	Speaker(s)	Message Unit	Surface Level		Underlying Level		
			Conversational Function	Location of Knowledge	Conversational Function	Location of Knowledge	Argument Elements
124		You guys know this.	Elaborating the question	Teacher	Illustrating a counterargument	Jointly held	Grounding
125	Camika	California ↑	Response	Teacher	Illustrating a counterargument	Jointly held	Grounding
126	Ms. Wilson	no	Evaluating response	Teacher	Illustrating a counterargument	Jointly held	Grounding
127	Janet	New York	Response	Teacher	Illustrating a counterargument	Jointly held	Grounding
128	Student	Chicago	Response	Teacher	Illustrating a counterargument	Jointly held	Grounding
129	Student	I dunno	Response	Teacher	Illustrating a counterargument	Jointly held	Grounding
130	Ms. Wilson	I was born in New York and moved to California.	Evaluation/Giving information	Teacher	Illustrating a counterargument	Jointly held	Grounding
131	Theresa	Yea that's where you grew up	Acknowledgment	Teacher	Illustrating a counterargument	Jointly held	Grounding

	Speaker	Utterance					
132	Ms. Wilson	When I moved to California I was teased when I was little because people told me I talked white	Giving information	Teacher	Illustrating a counterargument	Teacher	Grounding
133		How many of your ever heard that phrase *you sound white* ↑	Requesting information	Students' experience	Illustrating a counterargument	Jointly held	Grounding
134	Students	XXXXXXXXX	Response		Checking that interlocutors are paying attention		
135	Ms. Wilson	Now	Evaluation/New Interaction		Connecting to next phase of the argument		
136		How come white people never hear that phrase *you sound white* ↑	Request for inference	Teacher	Statement of fact/establishing the experiential basis for an argument about "white" language and "Black" language	Teacher	Warrant
137	Camika	Cause we tell them they sound they wanna be Black	Response	Teacher	Agreeing	Student	Warrant

(continued on next page)

TABLE 2.2 (*continued*)

Line No.	Speaker(s)	Message Unit	Surface Level		Underlying Level		
			Conversational Function	Location of Knowledge	Conversational Function	Location of Knowledge	Argument Elements
138	Ray	Cause they do XXXXX	Response			Student	
139	Theresa	I've heard *you sound country* but not white	Response	Teacher	Contesting statement of fact		Grounding
140	Ms. Wilson	OK	Evaluating/ Beginning new interaction	Teacher	Connecting to the next phase of the argument		
141		John	Designating turn		Designating turn		
142		Could you *possibly* explain this concept to me maybe ↑	Requesting for explanation	Teacher	Challenging argument	Student	Seeking backing
143		What is "sounding white"	Request for definition	Teacher	Challenging argument	Student	Seeking backing
144	Students	XXXXXXXXXXXXXX	Response	Teacher			
145	Ms. Wilson	I'm asking John	Designating turn	Teacher	Designating turn		
146		No ↑	Evaluating response	Teacher	Challenging argument	Student	Backing
147		You have no idea	Evaluating response	Teacher	Challenging argument	Student	Backing

148		Who can explain to the concept of sounding white ↑	Request for definition — Teacher	Challenging argument	Student	Seeking backing
149	Maria	OK I have an example	Bidding for a turn	Initiating a narrative	Student	Backing
150		When I be at lunch and I say like	Response	Telling a story	Student	Backing
151	Andre	When I be *laugh*	Interrupting response — Student	Challenging application of an illustration		Shifting the argument
152	Ms. Wilson	*Wait a minute*	Admonishing the interruption of a response — Teacher	Exploring the challenge in line 151		
153		I'm sorry	Politeness marker in shifting the turn from Maria to Andre	Exploring the challenge in line 151		
154		When you said | when I be | Andrew said *when I be ha ha ha*		Exploring the challenge in line 151	Jointly held	Grounding
155	Students	XXXXXXXXXXXXX XXXXX	Side comment	Side comment		
156	Drake	That don't make no sense.	Evaluating response — Rules of standard English	Exploring the challenge in line 151	Student	Evaluating the warrant

(continued on next page)

87

TABLE 2.2 (continued)

Line No.	Speaker(s)	Message Unit	Surface Level		Underlying Level		
			Conversational Function	Location of Knowledge	Conversational Function	Location of Knowledge	Argument Elements
157	Ms. Wilson	Hold on	Evaluating line 151	Teacher	Exploring the challenge in line 151		
158		I heard you say I be Ms. Wilson is looking at Drake	Evaluating a response	Rules of standard English	Exploring the challenge in line 151	Jointly held	Grounding
159		What does I be mean ↑	Requesting a definition	Teacher	Exploring the challenge in line 151	Teacher	Grounding
160		What is that	Reiterating question	Teacher	Opening up a turn at talk	Student	Seeking backing
161	Students	XXXXXXXXXXX					
162	Ray	Stupid	Response	Student	Side comment		
163	Student	It's like figure of speech	Response	Teacher	Informing	Student	Backing
164	Drake	When I am	Response	Teacher	Defining a linguistic form	Student	Grounding

Line	Speaker	Utterance	Function		Function		Analysis
165	Ms. Wilson	I really wanna hear this because your intellectualism is dazzling me	Managing classroom behavior/allocating turns		Locating argument with the students		
166		I mean *I'm dancing now*	Managing classroom behavior/allocating turns		Validating locating argument with the students		
167	Drake	Like when I'm at lunch	Correcting a student response	Teacher	Restarting the argument	Student	Backing
168		She says when I be	Correcting a student response	Teacher	Elaboration	Student	Warrant
169	Theresa	Why are you correcting someone when you say it yourself	Correcting a student	Assumed shared morality	Statement in form of a question	Student	Contesting the argument in lines 167–168 and 151
170	Ms. Wilson	Do I ever say that ↑	Evaluating responses in lines 162, 163, and 164/Requesting information	Teacher	Question	Student	Contesting argument in lines 167–168
171		Have I ever said *I be you be he be he be she be we be * ↑	Requesting information	Teacher	Question	Student	Grounding
172	Theresa	You don't make mistakes	Response	Teacher	Statement	Student	Warrant

(continued on next page)

TABLE 2.2 (continued)

Line No.	Speaker(s)	Message Unit	Surface Level			Underlying Level		
			Conversational Function	Location of Knowledge		Conversational Function	Location of Knowledge	Argument Elements
173	Ms. Wilson	Is it a mistake ↑	Evaluating response/Requesting judgment	Teacher		Question	Teacher	Contesting the warrant
174	Theresa	It's not mistake	Response			Statement	Student	Transforming contesting in line 169 to a claim
175		It's how we talk	Elaboration of response	Assertion of moral justification		Statement	Student	Warrant for claim in line 169

ence of a particular student, but once that experience is made public the knowledge ceases to be located solely in that individual student. It can then be viewed as publicly or jointly held. One might also distinguish the location of knowledge from the location of the authority for knowledge. A student might state that people talk in a particular manner because that was how their parents taught them to talk, but it might be the teacher who authorizes that knowledge. In our analysis of Transcript 2.1, provided in Table 2.2, we found that the location of knowledge depended, in part, on what assumptions were made about what was happening in the lesson at a particular point. Two students in the same lesson but holding different views about what was happening in that lesson at a particular point might hold different assumptions about the location of knowledge at that point in the lesson. Indeed, we often found that the location of knowledge did vary depending on whether the interpretation was given at the surface level or at an underlying argument level. We also found that the location or locations of knowledge at a particular point might be determined only after examining how interlocutors reacted to the message unit. Furthermore, sometimes the location of knowledge at a particular point shifted as the lesson evolved and as subsequent interactions redefined the location (i.e., the location of knowledge was indeterminate; cf. Bloome, 1993). Multiple and differing views on the location of knowledge become a methodological problem only if researchers assume that knowledge has one "true" location. We do not make such an assumption. Because we view knowledge as continuously contested, dynamic, and indeterminate, we find the notion of multiple, parallel, and even competing locations of knowledge consistent with the social dynamics found in numerous classroom literacy events.

In our view, it is not the location of knowledge per se that constitutes continuity or change in a classroom literacy practice but rather the location of knowledge invoked within an interactional structure. For example, it is a well-established instructional practice to solicit students' background knowledge prior to teaching new knowledge. In doing so, one might claim that knowledge is located with the student and/or is a merging of academic knowledge and student knowledge. Some researchers might therefore characterize such an instructional practice as student centered and indicative of a change in traditional classroom literacy practices by relocating knowledge from teachers, textbooks, and authoritative academic sources to students. However, we argue that merely soliciting student knowledge does not in itself suggest a change in "established" classroom literacy practices, although doing so might be a novel move. Inasmuch as the solicitation of student knowledge is merely a tactic for teaching authoritative academic knowledge and skills, we do not view such instructional practices as representing a change in given classroom literacy practices. However, if student knowledge and experience are solicited for use as validation of academic knowledge, an inverse of the relationship of the two locations of knowledge, then there might be a substantive change in the nature of classroom literacy practices. In sum, continuity and change in classroom literacy practices may occur at multiple levels; analysis of classroom literacy practices therefore also needs to occur at multiple levels.

In the description that follows, Transcript 2.1 and Table 2.2 are narrated line by line, at a surface level and an underlying level. The surface-level narration describes the interactional moves that the teacher and students make in order to display those interactional forms that constitute "doing lesson"; that is, they create a public performance that matches the cultural performance models that they hold, and that members of the broader culture hold, for what counts as "doing classroom literacy instruction."

What we label as the *underlying* argument level describes the joint teacher and student construction of an argument (an enacted system of claims, warrants, reasons, groundings, and backings) about the relationship among language, race, and education, an argument validated not by its performance but by how the participants take up the substance (the system of claims, warrants reasons, groundings, and backings) of what is said and by what structures of coherence they use to connect ideas (the structure of the ideational content). In describing the construction of an argument, we adapt terminology offered by Ramage, Bean, and Johnson (2001), which is based on Toulmin's (1958) discussion of argument. Ramage et al. described seven elements of an argument: (a) the claim or premise, (b) the stated reason, (c) grounds or evidence supporting the claim, (d) the warrant, (e) backing for the warrant, (f) conditions of rebuttal, and (g) the qualifier. We found that there were difficulties directly applying this terminology to arguments that are constructed through classroom interaction (see Eemeron, Grootendorst, Jackson, & Jacobs, 1997, for a discussion of the analysis of argumentation embedded in conversational interaction). For example, in Table 2.2 Ms. Wilson often poses two contrastive claims to the class and asks students to provide and examine the stated reasons, warrants, and grounding of each. Sometimes, attention is focused on the definitional aspects of a warrant rather than on its backing or grounding, or what at first appears to be a discussion of the stated reason for a claim evolves into a discussion of another claim. Thus, rather than treat Ramage et al.'s terminology as fixed and mutually exclusive categories, we use the terminology as a heuristic to help describe what is occurring at the level of constructing an argument. We also found that there were differences as to which term (*claim, warrant, grounding*, etc.) different people would use to describe what was occurring at a particular point in the transcript. What one person would label a *claim* another would label a *warrant*. Such differences depended in part on whether a message unit was being viewed at the moment of its utterance or from a post hoc analysis. Given these difficulties of description, it did not seem reasonable to describe the argument level as a set of discrete and stable elements. Instead, we describe the argument level to highlight a dimension of the classroom conversation that might otherwise not be apparent. It is the presence of the dimension itself, rather than the presence of specific or discrete elements of an argument, that concerns us.

As suggested through our analysis of the underlying argument level, the argument was constructed in a manner that problematized easy, formulaic, and given understandings of language, education, and race. The terminology provided by Ramage et al. (2001)—and indeed most discussions of the rhetorical construction of an argument—is based on the assumption of presenting a coherent unproblematized argument. Thus, in our analysis of the transcript, rather than following the underlying assumptions of a categorical system, such as that offered by Ramage et al., we followed as best we could what was happening in the classroom conversation. To do so, we had to reject the procedure used frequently in educational research that compares what is happening in a classroom conversation to an external frame (e.g., a framework for constructing an argument) and notes deviations as a lack or deficit. Through recursive processes of analysis, we attempted to understand what it is that the teacher and her students were constructing. In Transcript 2.1, part of what they are constructing is the problematization of the relationship among language, education, and race.

In brief, at the surface level we examined how Ms. Wilson and her students act and react to each other in terms of the performance of classroom literacy lessons (doing classroom reading and writing), whereas at the underlying argument level we examined how Ms. Wilson and her students act and react to each other as they problematized how language, race, education, and power operate in their world (acting on their world). Although an argument can of course be a type of cultural model,[8] what we argue in the narrative analysis that accompanies Table 2.2 is that the particular argument Ms. Wilson and her students create is not the enactment of a given classroom literacy practice but rather adaptations of school literacy practices and, as such, is the creation of a change in "established" classroom literacy practices. Part of the adaptations concern where knowledge is located and the problematizing of given understandings of their world. More important than the question of whether what is occurring at the underlying level is a transformation or adaptation of "established" classroom literacy practices, however, is recognition that what they are doing is acting on the world by interrogating it, re-representing it, and problematizing it. The tension, therefore, is between accepting the world as given (including one's place within it) and acting on it to change.

---

[8]Ramage et al. (2001) similarly suggested in their discussion of a Rogerian argument, that arguments are cultural practices. They noted that some people view argument structures in gendered terms, with some argument structures being associated with male rhetoric.

The segment of the lesson represented in Transcript 2.1 and in Table 2.2 begins with Ms. Wilson telling the students that the poem is set in the year 1865. In doing so, she is providing them with additional information. She does so by asking a question; the rising tone at the end of line 02 signals the question. It may be that her question is a check of student attention and engagement rather than a request for agreement or disagreement. Regardless, the students give an affirmative answer that is implicitly evaluated as correct (through ellipses) as Ms. Wilson repeats the question and receives the same response. She then moves on to another question, gets an affirmative answer (it is an affirmative answer in the sense that the students agree with her, although the actual answer is "no"). At one level, the teacher and students are enacting a series of overlapping I-R-E sequences. Knowledge is located with the teacher, and the students are acknowledging that the teacher is providing knowledge.

An examination of the same lines at an underlying level suggests a different interpretation. Lines 01, 02, and 03 are viewed as challenging the interpretations of the poem that the students have already produced and publicly displayed. Ms. Wilson is establishing a conditional premise from which to create an argument: "If the time period of the setting of the poem was 1865, then ..." Of course, given that Ms. Wilson is establishing the conditional premise, it might be better viewed as data (or grounding) that Ms. Wilson and students can use to establish claims. Viewed at this level, the teacher is establishing a common grounding that guides (limits) arguments about the meaning of the poem. In this sense, knowledge about the poem is jointly and publicly held rather than being located solely in the teacher, although the authority for the grounding lies with the teacher. Support for such a view of the instructional conversation can be found in line 10, in which Ms. Wilson says "I'm still making my point." She says this in response to a student who tries to take the floor and create an argument by connecting the grounding (that the poem is set in 1865) with previous claims. Ms. Wilson does not allow the student to complete an alternative argument at this point in the instructional conversation, and in so doing she not only maintains control of the floor (which is the contribution at the surface level) but also establishes interactional norms for taking and holding a turn at talk, namely, that a person gets to make his or her argument before needing to yield the floor. Such a norm also comes into play later in the instructional conversation, when one of the students is making an argument and is interrupted by another student (line 151). At the surface level, line 10 appears to shift the location of knowledge from the student back to the teacher; however, at the underlying level line 10 does not shift the location of knowledge but merely maintains it as a set of jointly held data or grounding. The differences in what is happening at the surface level and at the underlying level can be seen in the side-by-side comparisons in Table 2.2.

At the surface level, lines 6 through 17 are Ms. Wilson's attempt to initiate (I) an interaction that opens a slot for a student response (R; line 21), to which she gives an implicit positive evaluation (E) through ellipses (line 22). However, at the underlying level, she can be viewed as making visible the warrant for a later claim (lines 16–22) and as connecting the argument being made to previous arguments. Line 16—"don't *quote unquote* *know* any better"—involves the use of a colloquialism that posits ignorance as an inherent condition of a person or people. Thus, in lines 16 and 17 Ms. Wilson is asking students to take either the nature or nurture argument with regard to language use. She does not follow up on the students' response to the choice she gave them; it becomes an accepted warrant for future claims.

Line 22, "now," both distinguishes one interactional unit and topic from another (which is how it might be viewed at the surface level) and, at the underlying level, can be viewed as signaling a connection among parts of an argument, various groundings repeated in lines 23 through 27. Ms. Wilson restates the groundings she previously made public, raises shared experience as a way to warrant a premise (about how people talked and talk), and connects the warrants and groundings to the poem (lines 26 and 27). In so doing, she can be viewed as modeling how to establish warrants and groundings for a claim (in this case, it is through shared experience and through illustration). Line 28, at the underlying level, can be viewed as a student contesting the warrants and claims that Ms. Wilson is making. At the surface level, line 28 is an unauthorized interruption negated by Ms. Wilson producing another request that closes out the student's interruption. In brief, she has not allowed the interruption to be connected to any part of the conversation.

Across lines 29, 31, 32, and 33, at the surface level, Ms. Wilson is producing an initiation (I) that will be followed by student responses (R) in lines 35, 37, 38, 39, 40, 41, 43, and 44, which are evaluated (E) in lines 45 through 49 (which can be viewed as a kind of "revoicing"). However, something else may be happening at the underlying level. What appears to be a question because of the intonation pattern of the message unit may also be a rhetorical question establishing a warrant about the relationships of language, race, education, and choice. Ms. Wilson, in lines 32 and 33, is separating the way people speak from being an inherent part of their race.

In this interactional unit (lines 29–49), at the underlying level, the teacher is problematizing the issue of choice and education. "Choice" is a moral issue—that is, analysis of previous lessons, and of students' statements in earlier segments of this lesson, show that students view "choice" as a moral issue; a person has a "choice" to speak properly or not, to act properly or not, and so forth. Similarly, the teacher has often associated "choice" with morality. For example, in talking with the students about homework, the teacher frequently told them that they made the "choice" not to do their homework and thus the consequences of that "choice" are of their own making (see lines 113–117 in Transcript 2.1 and Table 2.2). However, "choice" in sociolinguistic terms can exist at multiple levels. One can make a deliberate and conscious choice to use a particular phrase or word, but one may also choose to use a different register because of a change in the interpersonal setting, and such a choice may be less than deliberate or conscious. Ms. Wilson invokes such a sociolinguistic view of choice in lines 67 through 107 by asking the students whether they switch their language when they enter the classroom and whether they are conscious of doing so at the time (she contrasts "choice" as a deliberate, conscious activity with an automatic response in lines 91 and 92 in Transcript 2.1 and Table 2.2). Janet picks up on the issue of choice in lines 37 to 44. At the surface level, Janet is providing a response to the question (I) that Ms. Wilson produced in lines 22 through 33. However, a close look at what Janet has produced shows that she is making an argument—she is claiming that the people did not and do not have a choice because of how they were raised. She assumes, and takes as reasonable and shared common sense, that how one is raised precludes choice in the way people speak and that therefore there is no "choice." In brief, Janet produces a warrant with backing.

One can see in Table 2.2 that at the underlying level, by making the claim and its warrants public, they become joint knowledge and thus are open and available for interrogation by anyone. Thus, in lines 66 to 77, when at the surface level it appears that Ms. Wilson is asking a question, at the underlying level she is clarifying an argument, and when some of the students challenge the argument by denying an assumption about shared experience (lines 78 and 79), she challenges what the students have offered as experiential data or the grounding.

At the underlying level, in line 119 and then on occasion throughout the lesson, Ms. Wilson engages the students in a series of deconstructions of oppositional pairs (proper/slang, talking white/talking Black). Doing so is connected to previous arguments, including challenging the representation of experience; the relationship of language, race, and education; and what constitutes "choice" in language variation. Yet, at the surface level, teacher–student interaction could be described as a series of I-R-E sequences.

The interrogation of language continues and is highlighted in lines 137 through 167. Ms. Wilson begins by asking John (who is white) to explain the concept of sounding white (lines 141–143). This may appear to be a question requiring an answer (a surface-level interpretation), but it can also be interpreted as a challenge to the validity of the concept of "sounding white" (an underlying-level interpretation). John indicates (through nonverbal behavior off camera) that he does not know, and Maria provides an answer by offering an autobiographical story starting at line 149. She is interrupted by Andre at line 151 who, as an aside, mocks Maria's use of the habitual *be* in line 150. It may be the case that Andre did not intend his line to interrupt Maria's story, but he is heard by Ms. Wilson, who responds to his interruption.

There are at least two ways to interpret what happens after Andre's interruption. One interpretation is that the teacher is managing errant behavior. Andre was rude and talked out of turn, and he mocked a classmate. The other students' responses to Andre in lines 156, 161, 162, and 164 support such a view. They criticize Andre for not making sense and for being hypocritical.

However, at the underlying level, Ms. Wilson is exploring and challenging the implicit argument that Andre made. Andre's argument might be inferred as questioning the legitimacy of Maria's story as warranting a particular claim, a claim about the unfair nature of accusing someone of "talking white," because Maria uses a language form associated with "talking Black." By "talking Black," Maria, according to the argument we might infer from Andre's comment, has either invalidated the data she is presenting (because she does "talk Black"), or she has invalidated her claim to authority, because "talking Black" is not associated with authority.

Ms. Wilson asks Andre—and, by implication, the rest of the students (cf. Bloome & Theodorou, 1988)—what "I be" means. The answer they give her is based on a framework of proper versus improper language. They state that "I be" is synonymous with the "proper" form "I am." From a sociolinguistic framework, the students have overlooked much of the semantic content of "I be" (its reference to a habitual happening) and focus solely on its deficient use in contrast to standard English. In so doing, they give "I am" authority, an authority that lies outside of themselves or the teacher. In lines 170 through 175, Ms. Wilson raises questions about the association of authority with a form of language by asking the students whether she uses the form "I be." At an underlying level, this move simultaneously raises two important questions about making an argument about language. What data can and should be brought to bear in making an argument (e.g., should the teacher's use of language be considered in warranting a claim)? Also, what and who counts as authority in making a claim or in presenting data?

Concluding Comments on the 7th-Grade Language Arts Lesson

Ms. Wilson deliberately chose the poem *After Winter* because she could use it as a means of provoking a discussion about language. The discussion did not happen by chance, although the specific topics, stories, and arguments could not have been predicted. Ms. Wilson engaged the students in using the reading of a poem as part of a classroom literacy lesson in a way that is different from dominant classroom literacy practices. The usual classroom practice for reading a poem is to focus on the interaction of a reader with the text of the poem. Whether one asks about the meaning of a line or about what feeling or image a poem evokes, at the center of the reading practice is the interaction of the reader and the written text. Even if one allows for the mediating influence of student background or context, the underlying cultural model of what the reading of a poem is focuses on the interaction between the reader and the text. However, although the teacher begins this lesson with classroom literacy practices that focus on reader–text interaction, the lesson moves away from that cultural model, and the text of the poem becomes a tool for engaging an analysis of the worlds in which the teacher and the students live. The poem in and of itself is not important—it is a backdrop for a discussion about language variations and race. Ms. Wilson presents the poem not for the purpose of explication or discussing rhythm, or even as means of teaching her students how to read (at least as learning to read is traditionally defined), but rather as a vehicle for understanding the world and oneself by confronting taken-for-granted and dominant assumptions about language, race, and people. Her questions are not about the content of the poem per se, or what feelings were invoked by the poem, but ones that require students to reflect on their own experiences and sociocultural histories. The poem is useful to the extent that it initiates and supports such an analysis. She problematizes and transforms the language arts curriculum by locating knowledge in and around people and their experiences and by discussing macro and micro level language issues as opposed to grammar and punctuation. Thus, an analysis of the poem as a coherent text to determine or construct a meaning for it is displaced by its usefulness in what Freire and Macedo (1987) called *reading the world*:[9]

> Reading the world always precedes reading the word, and reading the word implies continually reading the world.... In a way, however we can go further and say that reading the word is not preceded merely by reading the world, but by a certain form of *writing* it or *rewriting* it, that is, of transforming it by means of conscious, practical work. For me this dynamic movement is central to the literacy process. (p. 35, original emphases)

Inasmuch as analyses of the classroom literacy practices over time in this classroom show a consistent pattern in the use of literary text to prompt analysis of the worlds in which the students and teacher live and the ways in which it is represented, one could be argued that what the teacher is doing is providing the students with a model of how to read that contrasts with the cultural models of classroom literacy practices that dominate much schooling. She presents this model explicitly at the end of the lesson, saying:

---

[9]Although there are differences in the instructional methodology of Freire (1970/1995) and Ms. Wilson, one could argue for similarities—for example, the selection of lexical items for dialogue and analysis that are significant to the students' daily lives, the use of lexical items for reflection on the students' world, and centering the pedagogy around dialogue between teacher and students (eschewing so-called "banking:" models).

Hold on, hold on hold on
Whatever it is I want you to marinate on your thoughts and then
Think about yourself in relationship to your comments.
Use
A lot of you are making excellent comments but they are devoid of you as a
person.
It's very easy to make generalizations about people or about other people
when you're able to take yourself out of it.
But when you put yourself back into your statements,
put yourself in relationship to your comments you're making,
and then see if the comment still works.

CONCLUDING COMMENTS

In this chapter, we have shown that analysis of classroom literacy practices involves more than listing the literacy practices in the classroom being studied. We also have shown the importance of multiple-level analysis, and especially of describing what is happening in a classroom by examining both structure and substance. In the analysis presented in this chapter, there were at least two concurrent levels. It may have been that the students and teacher were engaged at both levels throughout or that, at times, different students and the teacher moved across levels. Although we do not claim that all classroom literacy events involve multiple levels in the way that the instructional conversation described in this chapter did, we would argue that as a matter of methodology, attention is requisite to the possibility of multiple levels of a literacy events (by *possibility* we mean as an interactionally constructed resource for creating meaning and social significance).

We have argued that classroom literacy practices cannot be understand in isolation but rather need to be located within the context of the events in which they occur and within the historical locations of those events; that is, classroom literacy practices need to be understood as part of a process of continuity and change over time and place. Both continuity and change require work; people in interaction with each other must interactionally work to construct continuity and similarly so with change.

We have suggested that any cultural practice is inherently at a nexus of continuity and change. The key question for researchers involved in discourse analysis of classroom literacy events is: What are the dimensions of continuity and change within a particular classroom literacy event? Although a researcher might be informed by previous scholarship on classroom literacy practices, it is through exploration of the multiple contexts of classroom literacy events and through detailed analysis of the classroom literacy practices themselves that dimensions of continuity and change can be identified. This may require multiple "false starts" and recurrent analysis. It may also require collaboration with teachers and students in reviewing videotaped events or other classroom data. It is also important to note that in identifying dimensions of continuity and change, researchers are identifying not *the* dimensions of continuity and change but only a subset—or, perhaps more accurately stated, only one perspective on the dimensions of continuity and change.

We have discussed in this chapter various tools for engaging in a moment-by-moment discourse analysis of classroom literacy events. In the analysis presented in this chapter we have used transcripts, multilevel transcript descriptions showing interactional structure juxtaposed with argument structure, and graphic–symbolic maps that displayed the locations of knowledge across the lesson at both the surface level and an underlying level. These tools were adaptations of tools developed by Green and Wallat (1981), Bloome and Theodorou (1988), and Bloome (1989), among others. We argue that it is almost always the case that a previously existing tool must be adapted to each new research endeavor. As the research questions change, and as what is occurring in each classroom varies (and thus as the demands of description change), the researchers' intimacy with what is occurring in the classroom needs to guide the adaptation of existing tools and the creation of new tools.

Microethnographic Discourse Analysis and the Exploration of Social Identity in Classroom Language and Literacy Events

In this chapter we use a microethnographic approach to discourse analysis to illuminate issues of social identity in classroom language and literacy events. *Social identity* has many meanings. Traditionally, social identity has been used to refer to the social group to which an individuabelongs, such as an ethnic group, gender, racial group, economic class, and so on. Within a classroom, a student's social identity might also include membership in a reading group or a friendship group. A student might have a social identity as a "top student," a "troublemaker," a "teacher's pet," and so on. *Social identity* has recently been used to describe more subtle, situated, and dynamic social relationships. Instead of fixed, predetermined, and stable, social identities (also described as *social positions*) are viewed as being constructed through the interactions people have with each other (sometimes referred to as *social positioning*) and as a consequence of the evolving social structures of social institutions.

In this chapter we focus on how microethnographic analysis can contribute to a better understanding of the dynamics of social identity in and through classroom language and literacy events—that is, how microethnographic analysis can help theorize the dynamics of social identity and the relationship of social identity to classrooms and to literacy events and practices. Stated simply, we are interested in how participation in classroom language and literacy events affects "who you are" and how "who you are" affects your participation in classroom language and literacy events.

As we have described in chapters 1 and 2, it is necessary to work back and forth across theoretical concerns, methodological issues, and findings, and we have found this to be the case with regard to the discourse analysis of social identity in classroom language and literacy events. Therefore, we have organized this chapter to reflect the recursive processes involved in microethnographic discourse analysis. We take the reader through the recursive process, beginning with a discussion of theoretical and methodological issues (what we call *Round 1*). We then shift to a microethnographic analysis of a storytelling event in a kindergarten, followed by a microethnographic analysis of three related events in a 6th-grade social studies/language arts lesson. We then return to a discussion of theoretical and methodological issues (what we call *Round 2*). By organizing the chapter in this manner, we illustrate how a recursive process can identify new questions and issues to explore and how it can lead to reinterpretations of data. The organization of the chapter emphasizes the importance of recursive design as a part of the microethnographic discourse analysis of classroom language and literacy events.

THEORETICAL ISSUES ROUND 1: SOCIAL IDENTITY AS APPELLATION AND PROCESS

One way to view social identity is as an appellation indicating membership in a particular social group or a social position within a social institution or social group. Thus, social identity would include appellations such as Jew, woman, middle class, student, teacher, banker, parent, quarterback, vice president, or some combination of these. For some theorists, social identities such as these are similar to various roles that a person might assume, metaphorically acting out a role like an actor in a dramatic production, with the real person hidden underneath the roles. At different times, a person/actor might act out different roles.

However, other scholars reject the dualism implied in this view of social identity (e.g., Butler, 1990; Hall, 1990, 1996; Hall & Gay, 1996). They claim instead that social identity defines the person, even if those definitions are multiple and conflicting and vary across situations. There is no "real" person hiding underneath various roles, waiting to express itself. There is no separation of the material existence of the body, social interaction, the social group, situation, social identity, and the person. How people interact with others, how people are located historically and geographically[1]—these visible features of social life simultaneously define social identity and who and what people are.[2] Thus, one does not merely act out the drama-

---

[1]By *geographical location* we are referring to more than a person's street address, city, and country; we are also referring to the social institutions in which people are located.

[2]The rejection of dualism does not necessarily equate to a rejection of alienation; rather, *alienation* is redefined as derivative of social, economic, and historical processes (cf. Marx, 1998)

talurgical role of being a Jew, a woman, and a teacher; in a particular situation one is a Jew, a woman, and a teacher.

So far the theoretical issues we have raised with regard to social identity concern the relationship between an appellation of social identity and cultural ideologies. However, the process of appellation itself is a complex, dynamic, and problematic one. What is meant by an appellation such as Jew, woman, and teacher changes and is negotiated, and the assignment of these social identity appellations and their meanings are often contested. For example, does the appellation of Jew mean membership in a religious, cultural, ethnic, or biological group? Who decides? How is a decision made? Is it only in some formal or legalistic process, well defined and bounded, or is it assigned through how people act and react to each other in a broad range of informal and everyday situations? When and where does the appellation apply? Similar questions can and have been asked about the social identity of teacher. Is it just a job classification, or is it a social identity both within a social institution (school) and across social institutions? Does one maintain the social identity of teacher in one's family? In government? As a patient in health institutions? In romantic and sexual domains?[3] Does the social identity of teacher depend on the existence of persons who take on the social identity of student? Does it require proximity of social processes defined as "teaching" and "learning"?

As the preceding questions suggest, part of the difficulty with treating social identity as fundamentally an appellation is that doing so obfuscates the social processes involved in the production, evolution, and use of social identity. Rather than focusing on labels per se, attention can be focused on the processes involved in labeling and on the functions that labels provide (cf. Kress, 1996; Reisigl & Wodak, 2001; Rymes, 2001; Van Leeuwen, 1996). Among the functions labels provide are inclusion and exclusion (a member of the group or not a member of the group; see Rymes, 2001), backgrounding (a peripheral member of the group), designation of histories and social relationships, suppression (no existence of a social actor), impersonalization (representing someone or a group without the quality of being human), relationship (an identity based on a relationship to another), and abstraction (identity based on a quality associated with the person or group), among others (cf. Van Leeuwen, 1993, 1996).

The processes through which social identities are named and constituted are language processes; that is, it is through the use of language that people name, construct, contest, and negotiate social identities. Analysis of social identity, therefore, requires attention to language use. Building on Van Leeuwen's work, Reisigl and Wodak (2001) described how the process of predication is an essential part of the presentation of self and others.

---

[3]See Mitchell and Weber (1999) for a discussion of teacher identity and a discussion of teachers and sexuality.

"Predication" is the very basic process and result of linguistically assigning qualities to persons, animals, objects, events, actions and social phenomena. Through predication, persons, things, events and practices are specified and characterized with respect to quality, quantity, space, time and so on. Predications are linguistically more or less evaluative (deprecatory or appreciative), explicit or implicit and—like reference and argumentation—specific or vague/evasive. Among other things, predicational strategies are mainly realised by specific forms of *reference* (based on explicit denotation as well as on more or less implicit connotation), by *attributes* (in the form of adjectives, appositions, prepositional phrases, relative clauses, conjunctional clauses, infinitive clauses and participial clauses or groups) by *predicates* or *predicative nouns/adjectives/pronouns*, by *collocations*, by explicit *comparisons*, *similes*, *metaphors* and other *rhetorical figures* (including *metonymies, hyperboles, litotes* and *euphemisms*) and by more or less implicit *allusions, evocations* and *presuppositions/implications*. (pp. 54–55)

Labeling a social identity is a social and linguistic move, a move to establish a sense of permanence by establishing a shared (and named) category with presumably shared boundaries. The attempt to create a sense of permanence may apply to either the person being labeled or to the social structure from which the social identity was derived. For example, when school officials label students as "Black," "white," "Hispanic," and so on, they are ascribing to students social identities intended to be permanent, and at the same time they are implicitly giving a sense of permanence to the social structure based on race and ethnicity. Of course, such moves may be contested. Students may protest such labeling because it does not apply (e.g., they may have multiple racial–ethnic identities and therefore not fit any of the categories) or because they disagree with a social policy that organizes people in terms of racial–ethnic identities. This is merely to say that although labeling may attempt to give a set of social identities a sense of permanence, it does not necessarily mean that either those social identities, or the social structure from which they were derived, will be permanent. Over time, the boundaries of an appellation may change (e.g., what counts as being "Black," "white," or "Hispanic" may change), the appellation itself may evolve and change, or, the social structure that generated the appellations might change (with the consequence of changing the meaningfulness and the use of the appellations of the social identities).

Beyond social identities with appellations are social identities that are not named. Consider a classroom in which the teacher has asked the students to sit in a group and read a poem silently. Assume that most of the students follow the teacher's directions but that a small number of students do not and that their behavior is visible to many, if not all, of the students. There is no extant appellation for this group of noncooperating students or for the others who observe them, yet their existence as two different social groups is evident as the teacher calls out "Those of you who aren't reading need to get going, and the rest of you need to put your eyes on the poem." Such social identities may lack a sense of permanence but nonetheless be powerful in orienting social behavior, assigning morality, and asserting a social structure. For example, by dividing the students into a group of cooperating students and a group of noncooperating students, the teacher is asserting a social structure based on a hierarchy of cooperative participation. The noncooperating students have been positioned as errant, as operating outside of the moral bounds of the reading group, and as at risk of negative consequences because of their membership in that social group.

These theoretical issues raise a series of methodological warrants, constraints, and complexities. Our discussion focuses attention on the processes involved in appellation; the relationship among social identity, social structure, cultural ideology, and personhood; and the tension between situated and evolving social identities and moves to promote permanence.

METHODOLOGICAL ISSUES

In this section we focus on three methodological issues: (a) the movement from the "givens" of social identity appellations as expressed in social theories to the processes of face-to-face interaction, and vice versa; (b) identification of the discourse processes involved in the production, evolution, and use of social identities; and (c) capturing, describing, and labeling social identities as they evolve within an event.

Among the most frequently used "givens" of social identity are the categories of race, ethnicity, gender, and class. These four categories are frequently treated as inherent to the human condition, as if they need no explanation as to what they are or how they are defined. In numerous studies, researchers begin with assigning these social identities to the people participating in the study. Then, findings are related to these given categories of social identity. Consistent with our earlier theoretical discussion, we reject such an uncritical acceptance of these categories of social identity and at the same time reject the claims of neoconservatives who argue that race, ethnicity, gender, and class do not matter and in fact do not exist.[4] In brief, we hold that racial, ethnic, gender, and class identities are social constructions (cf. Essed & Goldberg, 2002; Goldberg, 1990; Marx, 1998; Outlaw, 1990; Reisigl & Wodak, 2001). These social constructions, however, are not ethereal; neither are they matters of whim that an individual can change, the way one changes one's necktie or brand of soap. Rather, like social iden-

---

[4]A detailed discussion of the complexities and historical issues involved in the assignment of racial, ethnic, gender, and class identities is beyond the scope of this chapter. We refer readers to Goldberg (1990), Reisigl and Wodak (2001), Stavans (2001), and hooks (1994).

tities in general, they are material; they are built into how people act and react to each other; into social and governmental policy (Marx, 1998; Reisigl
& Wodak, 2001); into the architecture of the buildings and open spaces we
inhabit; into our social institutions of law, family, religion, business, health,
education, science, and so on. They are also built into the literacy practices
that dominate our social institutions, including schools.

We argue that two of the dynamics that distinguish "given" social identities such as race, ethnicity, gender, and class from other identities, such
as friend, good reader, author, problem child, and so on, are (a) the ubiquity and hegemony of the categories of race, gender, ethnicity, and class in
so many countries across the continents and (b) the vehemence with which
the categories of race, gender, ethnicity, and class are maintained and
their sense of permanence (including the maintenance of the rationale for
the accompanying inequalities, inequities, and suffering; cf. Balibar,
1990; Goldberg, 1990; Marx, 1998). Yet, we would claim that even given
the ubiquity and vehemence of the given categories of race, ethnicity, gender, and class, there has been resistance to these categories, and they have
been evolving as a result of people's resistance to how these categories
have been defined and of how people have lived their daily lives (Outlaw,
1990; Stavans, 2001).

The difficulty for researchers is that "given" categories of social identity
exist in the settings and situations being studied and in the traditions and
protocols of research. Schools use given categories of race, gender, and class
to describe students and teachers with a series of concomitant qualities.
Sometimes they get these given categories from folk theories of social life,
but others take them from the research and scholarly community. Regardless, these given categories are part of the social scenes and social interactions being analyzed, and a discourse analysis needs to take account of these
categories of social identity and that they are "given."

Researchers engaged in microethnographic analysis must ask, "What do
people make of these given categories?," in which *make of* refers to the construction and reconstruction of the given categories. From a practical point of view,
researchers can start with the given categories and bump them up against what
people do with them, or they can start with how people interact with each other
and how they constitute given categories. In either case, the constraint is to
work within the setting and event and with the people involved.

Consider these issues within the context of classroom language and literacy events. These events can be distinguished from nonclassroom language
and literacy events by the presence of school discourse (as discussed in chap.
2). Thus, writing a letter as part of a classroom lesson differs from writing a
letter or telling a story at home or at work, because in the classroom the activity is surrounded and permeated by school discourse. In writing a letter, the
student is involved simultaneously in an immediately present pedagogic
event and in an event involving the interaction of an author and an audience

mediated through the production of a written text. Stated more simply, the student is interacting with the teacher and students in the classroom, and the student is interacting with the people who will be receiving the letter (the addressee). Of course, it may be that there was never any intention to mail the letter, in which case the audience for the letter is an imaginary construction. Savvy students will recognize that in some classrooms they are really writing a letter to the teacher and, although they pretend to write the letter to some addressee they adjust the text they create accordingly. Even so, there is still the premise of (a) the schooling context and immediate, face-to-face event and (b) the context of author–audience for the written or spoken text being produced or consumed. In our view, it is always the case that the immediate, schooling event always contextualizes the author–audience event, and this is so whether the author–audience event is authentic or an artifice—which is merely to state that an author–audience event (the writing of a letter, the telling of a story, the reading of a novel) is constructed within and through the immediate, face-to-face, pedagogic event.

The complex relationship between the immediate, face-to-face pedagogic event and the author–audience event results in complex explications of social identity work in classroom language and literacy events. We illustrate part of this complexity through an analysis of the storytelling of a student, Shannon, in a kindergarten classroom (see Transcript 3.1). In this classroom lesson, students volunteered to tell a story to their peers as a precursor to writing down their stories.

Shannon begins telling a story that is structured the way many previous stories in the class have been structured. She tells about an activity that she (the protagonist of the story) and the teacher did (lines 05–09). Although fictional, it has the characteristics of a narrative report. Then there are major silences (lines 10–19) that indicate a transition and separation between the first story and the second one. The second story has some of the characteristics of a report, as if Shannon is telling about a sleepover party at her house. But the structure of her storytelling and her interaction with the audience make clear that the reporting is a weak artifice for identifying her friends in the classroom and entertaining her classmates by invoking a taboo topic (people sleeping with each other; lines 36–61). She is improvising a structure, adapting the reporting structure, perhaps importing structures from other stories she has heard, and in so doing creating a new story structure (at least new to this class and setting). She continues her improvisation as she counts the amount of money her mother gave the students (lines 68–83), encouraged by the positive response of the students. It may be that Shannon is building on call-and-response storytelling structures she has heard elsewhere, and she may be using structures from various children's counting books she has read.

Table 3.1 includes a moment by moment "map" of changes in the social identities and social positions of Shannon and the other students in the

TRANSCRIPT 3.1
Shannon's Storytelling in the Classroom

05	Shannon:	Me and Ms. Morgan
06	Bloome:	Uh huh
07	Shannon:	Ms. Morgan buy me a necklace
08		(Extended silence)
09		And then I said her tree looked pretty
10		(Extended silence)
11		and
12		Ms. Morgan took me to the park
13		(Extended silence)
14		and
15		(Extended silence)
16		ummmm
17		(Extended silence)
18		Nina came over my house
19		(Extended silence)
20		Ms. Morgan came over my house
21		Jasmine came over my house
22	Student:	(Nonverbal pointing to another student in the class)
23	Shannon:	I already got her
24		(Extended silence)
25		Felice coming over my house
26		(Extended silence)
27		Kelly came over my house
28		Sharon coming over my house
29		(Extended silence)
30		Mr. Bloome came over my house
31		(Extended silence)
32		My mama looked downstairs and saw all of us
33		She saw us making a pallet
34		He was playing downstairs
35		(Giggling from students)
36		Marcy was sleeping with Judith
37	Students:	Oooooooooo ooooooooooo ooooooooooo
38	Ms. Morgan:	[Undecipherable] a soap opera
39	Shannon:	Nancy was sleeping down the [undecipherable]
40	Students:	Oooooooooo ooooooooooo oooooooooo
41	Student:	I sleep with a girl

42	Shannon:	Joan was sleeping up top
43	Student:	Oooooo ooooo
44	Shannon:	I was I was sleeping by my own self
45		(Giggling from students)
46	Student:	(Undecipherable) sleep with a boy
47		(Giggling from students)
48	Ms. Morgan:	(undecipherable)
49	Shannon:	Sean was sleeping on the top bed
50		(Giggling from students)
51		and
52		Mr. Bloome was sleeping downstairs on the couch
53		(Giggling from students)
54		Ms. Morgan was sleeping on the other couch
55	Student:	So she can sleep (undecipherable)
56	Student:	(undecipherable)
57	Shannon:	Tamara and Judith was making them a (undecipherable)
58		(Giggling from students and various undecipherable comments)
59		And I was sleeping on the bottom bed
60		(Various undecipherable comments)
61		And I was sleeping
62		And momma woke up and saw all of us sleep
63		My momma woke up and took us to school
64		Quit coughing and get off of me David
65	Ms. Morgan:	(Undecipherable comment)
66		(Extended silence and background whispering)
67		And Danielle was playing to the park
68		My momma gave us a dollar
69	Students:	Ooooooo oooooooo
70	Shannon:	My momma gave us two dollars
71	Students:	ooooooo
72		(Extended silence)
73	Shannon:	Then my momma gave us three dollars
74	Students:	ooooooo
75	Shannon:	And then my momma gave us four dollars
76	Students:	ooooooo
77	Shannon:	All of my kids came over my house and got em four four dollars

(continued on next page)

78	Students:	Ooooooo ooooooooo
79		Student: (undecipherable comment)
80	Shannon:	and
81		and
82		(Undecipherable) five dollars
83	Students:	ooooooo
84	Student:	(Undecipherable whispered comment)
85	Shannon:	no
86		(Extended silence)
87	Student:	(Undecipherable whispered comment)
88	Shannon:	Can't tell you what to do
89	Ms. Morgan:	This is Sharon Shannon's story
90		(Extended silence)
91	Teacher:	Does your story have a happy ending what happens at the end of your story
92	Shannon:	We all came back to school
93		You took us to the dollar store the end
94	Students:	ooooooooo
95	Bloome:	Very good story

classroom during the storytelling event. The map reveals a number of language processes she used in creating a series of social identities for herself and others through the use of extant language and literacy practices and through improvisation. The table actually contains two parallel maps: The first traces the evolution of social identities of Shannon and her classmates within the narrative being told—that is, within the text world or situation model being created as the narrative is created, and the second map traces Shannon's social identity as a storyteller (the immediate face-to-face event). The two maps parallel the theoretical construct just discussed; namely, that classroom language and literacy events often involve an immediate, face-to-face pedagogic event (which in this case is the interaction of Shannon with her peers and her teacher) and an author–audience event mediated through the creation of a text world (situation model).

In line 05 Shannon creates a two-person group, she and the teacher (linked through the use of various conjunctions). They are friends who do things outside of school, highly valued activities such as the teacher buying her a necklace and going to the park, all of which give Shannon special social status. Defining a group and affiliating with highly valued activities are two strategies for constructing a social identity and social position.

TABLE 3.1

Mapping Social Identities in Transcript 3.1

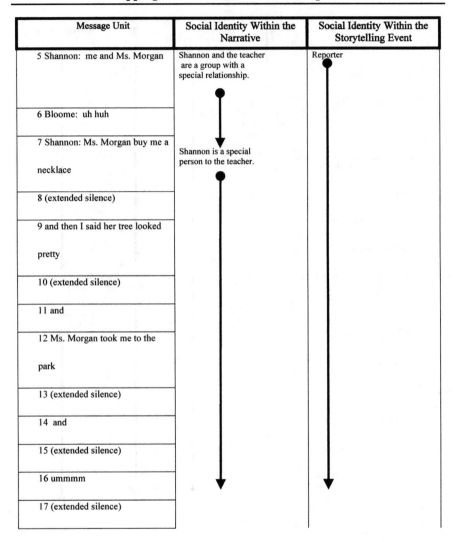

Message Unit	Social Identity Within the Narrative	Social Identity Within the Storytelling Event
5 Shannon: me and Ms. Morgan	Shannon and the teacher are a group with a special relationship.	Reporter
6 Bloome: uh huh		
7 Shannon: Ms. Morgan buy me a necklace	Shannon is a special person to the teacher.	
8 (extended silence)		
9 and then I said her tree looked pretty		
10 (extended silence)		
11 and		
12 Ms. Morgan took me to the park		
13 (extended silence)		
14 and		
15 (extended silence)		
16 ummmm		
17 (extended silence)		

(continued on next page)

TABLE 3.1 (*continued*)

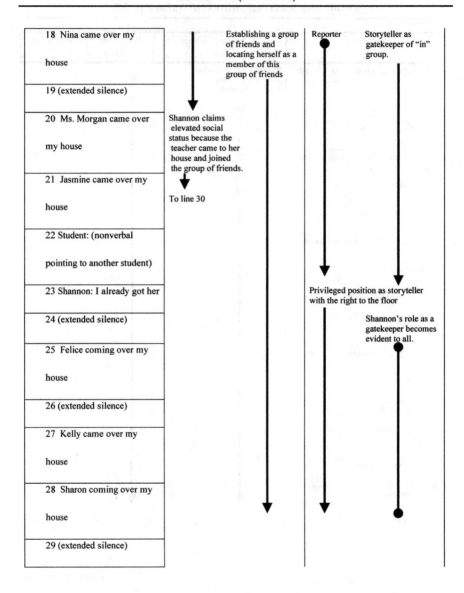

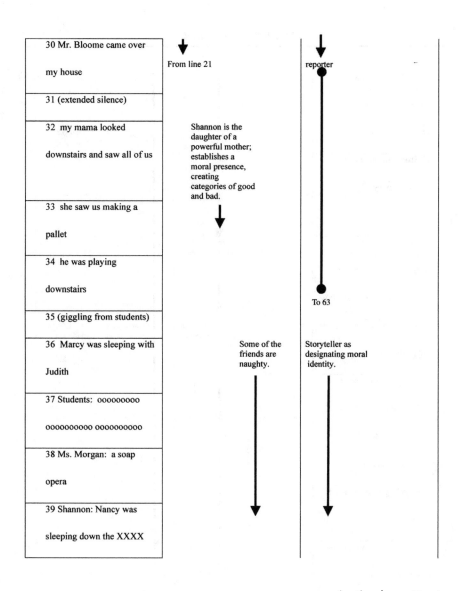

30 Mr. Bloome came over my house	From line 21	reporter
31 (extended silence)		
32 my mama looked downstairs and saw all of us	Shannon is the daughter of a powerful mother; establishes a moral presence, creating categories of good and bad.	
33 she saw us making a pallet		
34 he was playing downstairs		To 63
35 (giggling from students)		
36 Marcy was sleeping with Judith	Some of the friends are naughty.	Storyteller as designating moral identity.
37 Students: ooooooooo ooooooooo ooooooooo		
38 Ms. Morgan: a soap opera		
39 Shannon: Nancy was sleeping down the XXXX		

(continued on next page)

TABLE 3.1 (*continued*)

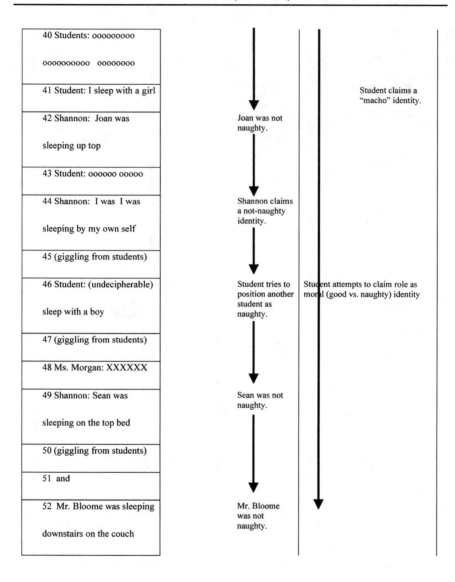

40 Students: oooooooooo ooooooooooo ooooooooo		
41 Student: I sleep with a girl		Student claims a "macho" identity.
42 Shannon: Joan was sleeping up top	Joan was not naughty.	
43 Student: oooooo ooooo		
44 Shannon: I was I was sleeping by my own self	Shannon claims a not-naughty identity.	
45 (giggling from students)		
46 Student: (undecipherable) sleep with a boy	Student tries to position another student as naughty.	Student attempts to claim role as moral (good vs. naughty) identity
47 (giggling from students)		
48 Ms. Morgan: XXXXXX		
49 Shannon: Sean was sleeping on the top bed	Sean was not naughty.	
50 (giggling from students)		
51 and		
52 Mr. Bloome was sleeping downstairs on the couch	Mr. Bloome was not naughty.	

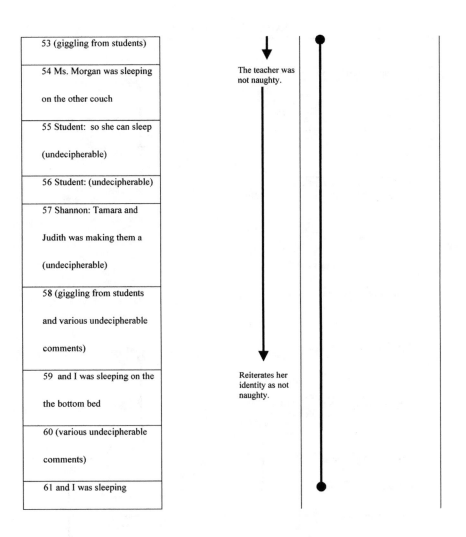

53 (giggling from students)	
54 Ms. Morgan was sleeping on the other couch	The teacher was not naughty.
55 Student: so she can sleep (undecipherable)	
56 Student: (undecipherable)	
57 Shannon: Tamara and Judith was making them a (undecipherable)	
58 (giggling from students and various undecipherable comments)	
59 and I was sleeping on the the bottom bed	Reiterates her identity as not naughty.
60 (various undecipherable comments)	
61 and I was sleeping	

(continued on next page)

TABLE 3.1 (*continued*)

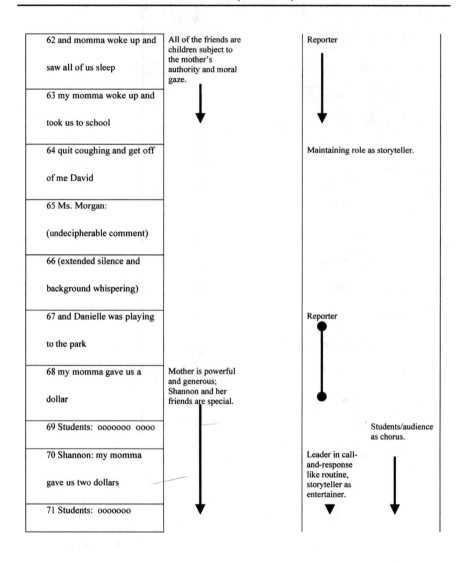

62 and momma woke up and saw all of us sleep	All of the friends are children subject to the mother's authority and moral gaze.	Reporter
63 my momma woke up and took us to school		
64 quit coughing and get off of me David		Maintaining role as storyteller.
65 Ms. Morgan: (undecipherable comment)		
66 (extended silence and background whispering)		
67 and Danielle was playing to the park		Reporter
68 my momma gave us a dollar	Mother is powerful and generous; Shannon and her friends are special.	
69 Students: ooooooo oooo		Students/audience as chorus.
70 Shannon: my momma gave us two dollars		Leader in call-and-response like routine, storyteller as entertainer.
71 Students: ooooooo		

72 (extended silence)
73 Shannon: then my momma gave us three dollars
74 Students: ooooooo
75 Shannon: and then my momma gave us four dollars
76 Students: ooooooo
77 Shannon: all of my kids came over my house and got em four four dollars
78 Students: oooooo ooooo
79 Student: (undecipherable comment)
80 Shannon: and
81 and
82 (undecipherable) five dollars
83 Students: ooooooo
84 Student: (undecipherable

(continued on next page)

117

TABLE 3.1 (*continued*)

whispered comment)		
85 Shannon: no		Maintains role and privileges as storyteller.
86 (extended silence)		
87 Student: (undecipherable whispered comment)		↓
88 Shannon: can't tell you what to do		Privileged position as storyteller with the right to the floor.
89 Ms. Morgan: This is Sharon Shannon's story		Shannon's position as storyteller is validated.
90 (extended silence)		
91 Ms. Morgan: Does you story have a happy ending what happens at the end of your story		Shannon as a child storyteller with an obligation to end the story with a happy ending.
92 Shannon: we all came back to school	She and her friends are moral people and students. ↓	Reporter
93 you took us to the dollar store the end	She and her friends are special students because they received a special privilege from the teacher.	
94 Students: oooooooo		

In lines 18 through 30, Shannon establishes a group of friends whom she names one by one. She uses a parallel linguistic structure in lines 18, 20, 21, 27, 28, and 30. In so doing, Shannon forms another social group and boundaries between those who can claim a social identity and social status as members of that group and those who cannot. Geography is a linguistic strategy that can be used to construct social identity. Within the storytelling event, Shannon has ceased being the reporter of what happened (whether fact or fiction) and has taken on the social position of gatekeeper, selecting who is in the group and who is not.

In lines 31 through 63, Shannon shifts her role as storyteller back to that of reporter, describing what happened at her house through the narrative text. Within the narrative text her social identity has shifted to that of "daughter" to her mother, who is a new character added to the story. Her mother is a powerful character who engages in a number of gazes (lines 32, 33, 62). The gaze is important because it is a control mechanism and a moral gaze. In line 36, Shannon begins assigning some of the students gendered and sexual social identities that are somewhat naughty. One student is sleeping with another. Although it is unlikely that the students have any substantive knowledge about sexuality, they appear to know that there are a series of taboo activities and domains, and by playing with these activities and domains they can assign to each other gendered and sexual identities. Shannon uses a taboo subject matter to create a line and by locating people across the line assigns to them a social identity as "adult," but at the same time, by locating herself on the "safe" side of the taboo (she is sleeping by herself; line 44), she assigns to herself a "respectable" social identity. This respectable social identity is contrasted with the social identity she created for herself by bringing up a taboo topic. So, whereas on one hand she is a respectable, good girl, on the other hand she is a slightly naughty child for bringing up a taboo topic. Thus, people can use already-established moral lines to construct social identities, and they can juxtapose various positions with regard to moral lines to create complex and nuanced social identities. During this phase of the storytelling event, Shannon is not just a reporter of events but also a moral commentator (as some of the students are sleeping with each other and some not). The students as an audience react by taking on a role that might be labeled the *chorus* or *partners*, in a call-and-response routine. The students are reacting to the narrative text, to the moral implications, and to the way the story is being told, and thereby they are assigning to Shannon the social identity of storyteller/entertainer and not just reporter.

Throughout the story, Shannon identifies herself as a daughter by invoking her mother as an actor in the story (lines 32, 62, 63, 68, 70, 73, 75). She then has her mother give money to her and her friends, increasing the amount as she tells the story. The step-by-step counting up provides increased social status and position to her mother, who has and gives the money, and to Shannon and her friends, who receive the money. The mother has the social position of authority in part because of the moral gaze and in part because she takes the friends to school. Shannon has become again the daughter within the narrative text. However, the students do not respond to her social identity as daughter but to the mother as a person who is rich enough to give them (the friends) money, the amount of which increases with each utterance. Within the storytelling event, the students again adopt the social position of chorus, commenting on the rich mother and on their increasing riches. People can construct social identities by invoking part of a complementary relationship (e.g., mother–daughter) and by invoking a quantitative scale.

Shannon maintains her social identity as the storyteller by guarding her rights to turn-taking and to determining the topic of her story. The teacher intervenes once to reassert those rights (line 89). Thus, social identity may, in some cases, depend on the process of delegation. The teacher delegates her social identity and social status as "owner" of the floor to Shannon, but it is also the case that maintaining one's social identity cannot be assumed and that it has to be defended. Shannon engages in such a defense by rebuffing a suggestion for including a student in a list of friends (line 23) by noting that the suggestion makes no sense (the suggested student was already included), by maintaining interpersonal distance (line 64, "quit coughing and get off of me David"), and explicitly stating a rule for the event (line 88, "can't tell you [me] what to do"). At the very end of the storytelling, the teacher invokes her authority within the context of the event and tells Shannon to end the story, which she does abruptly.

In both the narrative text and in the storytelling event, Shannon's social identity and that of the students continued to evolve and shift. By tracing social identities as they evolve on a moment-by-moment basis within a classroom conversation, researchers can make visible the interpersonal and language processes used by students and teachers to create themselves and each other. Shannon accomplished these social identities and their evolution through a variety of linguistic means, including conjunction structures; parallel structures across utterances; placing authority figures (mother, teacher) in the active case; using specific lexical items, including names, complementary pairs, places, and highly valued items; and combinations of these linguistic strategies. It appears that when Shannon found a linguistic strategy that produced engagement with her audience she repeated the linguistic strategy (e.g., the same combination of a linguistic structure and a lexical item).

The mapping in Table 3.1 shows that social identities are constructed at multiple levels within the multiple social contexts of the classroom event. Social identities shift and evolve; they are claimed, contested, and defended. The teacher plays an important role in validating certain identities and in creating the social rules for claiming, challenging, and defending the social identities claimed. As Gergen (1999) noted, social identities inherently involve others, and as one claims or is assigned a particular social identity others are inherently also assigned social identities. In part, such claiming and assigning are accomplished through given complementary relationships, such as mother and daughter. At other times the set of social relationships is manufactured through the assertion of dualisms, as in naughty and not naughty or morally appropriate or morally inappropriate. Such frameworks (whether consisting of dualisms or other structurations) can be constructed by invoking a figure whose personhood is understood by all to embody such a framework. When Shannon invokes her mother, she is also invoking a moral framework of right and wrong because such a framework is a shared understanding of the personhood of mothers (at least among the kindergarten students and teacher). In brief, both for participants and for researchers, the dynamic nature of social identity construction requires close attention to the linguistic give and take of an event and attention to social identity construction at multiple levels.

MICROETHNOGRAPHIC ANALYSIS OF THREE RELATED EVENTS IN A 6TH-GRADE SOCIAL STUDIES/LANGUAGE ARTS LESSON

The three events we analyze next occurred during a particular lesson in a 6th-grade language arts/social studies class early in the academic year. When we began the analysis of the lesson, we began with some "givens" of social identity. We described the students as African American or white, using the labels used by the school. We also described the students as coming from primarily low-income and working-class families based on the government's labeling of the school as a Title I school. In brief, we began with appellations of social identity established by the state.

The class was a participant in a research project involving cooperative learning. The emphasis on cooperative learning led to the organization of students helping students (as opposed to the teacher always needing to be in the teaching-and-helping position). The academic part of the school day was divided between two classes. One class focused on language arts and social studies; the other focused on math and science.

In the specific language arts/social studies class we examined, the students had previously written summaries about life in ancient Egypt in response to the question: "In ancient Egypt, how did the climate and geography affect the lives of the people?" Information for the summary was found in a textbook article provided to the students, which they had read in their peer reading groups. At the beginning of the target lesson, the teacher reviewed the process for writing summaries and the criteria that define a good summary. Writing a good summary was a goal of the school district curriculum. The summaries that had previously been written were returned to students, along with a separate sheet of paper containing written feedback from the teacher. The feedback was provided in the following format:

1. Does the summary meet the purpose?
   (Students received a check mark if 2 of the 3 primary points were made. Otherwise, an X was given.)
2. Does it only include information relevant to the purpose?
   (A check was given if only correct information relevant to the purpose was given. Otherwise, an X was given.)
3. Does it combine and condense details?
   (A check was given if any details were combined or condensed. Otherwise, an X was given.)
4. Does it restate information in the summarizer's own words?
   (A check was given if the summary was written in the student's own words, even if it was rewording sentences from the passage. Otherwise, an X was given.)
5. Does it make sense?
   (A check was given if it made sense, even if it wasn't relevant to the purpose. Otherwise, an X was given.)

In addition to the checklist, a space was provided for written comments. After receiving the feedback forms, students worked at their desks to revise their summaries based on the teacher's written feedback. It is important to note that multiple activities occurred at one time in the classroom. One group of students might be engaged in a reading group; another might be at computers, pursuing research questions or writing results from their inquiries, and another group might be at their desks, working independently or with others. The teacher during this part of the class moved among the students, ensuring that students were on task and addressing any problems that might have been preventing the students from engaging in their work. In this computer technology rich classroom, problems with the computers or their connections to servers, and so on, often required either the teacher's attention or the attention of a member of the research team (often, a member of the research team was present in the classroom).

Our analysis focuses primarily on the interactions between Andrew, an African American male student, and Carol, a white female student. Near the end of class, the teacher asked those students who had completed their revisions to help those students who were not finished, and Carol went to Andrew's table to help him revise his summary. One researcher (Mr. West) also interacted briefly with Andrew and Carol. Our analysis focuses on three encounters between Andrew and Carol that took place near the end of the class.

The First Event: Analysis of Transcript 3.2

Transcript 3.2, which consists of three interactional units composed of 13 message units, reveals Carol and Andrew's first interaction, when Carol went to Andrew's table to help him revise the summary he had previously written. We parsed Transcript 3.2 into message units and then into interactional units (following procedures described by Green & Wallat [1981], and discussed at length in chapter. 1). We used the transcript to examine the linguistic evidence available, both verbal and nonverbal, to describe how language was used to construct social identities. In Transcript 3.2, Mr. West interacts with Andrew and Carol. It was common practice in this classroom for researchers to move around the room helping students, much as a teacher might, and therefore we treat Mr. West as a teacher-like participant in the event.

In the first interaction unit (lines 101–104), Carol is positioned as the delegated teacher, while Andrew is positioned as a nonparticipant in the conversation. In line 102, Mr. West addresses Carol using the first-person plural ("so let's"), signaling that Carol is a coteacher along with him. Because Mr. West and Carol are standing, while Andrew is seated, their body positions also signal the teacher–student relationship between them and Andrew. In addition, Carol is holding Andrew's feedback form. In line 103, Andrew is positioned as a nonparticipant in the conversation, as a person with no conversational rights. Andrew is discussed in the third person ("is this HIS feedback?"), although he is present. The question is directed toward Carol, and Mr. West points to the form that Carol is holding. Mr. West and Carol do not look at Andrew. Andrew is also being positioned as a nonreader. His feedback form, which must be read and interpreted, is controlled by Carol and Mr. West. In line 104, however, Andrew resists being positioned as a nonparticipant by responding to Mr. West's question with "yeah" even though he was not addressed and even though Carol and Mr. West do not shift their gazes toward him.

During the second interaction unit (lines 105–109), Carol continues to be positioned as the teacher and Andrew as the student, but both Carol and Andrew attempt to position one another as derelict in fulfilling their teacher and student obligations, respectively. In lines 105 and 106, Andrew, referring to Carol, says "She's supposed to be helpin me. She ain't helpin me." Although Andrew might be trying to fault Carol for the fact that his summary remains unrevised, we cannot know with certainty his intentions. But an analysis of his words indicates that he, too, is positioning Carol as the teacher and himself as the passive student. This is illustrated through the grammatical relationship between Carol as the subject and Andrew as the object: "She's [the person who acts] supposed to be helpin me [the person who is acted upon]." In other words, Carol is supposed to

TRANSCRIPT 3.2

Description of Social Identities, Lines 101–113, of the 6th-Grade Lesson

Line No.	Speaker	Message Units	Interaction Units	Nonverbal Behavior	Identities Signaled in Message Units	Linguistic Evidence for Descriptions of Identity	Uptake Across IU's
101	Mr. West	okay					
102		So let's		Carol and Mr. West are standing. Andrew is sitting. Carol is holding Andrew's feedback form.	Mr. West positions Carol as teacher/teacher's helper	Body positions signal student/teacher relationship. Use of first-person plural by Mr. West signals that Carol is a teacher/teacher's helper.	
103		Is this his feedback?		Mr. West points at the form Carol is holding. Question is directed to Carol. Carol and Mr. West look at Andrew's form.	Mr. West and Carol position Andrew as nonparticipant in conversation (no conversational rights) and as a nonreader.	Andrew is discussed in the third person, although he is present. Carol and Mr. West do not look at Andrew.	
104	Andrew	yeah		Mr. West and Carol direct their eye gaze toward the feedback form.	Andrew resists being positioned as nonparticipant.	Andrew responds even though he wasn't addressed. Mr. West and Carol do not respond to 104.	

124

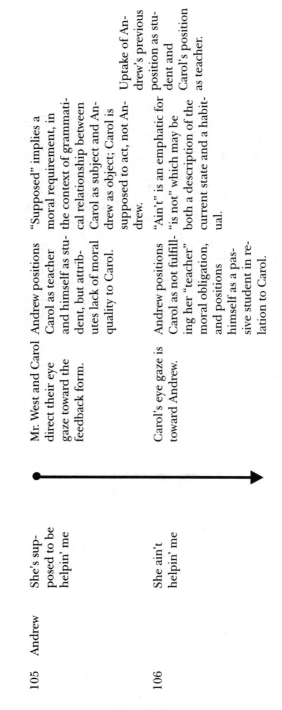

105	Andrew	She's supposed to be helpin' me	Mr. West and Carol direct their eye gaze toward the feedback form.	Andrew positions Carol as teacher and himself as student, but attributes lack of moral quality to Carol.	"Supposed" implies a moral requirement, in the context of grammatical relationship between Carol as subject and Andrew as object; Carol is supposed to act, not Andrew.
106		She ain't helpin' me	Carol's eye gaze is toward Andrew.	Andrew positions Carol as not fulfilling her "teacher" moral obligation, and positions himself as a passive student in relation to Carol.	"Ain't" is an emphatic for "is not" which may be both a description of the current state and a habitual. Uptake of Andrew's previous position as student and Carol's position as teacher.

TRANSCRIPT 3.2 (*continued*)

Line No.	Speaker	Message Units	Interaction Units	Nonverbal Behavior	Identities Signaled in Message Units	Linguistic Evidence for Descriptions of Identity	Uptake Across IU's
107	Carol	What were you doing			Carol positions Andrew as not fulfilling his student obligations and as actively derelict.	Question that takes the form of a statement. Emphasis on "you" juxtaposed with "doing" positions Andrew as having taken an action, contesting his claim in 105 and 106 positioning him as passive.	
108		How was I going to help you			Carol resists being positioned as not fulfilling her "teacher" moral obligation.	"How" acts as a causal conjunction ("if-then") with 107, and question form is rhetorical, dismissive of moral obligation.	
109		When you (indecipherable)					

#	Speaker	Utterance				
110	Andrew	here	Carol is holding feedback form.			
111		(Indecipherable) let me read it		Andrew positions himself as student and Carol as teacher. Andrew also positions himself as a reader.	Message is framed as a request, not a directive, providing Carol with opportunity to make the decision.	Continued uptake of Carol as teacher and Andrew as student. No uptake on Andrew's previous positioning of himself as a reader.
112	Carol	I'm not helping you	Carol throws Andrew's feedback form on the table and walks away.	Carol positions Andrew as student not worthy of help, and reiterates her position as helper/teacher and as having the "power" to help or not help, dependent on Andrew's behavior towards her.	Grammatical structure makes Carol active, Andrew passive. She acts on him, not vice versa, and they do not act together.	
113	Andrew	Bye		Andrew rejects Carol's positioning of him as worthless and helpless.	Use of sarcasm; Carol has already left, so there is no ratification.	

127

act on Andrew. However, Andrew also positions Carol as not fulfilling her moral obligations as a teacher. The word *supposed* implies a moral requirement, and in line 106 Andrew continues to position Carol as derelict: "She ain't helpin me." We interpret *ain't* as an emphatic and potentially as a habitual; therefore, we can speculate that Andrew might be attributing to Carol an ongoing lack of moral quality.

In lines 107 through 109, Carol resists being positioned as not fulfilling her teacher obligations and positions Andrew as not fulfilling his student obligations. Carol's question of "What were YOU doing" takes the form of a statement. The emphasis on *you* juxtaposed with *doing* positions Andrew as someone who is engaged in an action, thus contesting his claim in lines 105 and 106, that he is the passive participant in this relationship. Carol goes on to say, "How was I going to help you, when you (indecipherable)?" Carol here resists being positioned as not fulfilling her teacher obligations. She uses *how*, which acts as a causal conjunction with line 107 by establishing an if–then relationship. In other words, "if" Andrew is derelict in his obligation as a student, "then" Carol cannot help him. Once again, in line 108, Carol uses a rhetorical question, which is dismissive of the moral obligation that Andrew first brought up in line 105.

During the third and final interaction unit of this transcript (lines 110–113), Carol and Andrew continue to be positioned as teacher and student, respectively. In lines 110 and 111, Andrew tells Carol, who is still holding his feedback form, "Here (indecipherable) let me read it." Once again, Andrew positions himself as the student and Carol as the teacher by asking her for permission to read his feedback form. The message is framed as a request ("let me"), not a directive, providing Carol with the opportunity to make the decision. But Andrew also positions himself as a reader in lines 110 and 111. During the first interaction unit of this transcript, Carol and Mr. West read Andrew's feedback form as if Andrew were a nonreader, but here Andrew attempts to position himself as a reader by asking to read his own feedback form. Carol responds to Andrew's request by saying, "I'm not helping you," as she throws his form on his desk and walks away. In doing so, Carol positions Andrew as a student not worthy of help and reiterates her position as teacher, and thus as having the power to either help him or not, depending on Andrew's behavior toward her. The linguistic evidence from which we argue is that the grammatical form positions Carol as active and Andrew as passive (I'M not helping YOU). Carol acts on Andrew, not vice versa; neither do they act together.

An analysis of uptake across interaction units reveals that in Interactional Unit 2 (lines 105–109) and Interactional Unit 3 (lines 110–113), there is uptake of Andrew's position as student and Carol's position as teacher. Both Carol and Andrew accept these positions. There is no uptake, however, of Andrew's attempt to position himself as a competent student and as a reader. Carol does not accept this positioning of Andrew and even refuses to help him when he asks to read his own feedback form. Thus, although Andrew may make a bid for social identities as a reader and as a competent student, his bid is not interactionally validated. We argue that the failure to interactionally validate Andrew's bid for social identities as a reader and competent student involve more than a default inattention to his bid. Rather, the ignoring of his bid is overt and visible. In other words, it is not just that there is no uptake on his bid to establish himself as a reader and as a competent student—his bid is rejected.

The Second Event: Analysis of Transcript 3.3

Transcript 3.3 represents an interaction between Andrew and Carol that happened a few minutes after Transcript 3.2 and during the same class. Carol had returned to help Andrew revise his summary. Unlike in Transcript 3.2, where we parsed the interaction into message units to determine the identities signaled, in Transcript 3.3 we parsed the interaction into turns at talk. In Transcript 3.3 the structure of the turn-taking provides evidence and a picture of the social dynamics involved in the construction of social identity. We are interested here in analyzing who gets the floor, who participates in the conversation, and in what ways they participate. Thus, as an aside, the form of a transcript (e.g., the number of columns, the headings, the level of detail, which units are highlighted) varies depending on its intended use.

The event in Transcript 3.3 involves three people: Andrew, Carol, and Maria (a student seated next to Andrew). In this event, the duration of which is approximately 100 seconds, Carol spends most of the time either reading to Andrew or reading silently (see Table 3.2). Carol spends a total of 68 seconds reading, with 15 seconds devoted to Andrew's feedback form and 53 seconds allotted to his textbook. Carol directs a total of eight directives and imperatives toward Andrew, such as "Look," "You don't need that," and "Listen." Carol makes no comments to Andrew other than directives and imperatives. These unmitigated directives have the effect of positioning Carol as someone with authority and Andrew as having no choice but to obey (see Diamondstone, 1998, for a similar but more detailed discussion of the use of directives and power relations). There are four visible instances of Andrew's responding to Carol's directives, when she says "Look" and he directs his gaze toward her or the textbook. There are no visible indications that Andrew is responding to the content of the reading, however, and he initiates no comments toward Carol. There are several visible indications of nonparticipation by Andrew. On at least six occasions, Andrew looks away from Carol and the textbook, and three times he speaks to someone else seated at the table. Andrew never initiates conversation with Carol or responds in any way other than to look in her direction when she orders him to do so. He does say, "I'm listening," near the end of the event when she

Carol:	Okay, look. (Andrew looks at Carol.) (Carol reads from Andrew's feedback sheet) It says, "you're right that the Nile River flood, um flood, huh, you're right that the Nile River's flooding (Andrew looks in opposite direction, away from Carol) allowed them to grow more food. Can you think of another way that the land, the Nile River, the weather affected their lives?" Okay. (Andrew looks back at Carol. Carol picks up Andrew's textbook article.) It says right here. (Carol reads from textbook) The land was mostly desert except for the Nile River. The Nile River flooded, blahblahblah." (indecipherable) Okay, okay. (Andrew looks away from Carol. Carol reads from textbook) "The Nile River Valley" Look. (Carol touches Andrew's arm. Andrew looks back toward Carol.) (Carol reads from textbook) "Most of the people lived in the Nile River Valley because it provided water and land for growing food. The desert made it hard for other people to invade ancient Egypt." The desert. Because it was so much of it desert. You can write about how it made it hard for other people to invade and why the valley and why the people, most people lived over there. It was because of the water. (Carol reads from textbook) "The Nile River flowed a distance" Okay, you don't need, you don't need that. (Carol reads silently) Okay. (Andrew looks away as Carol read from textbook) "The Nile River flooded each year. The flooding started in July. When the rainy season began to central Africa, the rain raised the level of the river. The Nile River flooded northwards, though. Um. Flood waters usually went down in September, leaving a (indecipherable)." Okay, okay, look, look, look.
Andrew:	You're not supposed to be in that chair (directed to Maria).
Carol:	(Reading from textbook) "land. The average (indecipherable)"
Andrew:	You're not supposed (directed to Maria).
Carol:	(Reading from textbook) "of each side"
Andrew:	You're not supposed to be in that chair (directed to Maria).
Carol:	(Reading from textbook) "of the river. The first (indecipherable)." (Directed to Andrew) Listen, or I'm not helping.
Andrew:	(Andrew looks back toward Carol) I'm listening.

says, "Listen or I'm not helping," but on no other occasion does he verbally respond to what she is reading or to her directives. There is no uptake during this interaction of Andrew's previous attempt to position himself as a reader and as a competent student. Carol does all the reading and only addresses Andrew as a teacher might. Their relationship is not one of mutual collaboration and cooperation; rather, there is continued uptake of Andrew as the passive student and Carol as the directive teacher.

It is worthwhile to give some attention to the directive "Look," to Carol's gaze at Andrew, and to Andrew's gazing. Earlier in this chapter, when we discussed Shannon's story, we noted that one of the ways that Shannon associated her mother with power and authority was to assign to her mother the power to gaze. Her mother looked at what the kids were doing to insure that they were behaving properly. The importance of gaze in power relations has been noted by Foucault (1965, 1980), among others. At the beginning of the second event, Carol directs Andrew's gaze toward her, modeling the correct academic behavior and providing information. Andrew looks away and Carol asks him a question, causing him to redirect his gaze to Carol. Andrew's gaze is one not of surveillance but of acknowledgment of his participation in the interaction with Carol; it is a response to Carol's gaze. As Carol begins to read from the textbook to provide Andrew with a

TABLE 3.2
Analysis of Transcript 3.3

Total Time of Transcript	100 sec
Carol's Activities	
Reading Andrew's feedback form	15 sec
Reading Andrew's textbook article	53 sec
Number directives and imperatives directed toward Andrew	8
Number comments directed toward Andrew other than directives and imperatives	0
Andrew's Activities	
Number visible indications that he is responding to the content of the reading	0
Number visible indications of nonparticipation	
Looking in another direction	6
Speaking to someone else	3
Number visible responses to Carol's directives	4
Number initiations to Carol	0

model for reading and with information (positioning Andrew as a nonreader and as an incompetent student), Andrew looks away. His looking away might be considered an act of resistance both to the positioning and to Carol's control of his gaze. Andrew turns his gaze to Maria and tells her that she is misbehaving: "You're not supposed to be in that chair." In a sense, he is doing to Maria what Carol is doing to him: observing what is being done and policing misbehavior. The interaction with Maria may be a way to resist the directives from Carol ("look, look, look"). Carol is intent on controlling Andrew's gaze and, in so doing, controlling who he is as well as models of behavior and knowledge. When Carol says to Andrew, "Listen or I'm not helping," the reference is more about Andrew's gaze than his listening, as a gaze is a visible display of listening and of cooperation. Andrew yields to her demand by redirecting his gaze toward her and stating that he is listening.

One of the issues raised by this interaction between Carol and Andrew is the importance of the gaze of the subordinated person. It is not just Carol's gaze at Andrew, or a teacher's gaze at students, that structures power relations between them but the demand that the subordinated person fix his or her gaze on the model and knowledge being directed toward him or her. In brief, although both the subordinating person and the subordinated person engage in gaze behavior, the meaningfulness and functions of their gazes are very different.

The Third Event: Analysis of Transcript 3.4

Transcript 3.4, which consists of three interaction units composed of 26 message units, represents the final interaction between Carol and Andrew during this classroom lesson. Like Transcript 3.2, this transcript is also parsed into message units. Carol has returned to the table to help Andrew, and she continues to claim the identity of teacher while positioning Andrew as an incompetent student. Andrew, however, contests Carol's position as teacher and the position of incompetent student.

In lines 301 through 305, Carol uses the imperative form and is direct with regard to the academic task. Carol's use of a nonconditional modal ("you NEED to") positions her as the teacher, the expert. She also sets the criteria for the academic task as "more" by claiming that Andrew needs to "write more" about the Nile River as a transportation route and telling him to write "a lot" about how the Nile River helped people grow food. Lines 301 through 305 signal the "teacher" identity for Carol as she continues to clarify the academic task and specify how it is to be accomplished. In line 306, Carol positions Andrew as an incompetent student by denigrating his previous work, claiming that he should refrain from the content of his previous summary. She slights his previous writing by not using a politeness form and by the use of "not."

TRANSCRIPT 3.4

Description of Social Identities, Lines 301 to 326 of the 6th-Grade Lesson

Line No.	Speaker	Message Units	Interaction Unit (IU)	Nonverbal Behavior	Identities Signaled in Message Units	Linguistic Evidence for Descriptions of Identity	Uptake Across IU's
301	Carol	You need to write more about how the Nile River helped	→	Carol standing, gesturing with her arms. Andrew sitting.	Carol claims identity as teacher and positions Andrew as student.	Body positions signal teacher–student relationship. Use of imperative. Use of nonconditional modal. Directive with regard to academic task: "more" sets the criteria.	
302		In the transportation route				Clarification and specification with regard to academic task.	
303		how				Clarification and specification with regard to academic task.	
304		It helped them grow food				Clarification and specification with regard to academic task.	

133

TRANSCRIPT 3.4 (continued)

Line No.	Speaker	Message Units	Interaction Unit (IU)	Nonverbal Behavior	Identities Signaled in Message Units	Linguistic Evidence for Descriptions of Identity	Uptake Across IU's
305		You can write a lot about that				Use of imperative. "Can" is a moral statement and an ability statement, and the criteria for the academic task is established by "a lot."	Continued uptake of Carol's position as teacher and Andrew's position as student from previous interactions.
306		Not about the (indecipherable)		Carol turns away from Andrew.		Carol denigrates Andrew's previous writing by the use of "not." Lack of politeness form.	
307	Andrew	I already I already wrote more about that			Andrew confirms Carol's position as teacher, confronts her positioning of him as poor writer.	Andrew confirms Carol's identity as teacher by responding to her assessment of the instructional task and his performance; he accepts "more" as the criterion.	Uptake of Carol's position as a competent teacher.
308	Carol	yeah				Carol is not responding to Andrew's statement; it is a way to regain and maintain the floor.	

134

309	Andrew	How they grow food		A continuation of line 307 and confirms academic task as defined by Carol in line 304.
310	Carol	okay		A reiteration to regain floor totally.
311		How it helped transportation route		
312		How it helped them grow food	Carol positions Andrew as incompetent student and nonperson.	Carol ignores Andrew's statement that he already wrote about growing food.
313		How it was good		
314		For people to get around better		
315		How the farming helped		
316		And they got rich soil from that		Lines 311–316: Carol lays out the topic outline for the summary, presenting an academic discourse genre, thus providing evidence that she is positioned as teacher. No uptake of Andrew's position as a competent student.

135

TRANSCRIPT 3.4 (continued)

Line No.	Speaker	Message Units	Interaction Unit (IU)	Nonverbal Behavior	Identities Signaled in Message Units	Linguistic Evidence for Descriptions of Identity	Uptake Across IU's
317		You need to write about that	→	Carol walks away to the other end of the table.	Carol positions Andrew as student who is outside of morally appropriate academic writing.	Carol is emphasizing what Andrew needs to write about, although he said he already wrote about food. Carol's walking away provides no opportunity for Andrew to negotiate, respond, or contest.	
318	Andrew	Now look	⊢		Andrew contests Carol's position as teacher.	Use of directive.	
319		It says		Referring to feedback form.	Andrew contests Carol's position as teacher.	Andrew refers to the feedback written by the teacher as the "expert" source, not Carol.	
320		All I need to write about	→		Andrew contests Carol's position as teacher.	Use of "all" denies Carol's previous advice.	
321		Is what (pause)					

322		Other ways the land, the river, and the weather affect their life	Reading from feedback form.	Andrew positions himself as a reader.	Andrew holds and controls the feedback form, not Carol.
323		That's all I gotta write about	Eye gaze directed to Carol.	Andrew contests Carol's position as teacher.	
324	Carol	yep		Carol positions herself in agreement with teacher.	
325		How it affected their life			
326	Andrew	It says land, the river, and the weather affect their life	Andrew reading from feedback form. Carol walks away as Andrew is reading.	Andrew contests Carol's position as teacher. Andrew positions himself as a reader. Carol positions Andrew as a nonperson.	Andrew reiterates what is in the feedback form instead of accepting Carol's interpretation. By walking away from Andrew while he is talking to her, Carol denies Andrew's personhood in this classroom. No uptake by Carol of Andrew as a competent student.

In lines 307 and 309 Andrew says, "I already, I already wrote more about that, how they grow food." Andrew affirms Carol's identity as teacher by responding to her assessment of the instructional task and his performance. In other words, he accepts her criteria of "more" as the criteria for the task, but he also confronts her positioning of him as a poor writer. Although Carol responds with "yeah" in line 308, she is not responding to Andrew's assertion that he wrote more about food. Instead, it is a way for her to regain and maintain the floor. This is indicated in lines 310 to 316 when Carol simply reiterates the task. In line 312, when Carol says, "how it helped them grow food," she ignores Andrew's assertion that he has already written more and positions him as an incompetent student and as a nonperson. In lines 311 to 316, Carol lays out the topic outline for the summary, thus presenting an academic discourse genre for summary writing and providing more evidence that she is positioning herself as the teacher. Just before she walks away from Andrew to the other end of the table, Carol says to Andrew, "You NEED TO WRITE about that," positioning Andrew as a student who is acting outside of morally appropriate academic writing. Carol is emphasizing what Andrew needs to write about, although he says that he already wrote about food. Andrew, however, contests Carol's position as teacher. Using the classroom teacher's comments on his feedback form as the expert source ("it says"), Andrew contests Carol's position as the teacher or expert. Andrew also positions himself as a reader and as a competent student by taking control of his feedback form and reading from it himself. Carol does not confirm Andrew's attempt to position himself as a reader or a competent student, and by walking away while Andrew is reading from the feedback form she positions him as a nonperson.

Across the Three Events

In chapter 1 we discussed thematic coherence within and across events. The three events we just analyzed above provide an illustration. In each event there is the similar assignment and validation (and nonvalidation) of social identities for Carol and Andrew. The three events are related by their content, proximity in time, and location, of course, but they are also related because they build on each other's assignment of social identities.

Part of what we find interesting in the analysis of the three events is Andrew's complicity in the power relationship with Carol. Although he rejects her attempt to position him as a nonreader and as an incompetent student (which occurs in all three events), he accepts her social identity as teacher and his complementary identity as student. Although the explicit instructional philosophy of the instructional program was for peers to help each other, Carol and Andrew do not interact as peers. It is a teacher–student interaction, despite the fact that Carol is a student in the class.

In looking across the three events, one theme that emerges is the recurrence of the assignment of the social identity of a nonperson. In the first event, Mr. West and Carol talk in front of Andrew as if Andrew were not there. In the second and third events, Carol's ignoring of Andrew's attempts to position himself as efficacious may be a way that Carol invokes the potential of again positioning Andrew as a nonperson; that is, by strategic ignoring of Andrew's interactional efforts, Carol keeps on the table the possibility that Andrew is a nonperson. Indeed, one might interpret Andrew's isolation at the end of the second event as such a threat or perhaps even the enactment of ascribing to him the social position of nonperson. It seems to us that the potential to position someone as a nonperson, just the threat itself, may be a way to exercise power and control.

Theoretical Issues Round 2: Social Identity as Appellation and Process

As we noted at the beginning of this chapter, there is a recursive relationship of theory, method, and findings in the conduct of discourse analysis. Thus, we return to theoretical issues involved in the discourse analysis of social identity in classroom language and literacy events.

Consistent with our earlier discussion, our analysis showed that the appellation of social identity and the processes involved in constructing social identity were inseparable. Similarly, we found that social identities evolve and can be contested within and across events. Students can be positioned in various ways through language (e.g., the enactment of teacher didacticism through delegation to a student).

It is clear during the classroom literacy events analyzed in this chapter that students were positioned in various ways by others, but the micro-level interactions among students were played out against a background of specific macro-level educational issues. In Carol and Andrew's classroom, as in many classrooms, students were evaluated and positioned by their level of academic success—in other words, by how well they participated in the cultural practices of school (see Gee, 1996). The class was located in a school district that had just mandated a core knowledge curriculum. For all academic subjects, explicit goals, content, and skills were outlined for each grading period, and teachers felt pressure to see that students met those goals. Because Andrew's first summary was judged to not meet the standards defining good summaries, he was positioned as a poor writer, whereas students like Carol were positioned as good writers.

In his analysis of how people can be positioned by certain types of discourse, Fairclough (1989) demonstrated how a patient in a medical interview can be positioned by the scientific discourse of modern medicine as a "case" instead of as a person. Similarly, we suggest that Andrew was sometimes positioned as a nonperson. Egan-Robertson (1998a) demonstrated that a group's definition of the term *person* is a powerful concept: "Personhood is a dynamic, cultural construct about who is and what is considered to be a person, what attributes and rights are constructed as inherent to being a person, and what social positions are available within the construct of being a person" (p. 453). Personhood involves those shared, but continually negotiated and renegotiated, ways that a group of people have for behaving, interacting, valuing, thinking, and feeling. These dimensions help to determine the expectations that accompany various social positions.

Because of the social construction of Andrew as an incompetent student and poor reader and writer, he was sometimes constructed as a nonperson in the classroom, and the threat of being constructed as a nonperson may have extended across events. When Carol first began to help Andrew, Mr. West said to Carol "Is this his [Andrew's] feedback?" as though Andrew were not present. When Carol returned to help Andrew, she told him to write about how the Nile River helped the people of ancient Egypt with transportation and the growing of food. Andrew replied, "I already wrote about that," but Carol ignored him as if he were not there.

Walkerdine (1990) argued that people are "not unitary subjects uniquely positioned, but are produced as a nexus of subjectivities, in relations of power which are constantly shifting, rendering them at one moment powerful and at another powerless" (p. 3). Although Andrew accepted Carol's position as teacher and his position as student, he did not accept being positioned as a nonreader and an incompetent student and writer. Although Andrew contested being positioned as an incompetent student and poor writer, there was no uptake during the interactions we have analyzed to confirm that Carol recognized Andrew's attempt to reposition himself. Some discourse analysts argue that it is difficult for individuals to contest the social positions that are sometimes constructed for them. Ivanič (1998), for example, wrote:

> A critical view of the social construction of identity not only recognizes the powerful influence of dominant ideologies in controlling and constraining people's sense of themselves, but also recognizes the possibility of struggle for alternative definitions. For individuals alone contestation of damaging construction of their identities may well be doomed to failure, but struggle as a member of an oppressed group has the potential for producing change, as political action during the late 1980s, most notably in South Africa, has shown. (p. 13)

For Ivanič, although there is the possibility for "alternative definitions," the emphasis is on resistance, on "contesting dominant constructions of the self" (pp. 13–14), and even then, individuals are viewed as unlikely to successfully contest particular constructions of their identities.

Although we do not deny that powerful discourse practices can position students in particular ways, we believe that individuals are more than simply pawns who are either manipulated by or crushed by powerful social forces, and we believe that people have the power to transform how they are positioned by various discourses. There are powerful forces at work that sometimes drive the construction of social identity, but it is limiting to assume that social identities and subject positions are generally only adopted or resisted. The work of feminist theorists such as Walkerdine (1990, 1997) has produced a more empowering view of resistance: "Resistance is not just struggle against the oppression of a static power (and therefore potentially revolutionary because it is struggle against the monolith); relations of power and resistance are continually reproduced, in continual struggle and constantly shifting" (Walkerdine, 1990, p. 4). Because power relations are in a continual state of flux, "relations of power are not invested in unitary individuals in any way which is solely or essentially derived from their material and institutional position" (Walkerdine, 1990, p. 5). In other words, students and their teachers—even though they might sometimes appear to have little economic or institutional power—are capable of, and engage in, both resistance and transformative behavior. In the next chapter we take up in detail the issue of power relations and discourse in classroom language and literacy events.

In the discussion of theoretical issues at the beginning of this chapter, we discussed differences in perspectives about whether a social identity was more like a role enacted by an actor in a play or whether the social identity was the person. The analyses of Transcripts 3.2, 3.3, and 3.4 suggest a complex picture. On one level, and in that classroom event, Andrew is the person he is co-constructed to be: a nonreader, incompetent student, and potentially a nonperson, who is remiss in his obligations to appropriately engage in his academic work even when provided help. Or, at least Andrew has this social identity to others and they act toward him in terms of this social identity. Carol is a teacher by delegation, and this social identity is validated even by Andrew. However, Andrew contests the social identity ascribed to him. He attempts to position himself as a reader and as a competent student. However, there is no interactional validation of this social identity. So where does this leave Andrew? Is he a nonreader, an incompetent student, a derelict nonperson—or is he a reader and competent student? Is he (can he be) both? The theoretical answer to these questions may have less to do with the struggles among Andrew, Carol, and Mr. West than they do with the social institutions and cultural ideologies that govern how reading and academic competence are defined—that is, if the manifest definition of reading during the classroom lesson is one that allows for Andrew to be both a nonreader and a reader, then perhaps he can be both. However, if the manifest definition of reading does not allow for multiple definitions of being a reader then he is either a reader or a nonreader, and whoever controls the criteria for such a decision is who determines Andrew's social identity in that classroom event (and perhaps across events).

The struggle over Andrew's social identity raises the possibility of multiple concurrent and opposed social identities and suggests that the explication of social identity in classroom language and literacy events needs to allow for a broader range of possibilities than often considered. This relates, we believe, to questions about Andrew's ownership of his work. Andrew did not control his work. Either Carol held it, or Mr. West held it. Carol read Andrew's textbook to him, and she took over his composing process. The lack of ownership over his own work suggests that there are issues of alienation that need to be investigated in this classroom language and literacy event and in perhaps others. Although alienation has been a concept discussed with regard to adults and their labor and in research on psychological problems, it has not been examined with regard to classroom language and literacy events. Our purpose is not to begin such a theoretical discussion here but rather to illustrate one way in which a recursive design of working back and forth across theoretical issues, methodological issues, and findings can lead to fruitful questions and avenues of research.

Another theoretical issue we raised at the beginning of the chapter concerned the direction of research design in moving between givens of social identity and the micro-level discourse processes that maintain, refine, modify, contest, or transform those givens. In the classroom language and literacy events in this chapter, Andrew and Shannon were identified as African American and Carol as white. These ethnic and racial categories were givens, given to them by the researchers as part of usual social science research practice and given to them by their schools as part of the schools' system for classifying students. But what can be said of the given social identities as part of what occurred in the various lesson segments presented in this chapter? One could, for example, look at features of Shannon's verbal and narrative performance and find characteristics from African American language. Similarly, an analysis of the phonology of Andrew's verbal performance would also show that he uses African American language, at least some of the time. An analysis of Carol's verbal performance would show that she does not use features of African American language but does use features of standard English associated with white communities. Also, there is certainly the fact of their physical presence, as Shannon's and Andrew's skin coloring identify them as Black and Carol's skin coloring identifies her as white. But what are we to make of their racial and ethnic background? What are we to make of their given gendered identities? Do we have to wait until a larger corpus of data has been collected and we can look at generalized patterns of interaction in classrooms to see whether white students like Carol are being disproportionally delegated as teachers and whether African American students like Andrew are treated as if they are nonreaders and incompetent nonpersons before we raise the importance and social consequence of the given categories of ethnic and racial identity?

We would argue "no." The fact that there is no explicit verbal reference or identified contextualization cue to mark the children's ethnicity, race, or gender does not obviate issues of ethnicity, race, or gender. Yet we cannot merely accept such appellations as unproblematic givens. We need to ask: To what degree, and how, do the given social identities of race, ethnicity, class, and gender influence what occurs? Second, how do the interpersonal dynamics involved in the coconstruction and contestation of social identities contribute to the nature and status of the given social identities of race, ethnicity, and gender? These questions raise methodological issues that we explore in the next section.

Methodological Issues

How might one explore the degree to which and how, the given social identities of race, ethnicity, and gender influence what occurs in the interactions between Carol and Andrew or in Shannon's storytelling? One approach, hinted at earlier, is to identify linguistic and cultural features associated with the racial, ethnic, class, and gendered backgrounds of the students and then to trace those features through the interactions and how people react to them. One might also trace the absence of reasonably expected features; for example, one might note in the interaction between Carol and Andrew the absence of expected politeness forms that might otherwise be found in the interaction between Carol and another white female of equal social status. Noting the absence of such politeness forms, as in the analysis of the third event, is not a precursor to asking why the forms are absent but rather focuses on the "social work" that the absence of those politeness forms does.

Other methodological approaches might include interviewing participants and reviewing videotapes of the event with members of different ethnic, racial, and gender groups, as a means to acquire a diverse set of perspectives on what is happening, what linguistic and cultural features are being used or are absent, and what potential meanings the presence or absence might have. The findings from such interviews can be used to enrich a discourse analysis (see Michaels, 1981, for a classic study that used such a methodology).

The second question—"How do the interpersonal dynamics involved in the coconstruction and contestation of social identities contribute to the nature and status of the given social identities of race, ethnicity, and gender?"—is perhaps more difficult to explore, especially when there are no explicit references to given categories of social identity such as ethnicity, race, class, and gender. We take the theoretical position that it is always the case that interpersonal dynamics in every event (the micro level) contribute to the nature and status of given social identities, including those of race, ethnicity, gender, and class. At issue is only *how*, not *if*, interpersonal dynamics contribute. Thus, the interactions between Carol and Andrew, as well as those between Shannon and her classmates, have implications for given categories of social identities. From a methodological perspective, the key questions are what evidence is available and what evidence would be needed to warrant a claim for how those interpersonal dynamics affect given categories of social identity.

Methodological approaches associated with the constructs of intertextuality, intercontextuality, and interdiscoursivity may provide useful ways to explore how interpersonal events at the micro level contribute to given categories of social identity at the macro level. We discussed intertextuality at length in chapter 2. *Intercontextuality* refers to the social construction of relationships among contexts, past and future. It can also refer to the social construction of relationships among social events (cf. Heras, 1993; Lin, 1993). *Interdiscoursivity* refers to the relationship among institutional discourses, most notably the penetration of one discourse into another or the encapsulating of one discourse within another (cf. Bloome, 1997; Bloome, Katz, Solsken, Willett, & Wilson-Keenan, 2000; Fairclough, 1992).

In brief, we take it as given that people, through their interactions, construct relationships between and among texts and between and among events. Intertextual connections, intercontextual connections, and interdiscoursivity need to be interactionally proposed, acknowledged, and recognized, and they must have social significance (see our previous discussion in chap. 2; see also Bloome & Egan-Robertson, 1993). The methodological demand, therefore, is to identify where, within an interaction, people are making connections between and among texts and between and among events. These connections can be made at multiple levels.[5] There is the level of the text, by which is meant that specific lexical items, semiotic forms and symbols, and grammatical forms and textual structures from one text are proposed to be juxtaposed with those of another text. There is the level of the event, by which is meant the face-to-face interactions of people with each other; that is, interpersonal events. Two events are proposed to be related. There is also the level of the social institution. By *social institution* we are referring to social structures that organize events, activities, social relationships, and cultural practices, such as schooling, law, church, family, and so on.

In the next section we illustrate how the constructs of intertextuality, intercontextuality, and discourse orders might be used to provide insight

---

[5]Within each level there can be multiple levels. Thus, at the textual level, intertextual links can be proposed at the level of lexical items, grammatical structures among words, genres, content, and so on. The same is true at the level of events and social institutions.

about how interpersonal dynamics at the micro level contribute to given categories of social identity at the macro level.

DISCOURSE ANALYSIS OF THREE RELATED EVENTS IN A 6TH-GRADE SOCIAL STUDIES/LANGUAGE ARTS LESSON

On the basis of the preceding theoretical and methodological discussions, in this section we use the constructs of intertextuality, intercontextuality, and interdiscoursivity to focus attention on how the three events involving Carol and Andrew might be implicated in given categories of social identity, namely race, ethnicity, class, and gender.

We begin by noting that in the three events there are no explicit markers of race, ethnicity, gender, or class; that is, none of the participants refer to each other with explicit appellations of racial, ethnic, gender, or class social identity.[6] Yet it is reasonable to assume that the given categories of race, ethnicity, class, and gender do have validity within the classroom, at least at the level of the social institution, if for no other reason than that the school classifies students on the basis of race–ethnicity, economic level, and gender. Furthermore, in assigning students to classrooms, care is taken to ensure that the proportion of Black students to non-Black students is within school district guidelines and that that the proportion of males to females is a reasonable representation of that of the school as a whole. Although economic level is not used to determine class placement, it is noted with regard to school lunch, and thus eligibility for the free lunch program is marked in teacher records.[7] Also, the school itself is designated as a Title I school, a label indicating the generally low economic level of the families of the students attending the school. In brief, the given categories of race, ethnicity, class, and gender have usage within the school as an institutional context providing part of what Gee (1996) called an *institutional identity*, although where, how, and what social significance these given categories of social identity have in any particular classroom conversation or in the three events described earlier in this chapter is not necessarily obvious or direct.

---

[6]It may be that the given categories of social identity of race, ethnicity, class, and gender are explicitly assigned and used in other events in the classroom and outside the classroom. To the extent that a researcher is interested in those specific categories of social identity and how they are manifest in a classroom, he or she might carefully select classroom events to analyze where there is explicit use of such given categories of social identity. However, to the extent that a researcher is interested in and selects for investigation a series of classroom events because of other research goals, and views the manifestation of given categories of social identity as one aspect of the events, then the approach may be different.

[7]The designation of a family's economic level through their eligibility to participate in the federal free lunch program does not necessarily indicate their class membership; that is, the members of the family and others around them may have no sense of class membership. Thus, we argue that before class membership can be taken as a given social identity, researchers need to have evidence that it is a category of social identity grounded in people's lives.

Shown in Table 3.3 is a series of intertextual and intercontextual connections and indications of interdiscoursivity within the third event (which is shown in Transcript 3.4). As shown in the table, intertextual, intercontextual, and interdiscoursivity connections are proposed at multiple levels. For example, in line 301 there are proposed links at the levels of text, event, and social institution. Carol's directive to Andrew that he needs to write more about how the Nile River helped Egyptians is not just a proposed link among the article on the Nile River that they read, her feedback sheet, and Andrew's feedback sheet; it is also a proposed juxtaposition with her previous discussion with Mr. West about Andrew's feedback sheet, her previous interaction with Andrew regarding his feedback sheet, and goals of the social institution (i.e., the school) with regard to curriculum and institutional ideology (a sorting procedure based on a meritocracy). Also as shown in Table 3.3, connections may be proposed, but they are not necessarily acknowledged or recognized by interlocutors. When connections are not acknowledged or recognized, they can be viewed as having failed to become manifest—that is, no intertextuality, intercontextuality, or interdiscoursivity is socially constructed. In Table 3.3, a number of proposed connections are not acknowledged or recognized. Just as important is that there are a series of proposed connections in which the processes of acknowledgment, recognition, and social significance are ambiguous. That is, their social construction is ambiguous both to participants within the event and to researchers. This ambiguity (or *indeterminacy* as Bloome, 1993, called it) can be a conversational resource as opposed to a constraint; that is, people in interaction with each other can use the indeterminacy of the social significance and meaning of an utterance, text, proposed intertextual connection, and so on, to construct a working consensus within an event and to provide a way for meanings to evolve and change. Or, as is the case in Table 3.3, people can construct a working consensus that allows the event to continue and run its course although the interlocutors may be referencing different meanings. That is, the event can proceed smoothly without people necessarily having to agree too specifically about what is happening or what meanings are being created. Carol creates connections to school writing as a genre, as a set of expectations or standards for the use of written language in tasks such as the one Andrew must complete. Andrew creates connections to the reproduction of specific textual items and not necessarily to the genre of school writing as Carol has defined it.

As shown in Table 3.3, Carol proposes a series of connections between the text Andrew is creating through the revision of his original feedback sheet and the institutional level (see lines 301, 305, and 311–317). Carol is using what might be called the *institutional demands* for a particular type of academic literacy practice. She describes it as "write more" and as including a series of reasons why the flooding of the Nile River benefited the people who lived in the flood plain. It is as if she is sharing with Andrew an

TABLE 3.3

Intertextuality in Lines 301–326 of the 6th-Grade Lesson

Line No.	Speaker	Message Units	Pro	Ack	Rec	Proposed Intertextuality, Intercontextuality, Interdiscoursivity	Social Significance	Commentary
301	Carol	You need to write more about how the Nile	X			Discussion with Mr. West (see Transcript 3.2, lines 101–104)		Although unacknowledged and unrecognized, one of the "deep" principles to be learned in the unit was the adaptation of people to the environment. Neither Carol nor Andrew is explicitly making connections to this goal.
		River helped	X			Previous interaction regarding feedback sheet (see Transcript 3.2, lines 105–113)		"Write more" may reference an ideology about making it through school rather than an ideology about the learning of social studies. Writing
			X			Article on the Nile		"more" may also reference a "shared" expectation about school writing (writing more = higher grade).
			X			Carol's feedback sheet		
			X			"Community of Learners"	As part of the explicit instructional organization, students are supposed to help and seek help from other students.	
							Grading	Although not explicitly noted, students receive grades on their written work.
				X		School writing		

TABLE 3.3 *(continued)*

Line No.	Speaker	Message Units	Pro	Ack	Rec	Proposed Intertextuality, Intercontextuality, Interdiscoursivity	Social Significance	Commentary
302		In the transportation route	X					Andrew is positioned as someone who is able to write more and therefore be successful but who does not do so.
303		how	X					
304		It helped them grow food	X					"That" is an ambiguous reference, as it may refer to the list of topics in lines 301–304, or it may refer to the instructional theme of the many ways that people adapted to their environment.
305		You can write a lot about that	X			Connects with "more" in line 301	Andrew is capable of writing more.	Writing a "lot" also refers to a norm of school writing.

148

Line	Speaker	Utterance						
306		Not about the (indecipherable)	X			Andrew's feedback sheet	Andrew was a misguided student.	Andrew is not a capable student on his own.
307	Andrew	I already I already wrote about that	X	X	X	Previous writing events	Intertextual connection at the text level.	Contests social positioning in lines 305 and 306.
							Intercontextual link to previous writing event.	"That" references the last item on Carol's list (line 304)—"food." The intertextual link to the instructional theme is not taken up.
308	Carol	yeah		X	X			Ambiguous reference; can be taken as acknowledging and recognizing proposed intertextual link to 307 and revised feedback response or as referencing her own previous utterances and intertextual proposals.
309	Andrew	How they grow food	X	X	X	Reference to line 304 and article on the Nile River	Argument that the feedback text is already adequate (with the concomitant argument that he is a competent student and writer).	Andrew is proposing an intertextual link among what he wrote on his previous feedback sheet, Carol's comment in line 304, and the article on the Nile. He is not necessarily linking to the school genre of writing (school writing), which is the link proposed in line 304 by Carol.

TABLE 3.3 *(continued)*

Line No.	Speaker	Message Units	Pro	Ack	Rec	Proposed Intertextuality, Intercontextuality, Interdiscoursivity	Social Significance	Commentary
310	Carol	okay	X		X		Begins new interactional unit. Signals intertextual link between Andrew's feedback text and the article on the Nile. Ambiguous reference, as it may refer to line 309 and its implied meanings, or it may be a conjunction linking to the list in lines 311–316, a device to get the floor, or a marking of a new interactional unit.	"Okay" is ambiguous, as it may be interpreted as a demarcation between interactional units or it may be interpreted as signaling acknowledgment and recognition. Even if taken as acknowledgment and recognition, it may be referring not to the connections proposed by Andrew but to the connections Carol proposed in line 304 to the school genre of writing.
311		How it helped transportation route	X			Article on the Nile, Carol's feedback sheet, school writing		

312	How it helped them grow food	X	Article on the Nile, Carol's feedback sheet, school writing	
313	How it was good	X	Article on the Nile, Carol's feedback sheet, school writing	Lines 311–316 constitute a list. Although intertextual links can be made to any specific line, the list also functions as a unit. Thus, in line 317, "that" may refer not to specific items but to the list. The reference might be to the writing of a list (which would be a definition of "more").
314	For people to get around better	X	Article on the Nile, Carol's feedback sheet, school writing	
315	How the farming helped	X	Article on the Nile, Carol's feedback sheet, school writing	
316	And they got rich soil from that	X	Article on the Nile, Carol's feedback sheet, school writing	

TABLE 3.3 (continued)

Line No.	Speaker	Message Units	Pro	Ack	Rec	Proposed Intertextuality, Intercontextuality, Interdiscoursivity	Social Significance	Commentary
317		You need to write about that	X			Andrew's feedback sheet, discussion with Mr. West, Carol's feedback sheet, grading, school writing	Andrew is positioned as not knowing what to do.	Carol is comparing Andrew's feedback sheet to an accepted model of school writing, perhaps based on her feedback sheet and the processes involved in creating it.
				X			Carol as teacher.	
							Genre of school writing.	Carol is connecting the writing to the expectations and standards for school writing and their relationship to grading.
							Andrew is positioned as aligning himself with a low grade.	
318	Andrew	Now look	X			Comments on feedback sheet	Andrew is using one of Carol's rhetorical techniques to direct attention and designate an authoritative frame; as such, Andrew is positioning himself as astute with regard to what the revisions should be.	"Now" signals both a new interactional unit and a redirection or resistance to the assumptions underlying the conversation about authority.
					X	Connection to Event 2 (Carol's imperative to Andrew to "look")		

	Utterance				Contextualization		
319	It says	X	X		Juxtaposing comments on feedback sheet with the model Carol is invoking (line 317) Grading	Andrew is contesting what Carol wants him to do and therefore is also contesting her authority and social position. The established authority is constituted by the written comments.	Focuses attention on the text itself (as opposed to the genre of school writing)
320	All I need to write about	X	X	X	Projected grading event, projected revised feedback sheet response, multiple enactments by Carol of her teacher role		Accomplishing the task adequately is defined by doing that which is explicitly outlined. Andrew's use of "need to" is a repetition of words Carol uses to invoke her authority as teacher. When Andrew uses these words he positions himself as supplanting her authority and role.
321	Is what (pause)	X					False start
322	Other ways the land, the river, and the weather affect their life	X			Juxtaposing projected feedback sheet with the written comments and with the list in lines 311–316	Defining the text to be written.	The connection is with a specific text and not with a genre of writing.

TABLE 3.3 *(continued)*

Line No.	Speaker	Message Units	Pro	Ack	Rec	Proposed Intertextuality, Intercontextuality, Interdiscoursivity	Social Significance	Commentary
323		That's all I gotta write about	X			Grading	Positions himself as in reach of being a competent student and writer. Andrew is within the proximity of receiving a respectable grade for his work.	The criterion for what needs to be done—the underlying ideology of being successful in the lesson—is the production of the text itself as opposed to the production of a text that represents the genre of school writing.
324	Carol	yep		X	X	The list generated in lines 311–317 or the text generated in lines 319–323	Establishing a working consensus that allows the conversation to continue although they may be talking about different things.	Ambiguous reference, as it could refer to lines 319–323 or merely indicate presence but not agreement
325		How it affected their life		X	X	The list in lines 311–316 Line 322 repeating "affect their life"	School writing, text of comments on the feedback sheet.	Ambiguous reference. Referring back to her previous description of what Andrew needed to do (line 301) or reference to Andrew's assertion in lines 322 and 323
326	Andrew	It says land, the river, and the weather affect their life		X		Comments on the feedback sheet. Article on the Nile	Text of comments on the feedback sheet	The proposed intertextual link is at the level of text rather than at a genre level.

algorithm for providing a display that can count as the needed academic literacy practice. From the larger ethnographic study of the classroom, we know that the explicit curriculum focused on the learning of deep principles of social studies, including how people adapted to their environments. Carol mentions not this deep principle but rather the characteristics of the needed academic literacy practice based on the success of her feedback form and on her conversation with Mr. West. who provided her with guidance in helping Andrew. Andrew does not acknowledge or recognize the connection to the academic literacy practice, the genre of school writing, or the need for display of either. Instead, he proposes a connection between the written text he is creating and the text written by the teacher on his original feedback form. Carol's response is ambiguous with regard to whether she is acknowledging, recognizing, and giving social significance to the intertextual connections Andrew made. In brief, the intertextual connection Andrew is proposing is at the level of text to text, whereas Carol is proposing a connection between text and a language practice that exists at an institutional level.

It also seems to be the case that both Carol and Andrew are indirectly raising the issues of grading; that is, Carol tells Andrew what he "needs to do" (lines 301 and 317) presumably to create an acceptable written text and receive a desired/passing grade. Later, Andrew uses the same words, "need to …" (line 320), to connect both to Carol's previous comments and to the goal of creating an acceptable written text and receiving a desired/passing grade. Thus, Andrew is also connecting their face-to-face interaction to an institutional level. However, he and Carol differ in their assumptions about the cultural ideology manifest at the institutional level. Indeed, there are at least three different manifest views of the cultural ideology of "doing school" at the institutional level. There is (a) the ideological view of the curriculum planners, who are concerned with the learning of deep principles and how it might be displayed; (b) the ideological view of producing academic texts that can count as displaying a particular set of academic literacy practices (what Carol calls "write more"); and (c) Andrew's view of "doing school" as doing what he has been told by the teacher that he needs to do. Stated more simply, Carol is responding to the cultural norms for literacy work associated with the social institution, whereas Andrew is responding to specific textual productions and not displaying socialization to the cultural norms of the institution for literacy work.

The identity work being done in Transcript 3.4 involves multiples levels, including face-to-face interaction and institutional. As shown in Table 3.3, the social identities constructed at each level are linked by Carol and Andrew, although in different ways. For Carol, they are linked as part of school enculturalization processes; for Andrew, they are linked in terms of gatekeeping and credentialing processes.

We argue that in the construction of their institutional identities (which may overlap only partially with the social identities they construct within specific face-to-face events in the classroom), both Carol and Andrew are accumulating a set of social identities, social positions, and attributes associated with the social institution's definition of personhood. The institution has assigned to Carol and Andrew given social identities of race, ethnicity, class, and gender. It has also assigned to Carol and Andrew the social identity and social position of student. Each of these given social identities constitutes part of the institution's manifest definition of personhood; a person has a race, ethnicity, gender, and economic class level, and is either a student or a teacher. The institution has also assigned to them differential attributes of personhood based on their academic achievement; Carol has even been given the social identity of "teacher." However, in order for Carol to take on the identity of teacher, she needs others to take on the social identity of student to her teacher. Andrew is often unwilling to do so. In Transcript 3.2, Carol as a teacher delegate makes it clear to Andrew that either he behaves in an institutionally sanctioned manner (taking on the social identity of student to her teacher) or she will ignore him and leave him to risk an even lower academic status. Andrew's low academic status has already put him at risk at an institutional level of being denied status as a person. Indeed, as we discussed earlier in this chapter, at the beginning of Transcript 3.2 Carol and Mr. West do ignore Andrew; he is not a person at the beginning of Transcript 3.2, and he has to assert being a person.

Returning to the question of how the given social identity categories of race, ethnicity, class, and gender are implicated in the three events analyzed in this chapter, one way to describe the process is that students are accumulating a series of institutional identities, some of which they are given by the institution and some that they construct within classroom conversations. Some may be resisted, others accepted and adopted. The social identities, social positions, and attributes of personhood they accumulate can be viewed as a collage that constitutes who they are within the social institution. In brief, as students and teachers engage each other in instructional conversations, they are always in the process of constructing and accumulating institutional identities for themselves and each other. Part of that institutional identity is given, and part is constructed through connections made between what occurs in specific classroom events and the institutional level. In brief, it is not so much the case in the events analyzed here that the given social identity categories of race, ethnicity, class, and gender influenced how Carol, Andrew, and Mr. West interacted with each other (at least, there is no explicit evidence of such influence), but rather how they interacted with each other contributed to their institutional identities (part of which were given) and to the social institution's definition of personhood. Among the social consequences of the institutional identities constructed and the definition of personhood held by a social institution are the distribution of educational opportunities made available to the students, the social status and privileges made available to them within the social institution (e.g., honor student, access to special academic programs), marginalization, removal, and denial of personhood status (e.g., referral to special programs, special schools, suspension, expulsion). Another consequence is the provision of available rationales for explaining student behavior within events. For example, Andrew's performance on the feedback form, his sulking, and his contesting of Carol's efforts to help him may be explained merely by designating his behavior as that of a "low-achieving," "reluctant," "Black" "male" student from a low-income community, all of which are social identities he has accumulated either through assignment or through face-to-face events in the classroom.

At issue, then, at a theoretical level and a methodological level, and with regard to specific findings, is the definition of personhood held by the social institution and how people within that institution use and contribute to that definition of personhood. Of concern are the social identities, social positions, and attributes of a person made available; the rationales provided to explain (or explain away) people's interactional behavior; the relationship between a definition of personhood and the distribution of opportunities, privileges, and sanctions; the ways in which the social dynamics of events at the face-to-face level contribute to institutional identities (and vice versa); and the spaces, events, social interactions, and social identities people create that eschew incorporation into institutional identities.

CONCLUDING COMMENTS

A microethnographic approach to the discourse analysis of social identity in classroom language and literacy events eschews a simple or unproblematized approach to the description of social identities. It neither allows given identities to determine social identity nor allows given social identities to be dismissed. Rather, it insists on documentation and description of the social construction of social identities from how people act and react to each other, from the ground up. It insists on material data interpreted through the frameworks established by the people who are themselves in interaction with each other.

We have illustrated in this chapter a recursive process that moves back and forth between theorizing and the close analysis of data from the social interaction of teachers and students. Other modes of analysis of the social interaction among students and teachers beyond those presented here are possible and warranted. At issue was not the generation of a definitive and encompassing statement about social identity in the two events described (the storytelling and the classroom homework revision) but rather the generation of one set of insights about how teachers and students managed and defined each other through their social interactions and their linguistic behavior.

One needs to ask why a researcher would be concerned with questions of social identity. Underlying and perhaps unstated in some investigations of social identity are assumptions about the relationship of social identity and psychological health. Do the social identities assumed by or assigned to students provide them with positive social identities from which to engage in learning? Underlying other investigations of social identity are questions of educational equity and social justice. Are the social identities assumed and assigned ones that provide students with equitable access to educational resources and opportunities? A micro-ethnographic approach to the discourse analysis of classroom language and literacy events can provide insight into investigations of social identity based on the two questions of (a) psychological health and (b) educational equity. However, the approaches we have discussed here are liable to problematize the constructs that underlie definitions of psychological health and educational equity along with problematizing static and given definitions of social identity. The approach described in this chapter focuses attention on the social construction of personhood as part of the process of socially constructing social identities within the moment-by-moment context of classroom language and literacy events. At issue is not simply the assumption, assignment, or construction of social identities and their evolution over time and events but what meaning these social identities have and what social consequences they have over time for both the individual and for all people involved in the process of socially constructing social identities. The agenda laid out here, therefore, is concerned with understanding social identities *in motion*, as part of a process of continuity and change within and across events, settings, and social institutions.

Microethnographic Discourse Analysis and the Exploration of Power Relations in Classroom Language and Literacy Events

Power is often discussed in studies of classroom language and literacy events either directly or by reference to related topics such as equity, democracy, freedom, justice, racism, classism, homophobia, sexism, and so forth. What is meant by *power* is often vague, undertheorized, or left as an unacknowledged empty sign. In this chapter we examine the potential benefits of microethnographic discourse analysis to sharpen the discussion and debate of what and how power is in classroom language and literacy events.[1]

One of our goals in this chapter is to show multiple ways to approach the microethnographic analysis of power relations by focusing on "how power is." We do not argue for a singular definition of power, or for a particular approach to the explication of power relations in classrooms; rather, we argue for approaches to microethnographic discourse analyses that are cognizant of the varied and complex definitions of power, remembering cautions by Barrett, Stockholm, and Burke (2001) that "power is not everything" (p. 473) and that "an abstract theory of power has little utility" (p. 473).

We begin by discussing three models for defining power, then we argue for a reflective stance in the microethnographic analysis of power relations in classroom language and literacy events. Finally, we examine the complexities of power relations in classroom language and literacy

---

[1]Further discussion of multiple definitions of power can be found in Street (1995b, 1996) and Sheridan, Street, and Bloome (2000).

events through the microethnographic analysis of two classroom literacy lessons: one from the 7th-grade language arts classroom we discussed in chapter 2 and one from a 6th-grade social studies classroom (a different one from the one we discussed in chap. 3). We use the two analyses to enable us to (a) discuss a broader range of issues than only one of the examples would have allowed and (b) to illustrate how a comparative perspective can provide additional insight.

MODELS OF POWER

Power as Product

When *power* is defined as a product, it is viewed as a commodity, an object; a measurable thing that one person has over another or more of than another. Money, physical strength, and weapons, are prototypical examples as having larger quantities of these commodities may place a person or a group in a position to coerce others. If power is viewed as a commodity, then it can be given, received, transferred, traded, and taken away.

For the definition of power as product to be grounded—that is, to have validity within the context of people's lives—people must act, value, feel, believe, think, and use language[2] in ways defined as rational within the paradigm of a *market economy*. That is, within a market economy, exchanging commodities must be viewed as a valid and reliable activity, acquisition must be a desirable activity, self-interest (either as an individual or a group) must be viewed as a legitimate motivation, and competition must be viewed as ethical and inherent in the human condition. Definitions of power as product cannot exist outside of an ideology about social relationships and personhood closely related to a market economy.

Literacy can be defined as power from the perspective of power as a product. When viewed as a set of skills, a collection of reading and writing tools, literacy becomes a quantifiable entity, measurable and transferable, and becomes analogous to the prototypical examples of money, strength, and weapons. One person can be seen as having better or more literacy skills than another and, as such, may be in a more advantageous position than others with regard to obtaining desired things or coercing others. Such an advantage may be direct, as when a person uses his or her literacy skills to obtain and mark property, or the advantage may be indirect, as when a person exchanges his or her literacy skills for economic or symbolic capital—for example, by obtaining a high-paying job because they have a particular set of literacy skills (e.g., knowing how to read and write like a lawyer) or by earning an academic degree that provides the social status neces-

---

[2]The six items—acting, believing, feeling, valuing, language, and thinking—are derived from Goodenough's (1981) definition of *culture*.

sary to obtain desired goods and to influence others. From this point of view, questions can be asked about which literacy skills provide "power" in the sense of access to goods and influence, as well as how much literacy skill is needed, who should receive it, and from whom. Although one would want to be careful not to push the argument too far, it is safe to presume that the more of the "right" literacy skills one has, the more access one has to desired goods and influence.[3]

When power and literacy are viewed as quantifiable commodities, *empowering* others comes to mean that the "powerless" or "illiterate" can be "improved" by giving them skills or cultural capital to allow them to be more powerful. Inherent in such a view is a deficit model (although the cause of the deficit—genetic, cultural, linguistic—may be debated). Also inherent in a product model of power and literacy is the implicit concept that a certain amount of power exists, and not everyone can have it at the same time. Power can be taken away; people can be left illiterate and powerless. Literacy education can be denied to someone's or some group's children. Even if literacy skills themselves are not viewed as a finite quantity (e.g., everyone can learn the American alphabet), they are made to act as if they are a finite set because of the competition for access to cultural, symbolic, and economic capital.[4] Thus, although everyone can learn the alphabet, children who learn it early and quickly may be identified as academically oriented or gifted and placed on a higher track, whereas children who learn it slowly are identified as deficit and are at risk of being placed in special education tracks. Viewed this way, the power-as-product model promulgates a deficit model of literacy that has the potential to be coercive.

From the perspective of power as product, questions about literacy can be asked regarding who has what literacy skills, who provides or denies access to literacy skills, and what one needs to do to gain access to literacy skills. Questions of equity and social justice revolve around questions of the distribution of literacy skills and who controls access to them.

Fundamental to the model of power-as-product is the assumption that this is the only way to define power. The model assumes that everyone orients toward power as a product, seeks power, and wants more of it. Yet there are numerous examples, both in daily life and on broader scales, of people not solely orienting toward power as product, not seeking power, and not being coerced by the power other people have accumulated. Viewing literacy from the perspective of power as product fails to take into account the social and cultural aspects of literacy; the dynamics of cultural identity; and people's sense of self, their knowledge, worldview, and epistemologies. These aspects of literacy lie much deeper in people's minds and cultures than at the level of technical skills, such that learning a particular literacy in-

---

[3]*More* refers both to a quantity and to a competition (i.e., "more than someone else").
[4]For one example, see Dore's (1976) discussion of the diploma disease.

volves a much larger commitment and a significant shift in self-concept, identity, social life, and ideology. In some classrooms, for example, teachers may relinquish the "power" they have to control the topic of discussion or determine the correctness of an answer, insist that each child be viewed as a poet and author on a level plane, and resist hierarchical assessments. Some adult literacy programs focus minimally on the acquisition of literacy skills *per se* and instead focus on engaging their students in community action projects or other projects closely connected to their lives. Instead of accumulating skills to be exchanged for cultural, economic, and symbolic capital, such students are learning new ways (additional ways) of being in the world and of defining knowledge. Although it may be possible to concoct explanations of the counterexamples just given using a power-as-product model (as in "literacy [or some other skill] is an alternative route to power"), such concoctions are unsatisfying because they overlook challenges to the literacy-as-power-as-product model. We prefer explanations based on alternative models of power, namely, power as process.

Power as Process

Another model of power is the *process* model, which takes the view that power varies among and between contexts rather than being a static product. Power can be viewed as a set of relations among people and among social institutions that may shift from one situation to another. In addition, power is not something accumulated (like money or weapons) as much as it is a structuration of interpersonal relations, events, institutions, and ideologies (cf. Giddens, 1979, 1984; van Dijk, 1996). The locus of power, therefore, is not an individual or group per se but the processes that structure relationships among people. From this perspective, power is always contested and dialogic. Each action is the process of bargaining and compromise, all parties contribute to the process of power, and ultimately we are all part of the human network (e.g., Janeway, 1981, Lips, 1991).

According to this definition of power, power relations are an inherent part of any set of social and cultural practices and, as such, those power relations are integral parts of our daily lived experiences. Thus, power is a process that characterizes virtually all social relationships, both among individuals and among larger social units (Radtke & Stam, 1994).

Consider, for example, classrooms in which reading achievement is evaluated by students demonstrating achievement on a predetermined set of hierarchically ordered skills. From a power-as-product model, a student who is progressing through the various skills may be viewed as gaining "power"—skills that are transformed into social status (through report card grades, awards, etc.) and economic access (through admission to educational opportunities that lead to higher paying jobs). However, it is the structuring of reading into a set of hierarchical skills, and the institutional mechanisms of assessing those skills, that provides the "power" by defining who is who (good reader vs. bad reader), and how cultural capital (reading skills) can be transformed into symbolic status (e.g., designations that range from valedictorian to high school graduate) and economic status (access to higher paying jobs; see Bloome & Carter, 2001).

Power also lies in the ways that the structuring is supported through mechanisms of surveillance and of the policing of teachers, students, and the school (cf. Foucault, 1980), as well as through the discourse of access and the manufacturing of consent (van Dijk, 1996). Individuals who do not align themselves with the structuring are liable to lose their jobs or to be designated as failures, learning disabled, or psychologically dangerous.

An important aspect of the power-as-process model is the naturalization of a discourse and a culture. A word, symbol, language, or way of doing things becomes an integral part of a culture, so much so that it is taken as common or shared, and people who are ignorant of its "common-ness" are seen as not having common sense. This hegemony of discourses privileges some words, languages, and cultures by making them appear natural or commonplace while at the same time marginalizing other words, languages, and cultures by making them appear unnatural and not having common sense. Naturalization makes it possible to distinguish the normal from the abnormal, the sane from the insane, the righteous from the criminal, and "us" from "them" and, once so defined, naturalization makes it possible to justify acts to marginalize, punish, and annihilate the "other." To define literacy as a hierarchical set of skills and then to declare it so, and only so (through "science," general acclaim, state mandates, etc.), is to make a bid for naturalization and thus for the marginalization and criminalization of people who disagree or appear to be different. The analysis of power in classroom language and literacy events, from this perspective, seeks to examine the processes of naturalization, revealed in part by what is taken to be "common sense" and what is "not reasonable," what is "acceptable" and what is not.

From the perspective of power as process, control comes in the form of information and knowledge, not as a quantity but as an interpretive framework—what is sometimes called a *discourse* or *paradigm*—for defining and acting in the world that pushes out other ways of interpreting and acting, thinking, feeling, believing, and knowing. By reinforcing a particular interpretive framework or way of knowing as a naturalized way of thinking and being (*naturalized* in the sense of seeming to just exist, without human manufacture or conniving), a dominant culture is reinforced and re-created without seeming to be coercive (nonetheless, some may experience brutal discipline; Schutz, 2004). Control of the reading curriculum is a good example. Whoever is in charge of the reading curriculum, whether it is a textbook company, a state department, a local school district, the teacher, the federal government, or some combination of these, chooses which information to share and which information to leave out. In doing so, they often appeal to what "the research says" or what "parents want" or what "the teachers want" or "what is tested." As a result, students are provided with a conception of reading and literacy that is reinforced by a system of choices and relationships (among the state, the schools, the mass media, the test and textbook makers, etc.). At the same time, alternative conceptions of reading and reading curricula are discounted, declared irrational, unscientific, and lacking common sense, and the individuals who advocate for alternative approaches to the teaching of reading are liable to find themselves accused of harming children, of engaging in "soft racism" and denying children access to the dominant culture and economy.

Power as Caring Relations

There are a series of discussions about power and social relationships that seem to us sufficiently distinguished from the preceding discussions of power to warrant a separate section, although one could reasonably argue that they fall within the power-as-process model. We are referring to feminist discussions of power, such as those by Noddings (1984, 1989, 1992, 1993), Kreisberg (1992), and Smith (1989, 1990), among others, as well as to discussions of education with similar themes promulgated by a number of African American female scholars (e.g., Collins, 2000; Foster, 1997; Gay, 2000; hooks, 1981, 1990, 1994, 2000; hooks & Manning, 2000; Ladson-Billings, 1994).[5]

Although feminist theorists and educators vary in how they define power, one way to characterize feminist discussions of power is that women's work and life experiences are viewed as the grounding for theory generation. As Smith (1989, 1990) has made clear, until relatively recently sociological theories overlooked women's labor and life experiences. When those experiences are taken seriously and made central, it is not just new theoretical constructs that emerge but new paradigms for understanding human experience. Thus, although one can find much in common between models of power as process and feminist perspectives (see Collins, 2000; Weedon, 1996), given their different historical roots it is helpful to distinguish models of power derived from feminist and related discussions of power from the models discussed in the preceding section. More simply stated, models of power that are derived from feminist and related perspectives provide another point of departure for researchers interested in the microethnographic analysis of classroom language and literacy events.

A model of power as caring relations requires a reconceptualization of "power." Instead of being viewed power as only a coercive relationship or

---

[5]Feminist scholars and African American female scholars are not the only ones to discuss power in terms of "caring" relationships; see, for example, Buber (1976).

as a set of constraining influences, power is viewed as having the potential to bring people together for mutual benefit, both with regard to social relationships and with regard to other accomplishments. Kreisberg (1992), building on Noddings's (1984) definition of *caring relations*, distinguished between models of power that were "power over" others and models of power that were "power with." The caring relations that are at the center of a power-with model are not defined as surface-level politeness, sympathy, or "just being nice" but, as Gay and Banks (2000) described as a reciprocal and multidimensional process involving action, effort, achievement, accountability, respect, self-determination for self, community, and others, and responsiveness.

A model of power as caring relations also requires a reconceptualization of personhood and community. Foregrounded is the notion that inherent to a person are emotional, caring connections to others and that these emotional, caring connections are neither frivolous nor optional; neither are they vacuous in the sense of not having implications for action (e.g., teaching and learning). Indeed, they are realized through action. In a similar manner, a *community* not only consists of shared goals, a location, a network, or histories but also implies a set of caring relationships that members have with each other. A classroom community requires a set of caring relations (a) between teacher and students and (b) among students.

With regard to language and literacy, viewed from the perspective of power as caring relations, questions are asked about the role of language and literacy practices in helping to establish caring relations and communities and how caring relations and communities define and enact language and literacy practices. Conversely, questions are asked about how language and literacy practices might alienate people from each other and strip them of affective dimensions. How do people use language and literacy practices to create situations of "power with" each other, rather than "power over" each other, and what do they do to language and literacy practices when they place caring relations at the center of their social relationships?

For example, consider a 9th-grade language arts classroom in which the class is discussing Sandra Cisneros's *The House on Mango Street,* a book that raises important issues about identity, friendship, family, heritage, and community. Rather than asking questions solely about what reading skills the students are gaining or how much they comprehend, from the perspective of power as caring relations questions might be asked about how the organization of the discussion has helped students gain a better understanding of themselves, of others, and of their families and communities. Questions are asked about how or whether the class's engagement with the book created bonds of affinity and care among the students in the class and between the students in the class and people outside the class. Questions might be asked about whether the lesson helps students learn to use written text to distance, coerce, and silence others or whether they are learning to use written language to create a community of caring relations.

Part of what is key to approaching literacy from the perspective of power as caring relations is what is foregrounded and what is backgrounded. For example, consider two classrooms in which both teachers are concerned with fostering caring relations among the students and with the students' comprehension skills. However, in one classroom the teacher foregrounds the acquisition of comprehension skills and views the promulgation of caring relations as merely an enabling condition that promotes comprehension, and in the other classroom the teacher foregrounds caring relations among the students and defines reading comprehension in a manner that supports the evolution of a caring disposition.

TOWARD A REFLEXIVE STANCE IN THE MICROETHNOGRAPHIC ANALYSIS OF POWER RELATIONS IN CLASSROOM LANGUAGE AND LITERACY EVENTS

We view a reflexive stance as important to excavating power relations in classroom language and literacy events because it is not just the power relations among teachers and students, administrators, school boards, politicians, and so on, that are at issue but also the relationships of social institutions such as schooling, business, government, and *educational research*. There is no escaping either the characterization of educational research as a social institution, with all of the grand narratives, structures, rituals and rites, language, and culture of any social institution; neither can educational researchers escape being implicated in power relations (and that includes us as well). Research, including microethnographic analysis, is not a power-free or politically neutral enterprise (see Gitlin, 1994, for further discussion).

The microethnographic discourse analysis of power relations in classroom language and literacy events cannot be reduced to a set of procedures to be followed or a set of extant theoretical constructs to apply. Microethnographic discourse analysis requires more than taking a model of power and laying it over an event. We prefer to view the microethnographic discourse analysis of power relations in classroom literacy events as a recursive and reflexive process in pursuit of new understandings about the relationships of people and institutions to each other that moves across (a) consideration of models of power, (b) the dynamics of language in use, and (c) the demands of research as a social institution including the ways in which the researchers are acting in and on their worlds and bridging worlds (see Fig. 4.1).

Viewed from this perspective, the discourse analysis of power relations in classroom literacy events does not provide an unassailed moral high ground from which to judge the righteousness and morality of what occurs

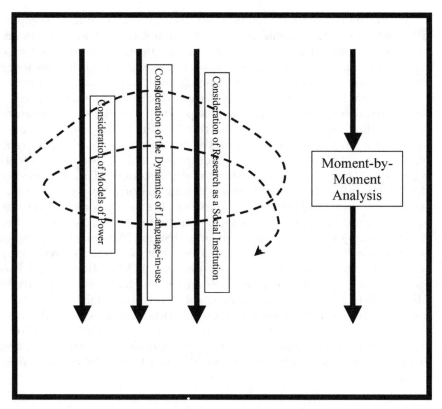

FIG. 4.1   Recursive and reflexive analysis of power relations in an event.

in classrooms. It only helps reveal, and only partially so, how we are all implicated in each others' lives and what we are doing to and with each other.

A DISCOURSE ANALYSIS OF POWER RELATIONS AND KNOWLEDGE IN A 7TH-GRADE CLASSROOM LITERACY EVENT

In chapter 2 we focused on continuity and change in classroom literacy practices and illustrated the tensions between continuity and change through a microanalysis of a 7th-grade language arts lesson. That micro-analysis involved a multiple-level analysis. We showed how at one level the classroom literacy practices appeared to be consistent with extant cultural models for classroom reading and writing, whereas at another level critical changes were occurring. We also showed that students variously participated at one level or the other or across the levels.

In the analysis of power relations, we are again faced with the complex task of revealing them on multiple levels. At a surface level, we could examine the differential distribution of cultural, linguistic, economic, and symbolic capital. Stated otherwise, we could examine whose cultural knowledge was valued in the classroom, whose language and ways of talking were valued, who had the economic resources to afford educational privileges (e.g., computers, special books, educational trips, etc.), what the social hierarchy was, and who filled which positions in that hierarchy. But doing so is more complex than it might initially seem. For example, consider the 7th-grade language arts classroom we described in chapter 2. There were 25 students in the class. The teacher and most of the students were African American. Most, but not all of the students, spoke African American language at home, in the community, and often in the classroom (including some of the white students). Most of the students came from the local area, a working-class section of a major city in the southern United States. (A detailed description of the class is provided in chap. 2). An analysis of the students' turn-taking behavior in one segment from one lesson (lines 1–32 in Transcript 4.1) is presented in Table 4.1. The analysis examines who had how many turns at talk, who determined turn-taking protocols, who initiated the topics of discussion, who interrupted whom, who revoiced whose comments, and so on.

By conducting an analysis such as that shown in Table 4.1, we would be implying that the distribution of turns, topic initiations, interruptions, and so on, could be readily interpreted—in other words, that the interpretation

TRANSCRIPT 4.1
Lines 01–32 7th-Grade Language Arts Lesson

01	Ms. Wilson:	We're talkin' about 1865.
02		And we're talkin' about a period of time when slavery was still instituted↑
03	SS:	Yes.
04	Ms. Wilson:	Was slavery still instituted↑
05	SS:	Yes.
06	Ms. Wilson:	Were blacks allowed the same type of education as whites↑
07	SS:	No
08	Theresa:	XXXXXXXX no
09		That's why...

10	Ms. Wilson:	[*Holds up hand*] I'm still making my point
11	Theresa:	OK go ahead
12		Just go ahead
13	Ms. Wilson:	OK
14		So if we know that slavery was still instituted
15		If we know that African Americans were not afforded the same education as other people
16		Is it a matter that they don't *quote unquote* know any better
17		Or they never had the opportunity to get an education
18	Camika:	They never had an opportunity
19	Ms. Wilson:	I'm not asking you [*Directed to students calling out responses*]
20		I'm asking the person who made comment [Theresa (T) had earlier made the comment Ms. Wilson was referring to, that black people talked "that way" in 1865 "because they did not know any better"]
21	Theresa:	They didn't have the opportunity
22	Ms. Wilson	They did not have the opportunity
23	Ms. Wilson:	Now.
24		Over a period of time
25		1865 all the way to 1997
26		There are still people who use terms and phrases
27		*De, fo', folks*
28		That are similar to what we read in the poem
29	Theresa:	Yea but..
30	Ms. Wilson:	Is that by choice↑
31	Theresa:	Choice
32	Ms. Wilson:	Or is that because *quote unquote* a lack of knowledge

TABLE 4.1
Analysis of Turns at Talk

	Turns at Talk	Interrupts	Initiates Topics	Revoicing	Determined turn-taking protocols
Teacher	20 message units, 9 turns	2	3	1	Establishes turn-taking protocol 3 times
Students	11 message units, 9 turns	0	0	0	0

is given in the analysis. That is, there is an unstated implication that the person or group with the largest number of turns, and so on, is the person or group with the most power. Furthermore, there is a "given" moral interpretation that the unequal distribution of turns (and the unequal distribution of valued cultural, linguistic, economic, and symbolic capital) reveals an inequity and a lack of social justice. In brief, we would find that the teacher dominates by controlling the floor, interrupting students, revoicing certain student comments, determining the topics of conversation, and so on. The teacher is powerful; the students are not.

Notice that such an analysis of power relations, like the one represented in Table 4.1, requires an undifferentiated definition of *power*. It does not take the particular situation, people, or history into account. It also fails to examine "what is happening" and "what is being constructed" and merely focuses on who has how much of what.

In our view, an analysis at the surface level alone is incomplete in a manner that may grossly distort what is happening in the classroom. We further argue that the example of microethnographic analysis presented in Table 4.1 reflects a power imbalance between the institution of educational research on the one hand and those who participate in classroom education (teachers and students) on the other hand. This imbalance is reflected not only in the fact that it is the educational researchers who determined the aspects of classroom life to examine, and that they conducted the analyses and connected the analysis with an interpretation, but also that in doing so they were imposing an ideology on what occurred in a manner that pushed out other cultural ideologies and definitions of power, including those at play in the event. That is, it is the educational researchers who present as common sense an equation between number of turns at talk and power, between number of topic initiations and power, between revoicing and power, and so forth. It is the educational researchers who present as common sense boundaries on the event as including simply the teacher and the students and thereby frame the question of power relations as one of equality with regard to who gets to share and explain their ideas. To the extent that the teacher inhibits the students from expressing their "voices"—and interrupting, controlling the topic of conversation, and revoicing might all be viewed as acts that inhibit students from expressing their voices—the teacher can be viewed as maintaining an inequitable and oppressive relationship with the students. But it is only by failing to examine their own relationship to the participants and to the classroom that educational researchers can make such claims about power in that classroom. Such educational researchers would have to ignore that they engaged in many of the same processes that they would be accusing the teacher of using in structuring power relations. For example, consider Table 4.2, in which we present an analysis of the interaction between the educational researchers and the teachers and students that resulted the analysis presented in Table 4.1.

It is the educational researchers who determined which topics would dominate the description, and it is the educational researchers who revoiced the lesson by describing it using their interpretive framework and specialized discourse as if it, and it alone, identified power relations.

Furthermore, the analysis presented in Table 4.1 is characterized by the difficulty we noted in chapter 1, namely, that attention to structure alone, without consideration of the content and substance of what is occurring, can distort what is happening in an event and can leave unexamined important aspects of the ways in which people act toward and react to each other and about how they act on their environments.

We argue for a more nuanced approach to the analysis of power relations in classroom language and literacy events. Rather than assume that, as educational researchers, we know who is in the event and what they are doing, or even what the boundaries of the event are, we begin by

TABLE 4.2

Comparison of Researchers' and Teachers' Activities

	Generated Dimensions of Analysis	Collected Data	Analyzed Data	Interpreted Data	Wrote Report	Determined Audience and Venues for Dissemination of the Research
Researchers	YES	YES	YES	YES	YES	YES
Teachers	NO	NO	NO	NO	NO	NO
Equivalent Conversational Function	Initiates topics	Determined valid knowledge	Determined valid knowledge	Revoicing	Turns at talk	Determined turn-taking protocols

problematizing the boundaries of the event, who is in the event, what is happening, and the relationship of the event studied to other events— that is, we assume that part of what occurs in classroom language and literacy events is a structuring of relationships among people and social institutions, the structuring of a history within which to locate the event, and the presentation and promulgation of an ideological justification for those power relationships.

For example, consider the 7th-grade lesson previously discussed in this chapter and in chapter 2. We began analysis of the lesson by identifying a small segment as an entry point. Underlying the process of identifying an entry point is a set of assumptions about classroom lessons (see Green, 1983, for a detailed discussion of these theoretical constructs). In brief, the events that make up a lesson are not monolithic; rather, they involve multiple phases and events. The 7th-grade classroom lesson lasted 60 minutes. We do not assume that the power relations that exist in one phase or one event within the lesson characterize the whole lesson. To create a description of power relations in the lesson as a whole, it may be necessary to analyze each phase of the lesson in depth, then one can examine how power relations are established, changed, maintained, or transformed across the phases of the lesson (and across lessons). We identified the segment in Transcript 4.1 as representative of one type of face-to-face interaction that occurred in the lesson, a particular cultural practice within this classroom. Thus, it provides one possible entry point.

After identifying an entry segment, we continue by asking who and what are *in* this event or phase of the lesson. For us, the warrant for a claim about who and what are in the lesson needs to come from material evidence, including what people say, how they act and react to each other, the tools they use (e.g., written materials), and the physical space they inhabit.

A quick analysis of Transcript 4.1 reveals that more than a teacher and students are *in* the event (although only they and the researchers are the people bounded by the walls of the classroom). A review of direct and indirect references to people include Black people as a collective (e.g., lines 02 and 06) and white people as a collective (e.g., "other people" in line 15, and by ellipses), people who speak African American language (e.g., lines 25–28), and all people involved in education (e.g., line 17). At yet another level, the "literary community" is involved in the event, including Sterling Brown, author of the poem *After Winter,* as well as the community of poets and literary theorists who have established and maintain the conventions for engaging literary works. Also a part of the event are the researchers, who are "hidden" by the conventions of research and by being located on the other side of the camera.

We do not view this list of event participants as complete; rather, it is a place to begin consideration of *who is acting on or with whom to do what*. Note that the identification of *who* is in the event requires analysis of complementary relations (e.g., teacher–student, parent–child, writer–reader, Black–white), those involved in the production and consumption of the texts used (e.g., publishers–consumers), and those involved in the administration and maintenance of the social institution (e.g., principals, politicians).

Notice also that power relations involve both acting *on* and *with* others. For example, considering just the teacher and the students: The teacher may be *acting on* the students (e.g., the teacher may be determining the instructional activities in which the students engage in the classroom); the students may be *acting on* the teacher (e.g., resisting participation in the prescribed instructional activities); and the teacher and students may be *acting together* on how language, literature, and race are understood (e.g., transforming how poetry is read in school, transforming how language variation is valued).

After an initial analysis of who is in the event, we ask "Where are the boundaries of the event?" In chapter 1 we discussed the importance of boundary making both as part of how people interact with each other and as part of research methodology. Here we are specifically concerned with the boundaries of the event being analyzed. One way to determine the boundaries of an event is through time; for example, at what time did the event begin, and at what time did it end? But doing this is more complex than looking at a clock. Determining temporal boundaries involves describing the time within which the interaction occurred, not the boundaries of the event. The boundaries of the event can be determined not *a priori* but by examining what the participants construct the boundaries to be. As an aside, we note that the methodological problem faced by researchers is not much different from that facing the participants. Participants must also decipher what the boundaries of the event are as they are establishing those boundaries.

For example, in Transcript 4.1 the teacher begins with (line 01) "We're talkin' about 1865. (Line 02) And we're talkin' about a period of time when slavery was still instituted ↑" Her use of the present tense suggests a continuation of an event rather than the establishment of a new event or, minimally, a connection to a previous event or phase of the lesson. The references to "1865" and to "slavery" link with previous discussions of those topics. Rather than attempt to resolve the ambiguity over whether the beginning boundary of the event begins with line 01 or with a previous interaction referenced in line 01, we argue that the ambiguity in lines 01 and 02 are also problematic for the students. They cannot be certain about the location of the boundaries of the event. However, the uncertainty that interlocutors have may not be problematic in the same way that it is for researchers. Researchers tend to want clearly defined boundaries and categories, but this need may not necessarily be shared by the people in the event. Indeed, it may be that ambiguous boundaries are a resource that interlocutors can use to create meaning (see Bloome, 1993).

On two occasions in Transcript 4.1 a student attempts to interrupt the teacher. The first time (line 09), the student is verbally rebuffed (line 10) and acknowledges the denial of a turn at talk (lines 11 and 12). The second time (line 29), the student is rebuffed by being ignored. Two ways to interpret the inability of the student to get a turn at talk and to raise topics and arguments that are presumably relevant are that (a) the boundaries of the event do not extend to either the topics she wanted to include or (b) they do not extend to the protocols for discussion she used. In brief, it is not that the student is off task but rather that her behavior and the content of her behavior are outside the event. Researchers can infer the boundaries of the event in a manner similar to the way participants discern the boundaries, from observing what happens when boundary lines are crossed. Thus, lines 09–12 and line 29 are instructive for both participants and researchers.

From the preceding discussion, one can see that boundary making is not just about the time interaction was initiated to the time it stopped but also about what substance is included in the event and what interactional behaviors are included. Stated more formally, the boundaries of an event include an *ideational* world, an *interactional* world, and a *textual* world (e.g., the world invoked by a written text).[6] One way to approach the analysis of power relations within an event is to first ask "What worlds are the people in the event creating?" and then "What are the social, cultural, and economic consequences of the worlds that have been created for the participants and for others?" Returning to lines 01 through 32 in Transcript 4.1, we can describe several worlds that are being created. There is the world of the classroom, with its particular set of social relationships and cultural practices (described in chap. 2), and there is the text world of the poem, which the teacher and students are co-constructing in their dialogue (lines 01–17), something cognitive scientists call a *situation model*. The teacher and students are also constructing a world of African-American Language speakers[7] (lines 22–32), asking 'Who are they? Why do they do what they do with language? What kind of education have they had?' In this lesson, the early interpretation of the poem that the students constructed in their groups is challenged by the teacher (as we discussed in chap. 2). She challenges them in at least two ways. First, she challenges the text world they created. She wants them to locate the poem in 1865, using the emancipation of people of African heritage from slavery as an interpretive framework for the

---

[6]We have taken the terms *ideational* and *interactional* from Halliday and Hasan's (1985) discussion about text and context, and we are building on many of their ideas. Although we clearly are influenced by Haliday and Hasan's work, there are important differences between our approach and theirs.

[7]In this classroom, both African American students and white students spoke African American Language in nonclassroom settings and, on occasion, in the classroom. The world of African American Language speakers is thus not limited solely to African Americans. Although the teacher, Ms. Wilson, does not explicitly make this point in the classroom discussion, she does mention it in an interview after the lesson.

text world of the poem. But she also challenges how they are engaging in the process of interpretation. She wants them to use the poem as a prop for gaining insight into the world in which they live. Notice lines 24–28, which directly connect the text world of the poem they have constructed, of the world of 1865, and of the world in which they live.

24		Over a period of time
25		1865 all the way to 1997
26		there are still people who use terms and phrases
27		*de, fo', folks*
28		that are similar to what we read in the poem

It is the teacher who makes this connection and who, by her question,

30	Ms. Wilson:	Is that by choice ↑
31	Theresa:	Choice
32	Ms. Wilson:	Or is that because *quote unquote* a lack of knowl-edge

makes it difficult for the students not to accept her linkages of the three world representations. To answer the question one has to accept the premises embedded within it, and in so doing one accepts the representations of the worlds presented. Thus, it would appear that the teacher is exercising *power over* the students in linking the world representations and making it difficult for the students to resist such a linkage. Furthermore, the teacher is framing the use of the poem as a prop for investigating issues of language variation, another example of *power over* the students. Also, if we were to leave the analysis here and view it as representative of the lesson as a whole, we might conclude that the teacher is exercising power over the students, albeit in service of a perspective of language we might share. But consider what happens immediately after Transcript 4.1. As we show in Transcript 4.2, the teacher creates a space for several students to give their interpretation of language socialization and code switching and then moves the discussion on to a consideration of the phrase "you sound white." She shares a personal narrative of being accused of "sounding white" and then asks the students what the phrase means.

Although most of the students have heard the phrase "sounding white," some have not, and the teacher's initial attempt to solicit a definition is unsuccessful. However, in lines 145 and 146, a student, Maria, begins to share a personal narrative about being accused of "talking white." Thus, in Transcript 4.2 the teacher and students are acting together to unpack the phrase "sounding white," using and sharing their own experiences to construct a world (a world of their own shared experiences) in which attitudes about language variation are sometimes hurtful and unfair. When the various phases or events of the les-

TRANSCRIPT 4.2

Lines 129–146 of the 7th-Grade Language Arts Lesson

129	Ms. Wilson:	When I moved to California I was teased when I was little because people told me I talked white
130		How many of your ever heard that phrase *you sound white* ↑
131	Students:	XXXXXXXXXX [*Many students talk at once and raise hands*]
132	Ms. Wilson:	Now
133		How come white people never hear that phrase *you sound white* ↑
134	Students:	XXXXXXXXXXXX [*Many students talk at once and yell out responses*]
135	Theresa:	I've heard *you sound country* but not white
136	Ms. Wilson:	OK
137		John
138		Could you *possibly* explain this concept to me maybe ↑
139		What is "sounding white" …
140	Students:	XXXXXXXXXXXXXX [*Many students talk and once and yell out responses*]
141	Ms. Wilson:	I'm asking John
142		No ↑
143		You have no idea
144		Who can explain to the concept of sounding white ↑
145	Maria:	OK I have an example
146		When I be at lunch and I say like

son are placed next to each other, the characterization of the teacher as exercising *power over* the students in Transcript 4.1 can be reinterpreted as part of an interactional process through which the teacher created the opportunity for herself and the students to act together (*power with*) to interrogate and gain insight into a shared set of experiences. A characterization of the lesson as either *power over* or as *power with* is too simplistic. From a theory–method perspective, analyses of power relations within any particular event need to be contextualized by what came earlier and what will come later.

Returning to analysis of the power relations in Transcript 4.1, we noted earlier that part of what occurs in classroom language and literacy events are the presentation and promulgation of ideological justifications for those power relationships. In this lesson, the teacher and the students are presenting various ideologies concerned with language and race. In Transcript 4.1, in lines 16 and 17 and then again in lines 30 through 31, the teacher is invoking two ideological stances about African American Language: (1) people speak African American Language out of ignorance and a lack of education, and (2) people speak African American Language because they choose to do so. It is perhaps important to note that the teacher did not place on the floor a third ideological stance about the speaking of African American Language, that speaking African American Language is a reflection of intellectual or linguistic deficiency, a view widely held by the general public. Such a deficit model can be detected in some of the comments made by the students; for example, Andre's mocking of Maria's use of the habitual "be" form instead of "I am" (which was discussed in chap. 2). Andre's statements can be mockery only if the habitual "be" is associated with a linguistic deficit.

One interpretation of lines 01 through 32 in Transcript 4.1 is that the teacher has objectified language ideology; that is, she has taken two (or perhaps three) language ideologies and placed them in front of students for exploration and interrogation. Among the ways that the teacher and students "objectify" African American Language are:

- Selecting lexical items from the poem related to African American Language as topics of discussion (e.g., line 27 in Transcript 4.1)
- Naming the phenomenon (e.g., line 419 in Transcript 1.4 ["Ebonics"]; line 216 in Transcript 1.2 ["talking Black"]) and distinguishing it from other phenomena (e.g., line 204 in Transcript 1.2 ["talking white"] and line 139 in Transcript 4.2 ["sounding white"])
- Illustrating the phenomenon (making it the object of a story; see lines 145–183 in Transcript 1.1).
- Placing the phenomenon into the objective case within the syntax of its discussion (e.g., line 129 of Transcript 4.2) and by so doing making it something that is acted upon or something that is used by someone or something to act on another object.

In this lesson the discussion of language ideologies is inseparable from a discussion of race ideologies. The teacher raises the issue of race ideologies by locating the poem in 1865 and explicitly noting that the time period corresponds to a time when slavery existed. Invoking the historical context of slavery in America raises the racist ideology of "white superiority" and "Black inferiority" with the corollary that not only is it bad to be Black, but it is also bad to "talk Black." The teacher seeks to connect race ideologies and language ideologies (e.g., line 133 in Transcript 4.2). Race ideologies are explicitly noted by several of the students (e.g., lines 55–58 in Transcript 2.1), and several of the students do connect race ideologies and language ideologies (e.g., lines 427–431 of Transcript 1.4, lines 201–216 in Transcript 1.2). For example, Camika struggles with the contradictory concepts of white people talking "higher" than Black people but white people wanting to act Black.

Camika:	OK
	Today y'all said that the poem was from 18 1885 …
Ms. Wilson:	1865
Camika:	65
	white people have always talked
	back then
	white people always talked ⌐h ⌐ …
Students:	⌊ higher.
Camika:	⌐ higher than we have
	we have always had XXXXXXX Ebonics
	From what I've seen
	most white people <u>wanna</u> be Black or act
	they don't wanna be
	but they act Black

Camika accepts that there is a difference in language but struggles with the contradictions in what that difference means with regard to hierarchy. "White talk," so-called "Proper English," is viewed as higher than Ebonics, but her experience—perhaps based on knowledge of white musical artists such as Vanilla Ice or Eminem—is of white artists imitating a Black musical genre or, perhaps based on her interactions with white people in her daily life, evidence of white people trying to act (and talk) Black. Camika is, of course, not the first to recognize that some white people in some situations have simulated acting Black; neither is she the first to recognize the complexity and contradictions of hierarchical language statuses.

We argue that making the language ideologies visible, presenting them for analysis, and suggesting that there are alternatives need to be viewed as part of the power relations at stake in this classroom event. That is, to the extent that language ideologies are invisible and exercise power in part through their invisibility, making them visible and an object of interrogation undercuts and transforms the extant power relations embedded in language ideologies. Furthermore, inasmuch as many of the students in the class (including some white students) and the teacher speak African American Language at least on some occasions, the ideological issues are not far from their own lives. They are examining (perhaps interrogating) power relations in their own lives. The teacher challenges the students to deconstruct the extant language ideology by asking them to examine how they position themselves and others within those ideologies (e.g., she challenges how Andre positioned Maria in Transcript 2.1). In addition, the teacher asks the students how those ideologies have come to shape their perceptions of the world by challenging students to deconstruct macro-ideologies (e.g., her challenge to them about how to define "proper" versus "slang," what constitutes a mistake, and how generalizations can be made from their experiences). The teacher creates a space for instructional conversations that allows students to bridge the macro to the micro by sharing personal experiences and deconstructing and reconstructing what race means. This, too, is a transformation of power relations—that is, it is not just the objectification of language ideologies or their interrogation that constitutes a transformation of power relations, it is the putting of the students' lives into the interrogation that is part of the transformation of power relations. The teacher creates a space in which the students' experiences (and those of their families, friends, and communities) play a prominent role in framing a critique of race and language ideologies.

With regard to the interrogation of language ideologies, there are at least four levels of engagement with power relations. The first concerns the relationship of "white talk" to "Black talk," the second concerns the schools' role in supporting and maintaining the hierarchical relationship (through the teaching of Standard English and by dismissing the use of other languages, including African-American Language), the third concerns who has the legitimacy to call those power relations into question, and the fourth concerns what counts as evidence and argument for calling power relations into question. The students are encouraged to use their experiences to call power relations into question; however, throughout the lesson the teacher makes clear that they are not allowed to use nongrounded statements or arguments (statements outside of their own experiences, arguments that are merely reiterations of stereotypes and taken-for-granted assumptions) without challenge.

The discussion of power relations in the 7th-grade classroom lesson highlights several important theory–method issues. Microethnographic analyses concerned with power relations often require multiple-level analysis. Researchers have to be cognizant of their own relationship to the participants in the analysis of power relations and not take themselves out of the analytic frame. Third, it may be that the boundaries of an event and who and what are in a classroom language and literacy event are difficult to discern. Researchers must be careful not to assume that such difficulties are also hindrances to the participants, because ambiguity may be a resource for meaning-making. Fourth, it is not sufficient to describe power relations simply as *power over* or *power with*; the substance of what is happening must be part of the interpretive frame for understanding those power relations, and the orchestration of power relations over time, phases of the lesson, levels, and situations must be considered. Analysis of power relations in one phase or event of the lesson may need to be understood in terms of what happens before or after that event. Finally, power relations are constituted not only by who coerces whom to do something but also by what worlds are constructed and how those worlds define people and their relationship to each other. Stated differently, power relations are both reflected in discourse processes and constituted by discourse processes.

In the next section we examine a lesson from a 6th-grade classroom. In one sense, the lesson from this classroom is similar to that in the 7th-grade classroom with regard to power relations. As we show, the teacher and students work together to transform given definitions of knowledge. However, there are also differences that are informative with regard both to understanding power in classrooms and with regard to understanding theory–method issues for the conduct of discourse analysis of classroom language and literacy events.

A MICROETHNOGRAPHIC DISCOURSE ANALYSIS OF POWER RELATIONS AND KNOWLEDGE IN A 6TH-GRADE CLASSROOM LITERACY EVENT

The 6th-grade social studies lesson from which Transcript 4.3 was taken was part of an instructional unit on Africa.[8] (Note that this class is not the same as the 6th-grade class discussed in chapter 3; neither was it in the same school). The teacher had divided the class into instructional groups, each taking a different topic about Africa. The students had created a large web of ideas related to Africa, and each group was given some guideline questions from the teacher and generated some of their own questions. They were to research the topic, prepare an oral presentation to give to the class, and turn a written report in to the teacher. The group of students in Transcript 4.3 were in the "family life" group. All of the students in this group were female; 4 were African American, and 2 were white. On the day of this lesson, the students were in the library for the second consecutive day.

On the day of the target lesson, the teacher asked a student from another 6th-grade class to join the group on family life. The student, Sanjo, was Nigerian and had only recently moved to the United States and entered the school that year. Although she was in the same grade and was known to the students in the class, they did not know her well. The students, and

---

[8]The analysis in this section was informed, in part, by a series of research articles, including those by Bercaw and Bloome (1998), Morris (1998, 2003), and Muldrow and Katz (1998). Members of the research team that conducted the study included Lynne Bercaw, David Bloome, Jerome Morris, and Ramona Muldrow. We gratefully acknowledge the U.S. Department of Education for a grant that supported, in part, the research titled "Academic Learning From a Whole Day Whole Year Perspective" (principal investigators: John Bransford, Susan Goldman, Ted Hasselbring, and David Bloome). The opinions expressed here do not necessarily reflect the opinions or policies of the U.S. Department of Education.

TRANSCRIPT 4.3

Lines 132–192 of the 6th-Grade Social Studies Lesson in the Library

Line #	Speaker	Message Units
132	Sanjo	But [*stands up and leans across the table, picks up a book*]
133		I think this says Africa
134		Not Nigeria
135		Nigeria
136		They don't use to do like this in Nigeria
137		Nigeria they
138		You see they did not wear a shoe
139		In Nigeria they would wear a shoe
140	Makeda	Go on Anthony
141	Sanjo	... [Inaudible] not this type of
142		Right there we wear
143		Like this [*points to another picture*]
144		But this is Africa
145		I forget [inaudible]
146	Karen	She got some cool stuff
147	Teacher	[*Enters*]: So
148		Sanjo are the
149		Are the clothes that are pictured here in the book
150		Do do you think they are pretty accurate to what you really wear
151	Sanjo	Not this
152		Not this type
153	Teacher	Not this style
154	Sanjo	Yeah
155		They asked for this in the picture
156	Makeda	This is stuff she told us
157	Makeda	This is the shirt this is the skirt
158	Makeda	And this is the little head thing
159	Teacher	Yeah
160	Makeda	And this is the little dress thing

(*continued on next page*)

Line #	Speaker	Message Units
161	Teacher	Ooooh
162		That's beautiful
163		That's soft too
164	Sanjo	Yeah
165	Sanjo	They use cotton to make it
166	Teacher	Did did um did you make this
167		Or did someone in your family make it
168	Sanjo	My grandmother
169	Makeda	Your grandmother made it
170	Teacher	Does she sew a lot with you
171	Sanjo	Yeah
172	Teacher	That's pretty neat.

Line #	Speaker	Message Units	Line #	Speaker	Message Units
173-1		[7 second silence: some students writing]	173-2		[*Cathy hands teacher an index card*]
174-1	Sanjo	We have this type in Nigeria too	174-2		[*Teacher reads the card*]
175-1		This is nice	175-2	Teacher	[*To Cathy*] Ok you might want to talk about a
176-1		Look at this	176-2		Make your question clear … the people
177-1		My brother carried this yeah	177-2		Make your question a little bit clearer
178-1	Karen	Your brother carved it?	178-2		[*Teacher walks over to Karen and kneels by her*]
179-1	Sanjo	Yeah wear it	179-2		[*To Cathy*] What kind of language do they speak?
180-1	Karen	Oh that one or another one?	180-2		[*To Cathy*] You may want to list these languages
181-1	Sanjo	Yeah	181-2		where
182-1	Makeda	Let me see it right quick [*pointing to a book Ruth has*]	182-2		What countries

Line #	Speaker	Message Units	Line #	Speaker	Message Units
			183-2		Remember because there are many countries in Africa
			184-2		[*Teacher talking to student*]
185-1		[*Sanjo, Makeda, Karen stand up*]	185-2		[*Ruth kneels between Sanjo and Cathy*]
186-1	Sanjo	This they use it yeah they put this	186-2		[*Teacher continues to speak to Cathy—inaudible*]
187-1	Makeda	Ah Sanjo			
188-1		Sanjo is this what you had [*Makeda refers to a picture of clothing in the book*]			
189-1	Sanjo	Yeah this is this is it look at look [*showing the book to the teacher*]			
190-1	Makeda	That's the little head thing			
191-1	Teacher	Can you show me I want you to show me how to wear that			
192-1	Sanjo	Ok			

Sanjo, were seated around a library table with many library books and notebooks on top of the table, as shown in Fig. 4.2.

The students were looking through the books to find information for their report on family life in Africa. Sanjo was looking over the books on the table.

Similar to the analysis of the 7th-grade lesson presented earlier in this chapter, we begin our discourse analysis by examining the data collected on the broader social context. It is difficult to provide a guideline on how much contextual information is needed or how broad social context should be defined, because it may be only during the analysis of the classroom language and literacy event itself that the need for absent contextual information becomes apparent. For us, the discourse analysis of classroom language and

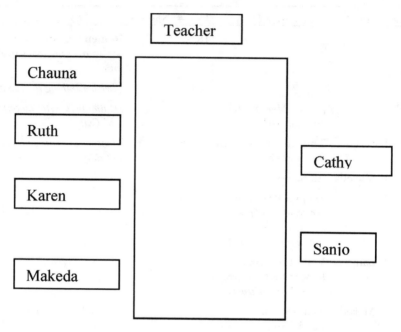

FIG. 4.2   Seating chart.

literacy events is often part of a larger ethnographic study, and hence a great deal of background and contextual data are available. However, on those occasions when a discourse analysis is not part of a larger ethnographic study, one technique that is often helpful is to share the data collected (e.g., showing the videotape of the event if it is available) and one's interpretations of it with one or more of the participants and ask about contextual knowledge that might better inform the interpretations (such interviews are sometimes called *videotape feedback interviews*). However, even with the use of such feedback, we have found that nonetheless it is often the case that one lacks at least a part of the contextual data that one might want. Furthermore, as time goes by, videotape feedback interviews or similar interviews may yield reconstructed memories based on subsequent experience rather than insights into the social and historical context at the time of the lesson. In brief, it is always the case that no matter how diligent a researcher is, he or she is always conducting a discourse analysis with partial contextual data and must take such uncertainty into account.

Also similar to the conduct of the earlier discourse analysis of the 7th-grade lesson, we identified an entry point to the 6th-grade lesson. To do so, we parsed the lesson into a series of phases or events. We based our parsing on procedures we described in chapter 1, looking for major changes in interactional patterns signaled by major changes in bodily configurations and participation structures of the group.

After watching the videotape of the lesson numerous times, consulting field notes taken during the lesson and other lessons, reviewing other data collected, and reviewing our research goals (in this case, a prominent goal was to better understand the relationship of classroom practices, literacy practices, knowledge, and social identity), we selected an event within the lesson as representative of the relationship of literacy, knowledge, and social identities constructed in the lesson. That is, the entry point we selected was our best guess at what was representative of the lesson as a whole with regard to our research goals. Such representativeness must be treated with a degree of open-mindedness, because further analysis might reveal that our "best guess" was wrong about the representativeness of the entry point.

The entry point we began with is shown in Transcript 4.3. The students had selected books from the library shelves from which to find information about their topic, family life. It had not taken them much time to find the books, because they had been in the library the day before and had located the section of the library where appropriate books could be found. They had laid the books out on the table in front of them and had opened their notebooks to begin looking at the guiding questions that they had received from the teacher. They began taking notes. Sanjo was sitting at the table where the group was working, waiting for the group. The teacher had already informed the group that Sanjo was from Africa and that she might provide them with additional information. The teacher was walking around the room helping students get materials and begin finding information and taking notes.

Just prior to the beginning of Transcript 4.3, Cathy sees in a library book a picture of women carrying water on their heads and comments that she would not be able to do so. Makeda asks Sanjo if she had to carry water on her head. Sanjo replies that she had done that, and the students begin to talk with Sanjo about the picture and carrying water. They notice that Sanjo has brought with her some clothing and ask her what the clothing is. She explains and shows them how she wears the head covering. The students comment on how "cool" the clothing is. Meanwhile, Sanjo continues to scan the books on the table, and some of the students continue to write information from the books. As Sanjo is putting aside the clothing, she stands up and leans across the table and comments "But, I think this says Africa, not Nigeria." This begins the particular language and literacy event that we are using as an entry point to explore power relations in this lesson.

As we did in our analysis of the 7th-grade lesson, we begin analysis of power relations in the classroom literacy event in Transcript 4.3 by asking who and what are *in* this event. Physically present are the 6 students in the group—Makeda, Karen, Cathy, Ruth, Chauna, and Sanjo—the teacher, and Anthony (who is not at the table but comes by later). Also present in the library are the other students in the class and the librarian. This second group of participants can be described as one level removed from the face-to-face event, physically present but outside of the boundaries of the conversation among the primary participants. Also physically present are the researchers. Although they did not participate in the turn-taking, they and the video camera are a part of the face-to-face interaction. On occasion, students made eye contact with the camera, indicating their awareness of the camera and the researchers even if that awareness is intermittent.

Also involved in the event are book and magazine publishers, media publishers (e.g., those who produce encyclopedias on CDs and CDs about Africa), the state (the project on which the students are working was a result of a curriculum mandated by the school board, what is available in the library is a result of school board funding and purchasing guidelines, state assessments of student achievement will be published in local newspapers), and universities (through the presence of the researchers and through the teacher education programs attended by the teacher). These participants are indirectly present; that is, although the people who actually published the books are not present, their books are. Although the members of the school board are not physically present, the policies they have passed are materially represented in the curriculum guide, by what is available in the library, and so on. Following Fairclough (1989, 1992, 1995), we argue that the context(s) of production is always a part of the context(s) of use; thus, the book publishers, school board members, and so on, are materially present in the event if not bodily. Of course, their presence is not unmediated; that is, how they are present in the event depends a great deal on what the teachers, students, and others do.[9] Additional participants who are indirectly present are invoked through comments made by participants. They include the church, popular media (e.g., television, movies), and family.

Beyond the participants identified in the event directly or indirectly through material manifestations is a set of historical participants. For example, Morris (2003) argued that the study of Africa by African American students requires asking how such study does or does not engage the students in an understanding of their cultural heritage and cultural identity. For African American students to study Africa without recognizing the connection to their heritage is, Morris argued, as visible a material manifestation as if they were to recognize it overtly, a sort of "erasure" (cf. Kaomea, 2003). If Morris's argument is accepted, then the historical debates about the relationship of African Americans to Africa are part of the event. We argue that

---

[9]Fairclough's insight about the relationship of contexts of production and contexts of use provides more than just a list of who is "in" the event; it also provides insight into the set of events that are related to each other, even if their relationship is mediated (e.g., the relationship of the events involved in the production of the textbook to the classroom event may be mediated by the teacher using the books in a manner not prescribed by the publisher, or by the presence and use of other books).

the students or the teacher need not be aware of the people involved in those debates, or of the debates themselves, in order to warrant their inclusion as part of the event. Rather, the warrant comes from how those debates have established and shaped the discourse about American history and African American history.

One question that researchers might ask of themselves is how we can know which historical participants and historical debates are to be included as part of the event, especially when it is the absence of those historical participants and debates that is meaningful. We argue that part of the background research needed in order to conduct discourse analysis of a classroom language and literacy event involves historical study of the communities from which the students and teachers come (even if researchers can only gain a partial understanding). Furthermore, the need for such historical and community studies argues strongly for research teams that are themselves culturally and historically diverse[10] and for collaboration with people who are either members of the community or who have close, insider knowledge of the community.

Of course, it may be that a beginning analysis of who and what are in the event has overlooked some people and social institutions. As one proceeds in a discourse analysis, additions or other modifications may be warranted. Even so, there is a limitation on our ability as researchers to know fully who and what are in an event. We can speculate on the basis of previous research and scholarly discussions, but such speculations cannot rise above the level of speculation unless warranted by material evidence from study of the event itself. As researchers, we must be aware that there are limits to the certainty we can have. This is one reason why we noted in chapter 2 that any discourse analysis comprises only a partial description and analysis.

By identifying who and what are *in* the event, we can focus attention on the power relations among them. Because the permutations are much larger than could be described in any discourse analysis, we as educational researchers have to make decisions about which sets of power relationships provide a good beginning point of entry. For some researchers, the decision will be guided by their research question (e.g., a researcher who is interested in teacher–student interaction might begin by focusing on the power relations between the teacher and the students); for others it might be guided by theoretical concerns about the nature of power (e.g., what is power in this classroom literacy event). In the former case the emphasis is on how power relations are a part of classroom literacy events; in the latter case the emphasis is on how classroom literacy events are a part of power processes. These

---

[10]The argument for a culturally and historically diverse research team is not based on the assumption that one of the members will have "insider" knowledge but rather that a diverse team will be able to bring to the research endeavor diverse and contrastive perspectives that can raise issues that might otherwise be overlooked.

two approaches are not mutually exclusive, but they do represent two different stances toward power relations.

As shown in Fig. 4.3, emphasizing how classroom literacy events are a part of power processes (a) frames research questions, theory–method links, and the interpretation of data as part of an inquiry about power relations and (b) defines classroom language and literacy events as part of the process and matrix of power relations. As shown in Fig. 4.4, foregrounded are questions about how what happens during classroom language and literacy events contributes to power relations, such as the reproduction of social, economic, racial, and gender hierarchies. Also foregrounded is resistance to extant power relations such as the ones listed earlier.

By contrast, as shown in Fig. 4.5, by emphasizing how power relations are part of classroom language and literacy events one foregrounds the premise that although power relations are part of what occurs in a classroom language and literacy event, they are not the only dimension of what is happening (i.e., it is assumed that the event is about more than power relations).

Foregrounded would be research questions, theory–method links, and the interpretation of data that sought to understand how power relations were related to and part of the accomplishment of classroom life. That is, as shown in Figure 4.6, the accomplishment of classroom life is not defined by power relations alone but by a broad range of dimensions of human relationships and endeavors and the meanings and import that people give to them.

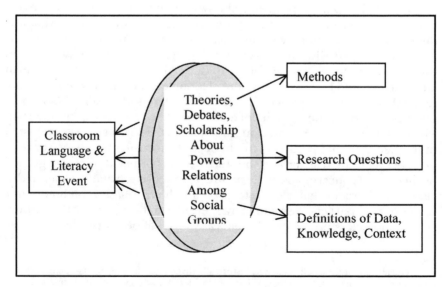

FIG. 4.3   Framing methods, questions, and definitions through a power relations lens.

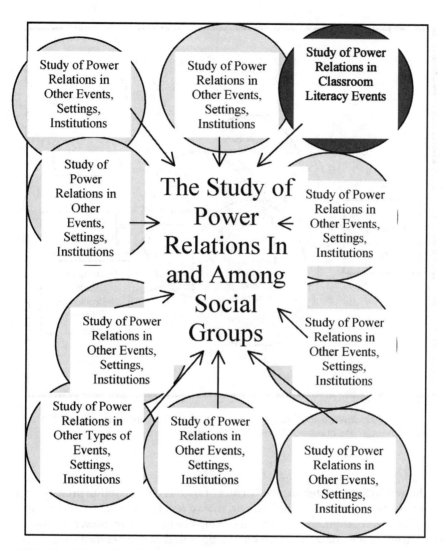

FIG. 4.4 The study of power relations in classroom literacy events to understanding power relations among social groups.

189

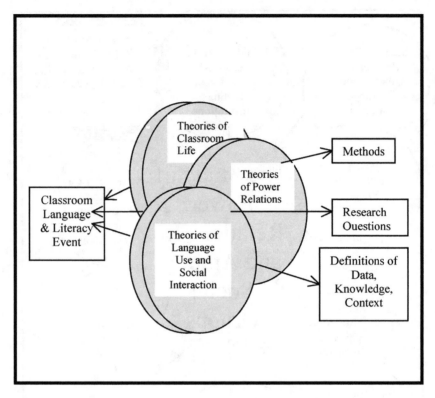

FIG. 4.5 Framing methods, questions, and definitions through multiple lenses to examine classroom language and literacy events.

Stated in simpler terms, the former stance is concerned primarily with power relations at both the micro and macro level and seeks to understand how classroom language and literacy events contribute to power relations. The latter stance immediately acknowledges that power relations are an integral part of classroom language and literacy events but does not use questions about power relations to totalize the interpretation of what occurs in classroom language and literacy events.

Building on our discussion on models of power at the beginning of this chapter, one way to approach power relations in the 6th-grade classroom lesson is to equate power with a quantity of knowledge (the power-as-product model). One could argue that traditional schooling is organized around such an equation (at least on the surface). The more knowledge one acquires, the greater the power one will have to exercise influence over one's life and the worlds in which one lives. From this perspective, methodology consists of de-

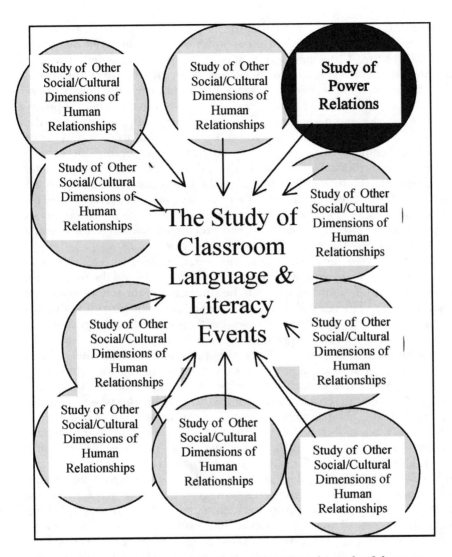

FIG. 4.6   The study of power relations contributing to the study of classroom language and literacy events.

scribing, cataloging, and quantifying the knowledge people have, the access to knowledge that they have, and what and how knowledge is exchanged.

In Transcript 4.3 we can identify at least two types of knowledge: factual and procedural. There is factual knowledge about the styles of clothing people in Africa wear, how they carry water, and so on, from the library books and from Sanjo's personal experience of living in Nigeria. There is procedural knowledge about wearing special clothes (e.g., Sanjo showing how the clothes are worn) and about how to put together a report. These types of knowledge come from a variety of sources: library books, an experienced-based authority on the topic (Sanjo), and the teacher. By having Sanjo present, the teacher has provided the family life group students access to knowledge they would not otherwise have had. By recording the information in their notebooks and later transferring it to a written report and oral presentation, the students can exchange knowledge for a grade and whatever privileges accompany the grade.

On the basis of our discussion of knowledge, there are at least three sets of power relations to examine: (a) between the students and the teacher, (b) among the students, and (c) between the students and the school as a social institution. The teacher fulfills the role of gatekeeper by providing the students access to knowledge and by assessing their knowledge acquisition. In this lesson, students are working cooperatively (or at least collectively) to display knowledge acquisition. Thus, although there might be hierarchical power relations among them in the process of acquiring the knowledge, from the perspective of their official assessment the students within the group are cooperative rather than competitive. Thus, the power relations among them might be described as equal. However, an analysis of interpersonal conversational strategies in Transcript 4.3 shows that Makeda used directives (lines 140 and 182-1), gave information (lines 156–160 and 187-1–190-1), and spoke for others (line 169), and that all of her conversational moves were validated by others. Such a pattern of conversational behavior among the students and teacher suggests that there may have been a social hierarchy among the students with regard at least to accomplishing the academic task. Thus, although the power relations among the students were equal from the perspective of exchanging knowledge acquisition for a grade, within the doing of the lesson there may have been an unequal relationship in terms of who directed behavior.[11]

Questions about power relations between the students and the school as a social institution are also important, although difficult, to address. Scholars have raised questions about schools as agents of cultural social-

---

[11]Although the relationship between Makeda and the other students may have been unequal with regard to turn-taking rights and processes, it is not necessarily the case that an unequal situation is an inequitable one, or an undemocratic one. Additional data and interpretive work would be needed to make the inferential leap from an unequal relationship to an inequitable or undemocratic one.

ization, social control, nationalism , racial hierarchy, and socioeconomic reproduction. In some instances, researchers interested in the detailed analysis of classroom language and literacy events have taken one or more macro-level social and political theories and processes and laid them over the language and literacy event—that is, they have treated the language and literacy event as an illustration of the macro-level social and political processes with which they are concerned. Illustration clearly has important value. However, as we have discussed earlier in this book, the approach we take here differs. Although we acknowledge macro-level social processes and keep them in mind as potential frames for helping with the analysis and interpretation of social phenomena within an event, we do not assume that a classroom language and literacy event is merely an illustration of them. As we noted in chapter 2, every event involves tensions between continuity and change. Thus, rather than begin with the assumption that we know what a particular event is about from macro-level social theories, we begin with the assumption that in every event the relationship between that event and the social institution(s) within which it occurs needs to be established (or re-established) by the participants.

With regard to the specific lesson being examined and Transcript 4.3, one question to address is whether there is any indication within the lesson or event that power relations between the students and the social institution of schooling have changed. For example, did students violate rules of location and place (e.g., did they skip school)? Did they resist the curriculum (e.g., refuse to research Africa and instead read a novel)? Did they challenge the school's authority to set and implement policy (e.g., organize a petition to allow banned books into the school library)? In our analysis of the lesson and Transcript 4.3 we find no evidence to suggest a change in power relations or a challenge to extant power relations between the students and the school—*at least at the surface level*. As we show later, questions can be raised about whether the conversation among the students, Sanjo, and the teacher strayed from the instructional goals of the curriculum and focused on the establishment of "caring" relationships among the students and teacher. If so, the relationship between the event and the social institution of schooling could be characterized as challenging the authority of the school to determine the content, use, and nature of all academic conversations. That is, if the students and teacher were engaged in an activity not oriented toward a knowledge–grade exchange, then their activity might be viewed as constituting a change in power relations with the school as a social institution.

To get beyond a surface-level microanalysis of Transcript 4.3, we need to shift from a model of power as product to a model of power as process. The discourse analysis presented earlier that was based on a power-as-product model left unaddressed questions about how knowledge works; that is, what social work occurs in and through knowledge. For example, questions can be asked about the import of the knowledge the students are accessing. Is it only for exchange for a grade, or does the knowledge *do* more? Questions can be asked about how the knowledge influences interpretive frameworks, social relationships, social and cultural identities, and cultural ideologies. What worlds are being created by and through the use of the knowledge in the lesson? Whose knowledge is taken as authoritative, and whose is discounted (perhaps not even counted as knowledge)? With specific regard to language and literacy, one can inquire about the role and use of spoken and written language with regard to the questions about knowledge listed earlier. These questions may be better addressed using a model of power as process.

Table 4.3 is a moment-by-moment analysis of Transcript 4.3 that shows how Sanjo, the students, and the teacher negate the authority of library book knowledge and build knowledge based on Sanjo's personal background experience.

From line 132 through 144 in Transcript 4.3, Sanjo challenges the knowledge in the library books and incorporates the students and the teacher in that challenge. At the same time, however, she also builds knowledge. She makes a distinction between Africa and Nigeria and describes the knowledge in the books as referring not to Nigeria but perhaps to somewhere else in Africa (lines 133–135). Sanjo focuses attention on the book, on the pictures in the book, and on the written text using a string of deictic references (lines 133, 136, 138, 141, 142, 143, and 144). Her deictic references to the book constitutes a type of text analysis, in which she identifies an object in a picture or a description in the written text and contrasts it with her own personal experience. In so doing, she repositions her relationship to the book: She, not the library book, is the authoritative source.

Part of what is interesting to note is that the building and acquisition of knowledge involve *identity building*; that is, by negating the authority of the library book knowledge and asserting her authority with regard to knowledge about Nigeria and Africa, Sanjo is taking on an identity. Briefly stated, the identity Sanjo is taking on is that of expert and tutor. But the issue of knowledge and identity goes further than just Sanjo; it would seem that it is always the case that people take stances toward knowledge (a stance toward what is valid knowledge and who is the authority for having and validating that knowledge) and do doing define themselves and others (as expert, novice, student, teacher, insider, outsider, etc.). In sum, identity and knowledge are inseparable constructs. They always implicate each other.

Notice also the role of written language in establishing authoritative knowledge in this event. The book is presented (by the library and the school) as having authoritative knowledge. Sanjo challenges not only the knowledge given but also the basis of the authority (which is its presentation as a school/library book). Although we do not view written language as having an inherent superiority over spoken language with regard to claims of authority of knowledge (see Street, 1995b, 1996, 1997), the literacy prac-

TABLE 4.3

Building and Contesting Knowledge

Line No.	Speaker	Transcript	Social Interaction	Building Knowledge		Comments
132	Sanjo	But [stands up and leans across the table, picks up a book]	Responding to academic activity and topic, takes the floor; shifts the focus of discussion from the book to herself.	Negating book knowledge →		
133	Sanjo	I think this says Africa	Mitigates assertiveness, creates group interaction with book/written text through use of deixis.	Negating book knowledge →		Critiquing the book through textual analysis (the domain is wrong).
134	Sanjo	Not Nigeria		Negating book knowledge →	Differentiating domains of knowledge (Africa vs. Nigeria) →	
135	Sanjo	Nigeria	Initiates topic.	→	Emphasizes the general topic →	Makes clear students' rights to initiate topics.

195

TABLE 4.3 (*continued*)

Line No.	Speaker	Transcript	Social Interaction	Building Knowledge		Comments
136	Sanjo	They don't use to do like this in Nigeria	Use of deixis to direct attention.	Negating book knowledge →	Focuses discussion on Nigeria →	Repositioning the relation between sources of knowledge; experiential knowledge positioned over library book knowledge.
137	Sanjo	Nigeria they	Initiates topic.		Initiating a new topic →	
138	Sanjo	You you see they did not wear a shoe	Use of deixis to direct attention.	Textual analysis for negating book knowledge →	Adding information from background knowledge →	Provides a model of textual analysis for repositioning students vs. a text.
139	Sanjo	In Nigeria they would wear a shoe	Maintaining role of expert and positioning the students as "informed outsiders" with regard to knowledge about Nigeria.		Adding information from background knowledge →	Repetition and use of conditional "would" emphasizes her claim to authority and her role as "expert" in the group.

140	Makeda	Go on Anthony	Maintaining group and gender boundaries, keeping others out.		Asserting ownership over knowledge and access to knowledge.
141	Sanjo	[Inaudible] not this type of	Use of deixis to direct attention.	Negating book knowledge →	Maintaining role of expert and positioning the students as "informed outsiders" with regard to knowledge about Nigeria.
142	Sanjo	Right there we wear	Use of deixis to direct attention, selecting text to designate validity.	Subordinating book knowledge → Adding information from background knowledge →	Maintaining role of expert and modeling a social relationship between a student and a text. Relocating book knowledge in personal experience knowledge.
143	Sanjo	Like this [points to a picture]	Use of deixis to direct attention.	Subordinating book knowledge → Confirming book information →	
144	Sanjo	But this is Africa	Use of deixis to direct attention.	Negating book knowledge →	

197

TABLE 4.3 *(continued)*

Line No.	Speaker	Transcript	Social Interaction	Building Knowledge	Comments
145	Makeda	I forget [inaudible]			
146	Karen	She got some cool stuff	Gives social status to Sanjo and invokes "teenage" social register for assigning value; assumes right to assign value within the "teenage" register. This may also be a reference back to earlier lines where Ruth talks about Sanjo having "cool" things.	Validates Sanjo's clothing as legitimate academic knowledge and Sanjo as an expert on the topic	
147	Teacher	So	Initiates social interaction, takes floor.		
148	Teacher	Sanjo, are the	Holds floor (positions Sanjo as a student who has important background knowledge).	Positions Sanjo as expert on the topic →	
149	Teacher	Are the clothes that are that are pictured here in the book	Positions the book as subordinate to Sanjo's knowledge and positions Sanjo as an expert in the group on this topic.	Subordinating book knowledge →	

	Speaker	Utterance			
150	Teacher	Do do you think they are pretty accurate to what you really wear		Subordinating book knowledge →	
151	Sanjo	Not this	Claiming social position as expert.	Negating book knowledge →	
152	Sanjo	Not this type		Negating book knowledge →	
153	Teacher	Not this style	Asking for confirmation and clarification from Sanjo as the expert.	Negating book knowledge →	
154	Sanjo	Yeah	Clarifying and confirming.	Negating book knowledge →	Claiming social position as expert.
155	Sanjo	They asked for this in the picture			

TABLE 4.3 *(continued)*

Line No.	Speaker	Transcript	Social Interaction	Building Knowledge		Comments
156	Makeda	This is stuff she told us	Makeda initiates interaction with teacher, assuming role of teaching the teacher; positioning the teacher as learner and Makeda as expert.	Repeating knowledge given earlier by Sanjo	→	Validating Sanjo's knowledge and clothing through repetition.
157	Makeda	This is the shirt this is the skirt		Repeating knowledge given earlier by Sanjo	→	
158	Makeda	And this is the little head thing		Repeating knowledge given earlier by Sanjo	→	
159	Teacher	Yeah	Not rendered as an evaluation of lines 163–165, but as a continuance and as a confirmation that she understands.	Acknowledging the importance of the knowledge	→	

160	Makeda	And this is the little dress thing	Makeda continues teaching.	Repeating knowledge given earlier by Sanjo →
161	Teacher	Ooooh	Rendered as an emphasized expression of emotion, as such interacting with both Sanjo and the other students. Rendered in a manner that is gendered marked.	Adds aesthetic dimension to the knowledge they are gaining about Nigeria, Africa, and Sanjo
162	Teacher	That's beautiful		
163	Teacher	That's soft too		→
164	Sanjo	Yeah	Sanjo claims floor.	→
165	Sanjo	They use cotton to make it	Interacts with teacher; responds to affective response with additional information.	Adding information from background knowledge →
166	Teacher	Did did um did you make this	Teacher changes topic, positions herself as learner and Sanjo and her family as skilled craftspeople.	Linking knowledge about clothing to knowledge about family →

TABLE 4.3 (continued)

Line No.	Speaker	Transcript	Social Interaction	Building Knowledge	Comments
167	Teacher	Or did someone in your family make it?			
168	Sanjo	My grandmother	Rendered in a matter-of-fact tone while leaning over the book.	Validates teacher's attempt to highlight Sanjo's family but downplays the importance →	
169	Teacher	Your grandmother made it?	Rhetorical questions, teacher maintaining topic, not allowing it to shift back to the book.	Emphasizing the importance of family relationships →	
170	Teacher	Does she sew a lot with you?	Continuing topic.	Adding knowledge to topic →	
171	Sanjo	Yeah	Confirmation.	Validates knowledge →	

Line	Speaker	Utterance		
172	Teacher	That's pretty neat.	Teacher changes tone, adding an affective dimension.	Adds affective dimension to the knowledge being shared

Lines 173-1 through 192-1 occur at same time as lines 173-2 through 186-2 as two simultaneously occurring conversations

Line	Speaker	Utterance		
173-1		(7-sec silence: some students writing; Cathy hands teacher an index card)		
174-1	Sanjo	We have this type in Nigeria too	Sanjo interacts with Makeda, initiates topic.	Adds knowledge, validates book knowledge	Sanjo continues role of validating or in-validating book knowledge.
175-1	Sanjo	This is nice	Sanjo interacts with book, speaking to no one in particular.	Adds affective dimension →
176-1	Sanjo	Look at this	Directive; use of deixis.	→

TABLE 4.3 *(continued)*

Line No.	Speaker	Transcript	Social Interaction	Building Knowledge		Comments
177-1	Sanjo	My brother carried this yeah	Use of deixis and personal knowledge.	Adds knowledge, relates to family, relates book knowledge to personal experience	→	Presents a model of text analysis, connects text with personal experience.
178-1	Karen	Your brother carved it?	Karen picks up on Sanjo's comments.	Gives Sanjo's knowledge and experience esteem	→	
179-1	Sanjo	Yeah wear it	Sanjo interacts with Karen.	Adds knowledge	→	
180-1	Karen	Oh that one or another one?	Request for clarification.		→	
181-1	Sanjo	Yeah			→	Sanjo misunderstands Karen's question.

182-1	Makeda	Let me see it right quick (pointing to a book Ruth has)	Directive.		Text reproduction, targeted by Sanjo's discussion	Makeda asserts control, interacting with Ruth and other students who are writing note cards.
183-1		(Sanjo, Makeda, Karen stand up. Ruth kneels between Sanjo and Cathy)				
184-1	Sanjo	This they use it yeah they put this	Sanjo interacts with book, speaking to no one in particular but available for all to hear.		Adds knowledge →	
185-1	Makeda	Ah Sanjo	Makeda initiates interaction and topic, continuing her role as group leader.			
186-1	Makeda	Sanjo is this what you had	Requesting conformation of knowledge.	Questions knowledge in the book	Repeating knowledge →	
187-1	Makeda	(Refers to a picture of clothing in the book)	Confirming.			

TABLE 4.3 (continued)

Line No.	Speaker	Transcript	Social Interaction	Building Knowledge		Comments
188-1	Sanjo	Yeah this is this is it look at look (*showing the book to the teacher*)	Sanjo shifts the interaction from Makeda and Sanjo to Sanjo and teacher. Sanjo takes on role of teacher and positions teacher as learner.		Repeating knowledge, Validates book knowledge →	
189-1	Makeda	That's the little head thing	Makeda reasserts role in conversation, positioning herself as teacher and teacher as learner	Validates and emphasizes previous knowledge from Sanjo	Repeating knowledge, validates book knowledge →	
190-1	Teacher	Can you show me I want you to show me how to wear that	Teacher maintains topic and roles but shifts interaction and initiates a subtopic.		Request for new "how-to" knowledge based on Sanjo's background experience	Shift from a listing of facts to procedural knowledge, how to wear something.
191-1	Sanjo	OK	Sanjo agrees to request.			
173-2 through 186-2						
173-2		(*Cathy hands teacher an index card*)			Procedural knowledge about how to do report →	Separate from knowledge being built in discussion with Sanjo.

	Speaker	Utterance	Action	Knowledge
174-2		(Teacher reads the card)		Procedural knowledge about how to do report →
175-2	Teacher	(To Cathy) OK you might want to talk about a	Teacher interacts with Cathy to help her write index cards and questions for her report.	Procedural knowledge about how to do report →
176-2	Teacher	Make your question clear ... the people		Procedural knowledge about how to do report →
177-2	Teacher	(To Cathy) Make your question a little bit clearer		Procedural knowledge about how to do report →
178-2	Teacher	(Teacher walks over to Karen and kneels by her)		
179-2	Teacher	What kind of language do they speak?		Academic procedures and knowledge of other topics related to the discussion

TABLE 4.3 (continued)

Line No.	Speaker	Transcript	Social Interaction	Building Knowledge	Comments
180-2	Teacher	(To Cathy) You may want to list these languages			
181-2	Teacher	where			
182-2	Sanjo	What countries	Sanjo interacts with Karen, positions Karen as naïve learner and herself as teacher.	Repeats distinction between Africa and Nigeria →	
183-2	Teacher	Remember because there are many countries in Africa		Repeats knowledge	
184-2	Teacher	(Talking to student)			
185-2		(Ruth kneels between Sanjo and Cathy)			
186-2		(Teacher continues to speak to Cathy—inaudible)			

tices valorized by the school are given that hierarchical relationship. Indeed, one might argue that one aspect of language socialization promulgated by schools such as the one attended by these 6th-grade students is to promote the authoritativeness of certain kinds of written language. Thus, one might claim that Sanjo's challenge to the knowledge in the library book and her challenge to the authority of certain kinds of written texts constitute a form of resistance to extant power relations between the students and the school as a social institution.

With regard to power relations among the students, consider how Makeda builds on Sanjo's authority to maintain leadership in the group. From line 156 through 160, Makeda repeats to the teacher the knowledge she acquired from Sanjo. From a theoretical perspective, this social dynamic is an interesting case of how symbolic capital (the value placed on various social identities) can be created and shifted. The symbolic capital that Sanjo has acquired because of her knowledge authority gives Makeda social status because Makeda acts as a self-appointed delegate for Sanjo. The identity one assumes based on the knowledge one has or acquires depends not solely on whether one has or does not have the knowledge but on whether one is in a situation in which having the knowledge allows one to shape particular kinds of social interactions with others. Sanjo took the initiative to create and shape a social interaction with the other students by negating the library book knowledge. Makeda took the initiative to create and shape a social interaction with the teacher. In both cases, they acquired symbolic capital by doing so.

It is interesting to note in Table 4.3 that one of the students, Karen, and the teacher insert affective dimensions to the knowledge that Sanjo is sharing. Karen states that Sanjo has "some cool stuff " (line 146), and the teacher states that the clothing is "beautiful" and "soft" (lines 162 and 163). The insertion of the affective dimension is not just a communication of opinion but a public valuing. In making a public valuing, both Karen and the teacher have put themselves, their "face," at risk. That is, if others viewed their public valuing as errant—if the clothing weren't "cool" or "beautiful"—then Karen and the teacher might be viewed as weird or aberrant, lose status among others, and be stigmatized as such.

Following the terminology of Baynham (2000), what may be occurring with the insertion of the affective aspects is a paradigm shift in the event. The event may be shifting from being about knowledge acquisition and validation to being about the construction of social relationships among the students based on a model of empathy. Shortly after noting that the clothing was "beautiful," the teacher asks Sanjo if someone in her family made it (line 167). The question and subsequent discussion reframes who Sanjo is. She is no longer the exotic Nigerian who has authoritative knowledge for the students' report, she is a granddaughter in a loving family who engages in activities similar to those with which the other students are familiar. Sanjo's world becomes less exotic and more accessible when shared with the students. Notice that the family theme reoccurs in lines 177-1 and 178-1 as Sanjo mentions her brother and Karen repeats the statement.

As we noted earlier in our discussion of power relations in the 7th-grade lesson, world creation is one of the ways of exerting power. It not only provides people with social identities, but it also creates a seemingly natural moral order and interpretive framework. The creation of the family world with regard to Sanjo stands in contrast to the exotic world of Africa as portrayed in many movies, television programs, and in the mass media. Indeed, this same exotic world is portrayed in the library books.

It is not just the representation of Sanjo as a member of a loving family that is key to a paradigm shift in Transcript 4.3 but rather the shift in social relationships among the people in the event. Sanjo is no longer an exotic outsider providing information for the students to complete an instructional task; neither is she just a member of a family similar to the families of the other students. She has become a member of the group.

One way to describe the group is that it is a type of "women's" group. By "women's" group we mean that the participants are defined in part by being "women." Makeda chases away Anthony, who wants to observe what is happening in their group, and she does so in full view of the teacher, who ignores what Makeda does. Later, boys will come back and try to participate in the group, but again Makeda chases them away, and the teacher supports Makeda in doing so. Indeed, Anthony will loudly comment "We [the boys] have to learn, too," but he is ignored by the teacher.

The exclusion of the boys creates one level of solidarity with Sanjo. There are other levels of connection between Sanjo and the other girls, including the sharing of the clothing and the sharing of experiences of cooking and baptism that occurs later in the lesson. The comparison of what Sanjo does with what the other students do (e.g., how they do baptism, what clothes they wear) provides personal connections and empathy. Another indication of the formation of group solidarity is that at the end of the lesson the students ask if they can continue to "interview" Sanjo in the next class period. When the teacher gives them permission to do so, on the condition that it is acceptable to Sanjo, the students speak for her and then go off together with Sanjo to the classroom. These behaviors are evidence that they have formed a group, of which Sanjo is now a member.

The creation of affective relations and group membership can be seen both as part of an agenda the teacher had with regard to the lesson and as part of a counterdiscourse about Africa and Africans. From interviews with the teacher, we learned that Sanjo had few friends in the school and was often isolated. Many students made derogatory comments about her. Some of these comments may have derived from negative images of Africa promulgated by the popular media (the "Tarzan" image of Africa). The derogatory comments made by African American students about Sanjo may reflect some of the ambivalent attitudes toward Africa that some people hold, and, it may reflect images portrayed in the popular media. Thus, creating social relationships among the students that foreground their similarities and that negate the "exotic" and "primitive" imaging of Sanjo and Africa can be seen as part of the creation of a counterdiscourse, an alternative worldview. This, too, would be part of the complex of power relations and processes in this lesson.

Subsequent analyses of other events in the lesson show that the group moves back and forth between working on the academic task and abandoning the academic task to explore similarities among themselves. For example, later in the lesson the topic of baptism arises. Given the discussion in Transcript 4.4, and given the social context of the specific community in which the students lived, we can speculate that religion is of great importance to the students. (We lack the specific data needed to go beyond speculation. Had we known that the discourse analysis would have taken us in this direction, we could have inquired about the importance of religion to each of the students but, as we noted earlier, it is often the case that needed data are recognized only after data collection has been completed and after it may be no longer possible to collect the needed data. Again, one is always conducting a discourse analysis with partial contextual information.) A line-by-line analysis of the noverbal behavior and social interaction of Transcript 4.4 is provided in Table 4.4.

As shown in Table 4.4, the students seek connections with Sanjo in lines 505–506, 509–512, 513–514, 528–532, and 535–537. In each case they find that Sanjo is like themselves. One way to interpret the conversation is that the students are reducing the distance between themselves and Sanjo through a shared religion and set of cultural practices (baptism).

We argue that the connections are more than cognitive or factual; they hold an emotional quality. In lines 504 and 534, Ruth states that the similarities are "cool." This is a public valuation. Through the students' nonverbal behavior (the eye contact Ruth makes with other students, the leaning back in the chair, tone of voice), and by the placement of the statement as a sort of coda at the end of a conversation sequence, Ruth's public valuation represents the group's public valuation. That is, although it is not clear what each individual person at the table thinks, Ruth's public valuation is positioned in such a manner that it stands for the group's public valuation. We also notice that during Transcript 4.4 the students are not writing information down in their notebooks. The academic task appears to have been eclipsed by the task of finding social and emotional connections.

There is an interesting discussion at the end of Transcript 4.4. The students have shifted from exploring similarities with Sanjo to exploring similarities and differences among themselves. Their baptism procedures differ depending on whether they are dipped forward or backward, fully immersed or only symbolically immersed, and so on. Part of what makes this interaction interesting is that there is a change in the turn-taking pattern, suggesting a change in what is happening in the event. Sanjo is no longer

TRANSCRIPT 4.4

Lines 501–546 of the 6th-Grade Social Studies Lesson in the Library

501	Sanjo	But I'm not a tradition
502	Sanjo	I'm a Christian
503		[Approximately 3 second silence]
504	Ruth	Cool
505	Makeda	So you a
506	Makeda	You a Christian
507	Sanjo	Yeah
508	Makeda	Oh
509	Ruth	Ya'll don't
510	Ruth	You don't do ah
511	Ruth	ummmh
512	Ruth	[*Points to a picture in the book*]
513	Makeda	Do the Christian mean the same thing does it me and here is it meaning ya'll
514	Ruth	Does it mean the same thing here as it does there
515	Sanjo	Yeah but there we have
516	Sanjo	Something we wear in Nigeria
517	Sanjo	Which is white, white, white
518	Sanjo	Some we put like this and they are [*picks up cloth on table*] there, like this
519	Teacher	The bead and sequins and
520	Sanjo	Yeah
521	Sm	How do ya'll
522	Sanjo	Look look good
523	Sm	How do ya'll
524	Sanjo	White white everything
525	Teacher	U-hum
526	Makeda	Why do ya'll
527	Makeda	How'd I mean
528	Makeda	How do you all become a Christian in Nigeria
529	Sanjo	Nigeria
530	Ruth	Like here we have to be baptized

531	Sanjo	Yeah
532	Ruth	Ya'll have to be baptized
533	Sanjo	Yeah
534	Ruth	Cool
535	Makeda	Are ya dunked in the water
536	Makeda	Not dunked in the water but
537	Makeda	Dipped in the water
538	Sanjo	Not that deep like this,
539	Sanjo	They would put someone
540	Sanjo	[*Puts one hand behind her head and the other hand pinches her nose and then leans forward*]
541	Makeda	We'd go back
542	Sanjo	I'm goin' to show them a picture
543	Karen	Yeah we go back
544	Makeda	We go the reverse way
545	Ruth	We go we go
546	Ruth	[*Tips backwards*]

the only information giver. Each student has taken on that role, and they are each sharing information about their own lives.

Earlier we noted that part of who and what were in the event included the relationship of African Americans to Africa and the various theorists and positions about that relationship. In the students' discussion of baptism and Christianity no mention is made of the colonization of Africa by European countries or the role that Christian missionaries played in that colonization. No mention is made of the history of Christianity in the African American community. The teacher does not take the opportunity to inform the students. The students, we speculate, are unaware of that historical knowledge. Instead, the conversation focuses on similarities and functions to strengthen Sanjo's membership in the "women's" group. Within the conduct of discourse analysis, what is to be made of the disjuncture between what happens in an event and the historical context?

For some people, the disjuncture signifies a political discourse that minimizes or hides the history of European and American colonialism. To the degree that making visible such a history is a political goal, the conversation in the 6th-grade lesson certainly does not contribute to that goal, and its silence might even be considered as contributing to the masking of

TABLE 4.4

**Nonverbal Behavior and Social Interaction in Lines 501–546
of Transcript 4.4**

Line No.	Speaker	Transcript	Group Nonverbal Behavior	Social Interaction and Commentary
501	Sanjo	But I'm not a tradition	All 6 students sitting at table; teacher standing, leaning in; Sanjo standing; all eyes on Sanjo.	Takes the floor.
502	Sanjo	I'm a Christian		Initiating topic; establishing identity.
503		(Approximately 3 second silence)	Teacher looks at Ruth; Ruth looks at teacher; teacher looks at Cathy.	
504	Ruth	Cool		Confirming and validating religious identity.
505	Makeda	So you a	All look back at Sanjo.	Bidding for floor.
506	Makeda	You a Christian		Asking question.
507	Sanjo	Yeah		Confirming identity.
508	Makeda	Oh		Confirming.
509	Ruth	Ya'll don't		Initiating topic.
510	Ruth	You don't do ah	Teacher looks at Ruth.	
511	Ruth	ummmh		Holds floor.
512	Ruth	(*Points to a picture in the book*)	Ruth points to book on the table; students look at book.	
513	Makeda	Do the Christian mean the same thing does it me and here, is it meaning ya'll	Makeda looking up as Sanjo finishes question by rolling her hand.	Makeda taking the floor; ignoring Ruth's previous question for Sanjo; positioning Sanjo as the expert.
514	Ruth	Does it mean the same thing here as it does there		Taking the floor to rephrase Makeda's question.

515	Sanjo	Yeah, but there, we have	Ruth, Cathy, and Makeda are all leaning in, looking at Sanjo (all others out of view of camera).	Confirming similar identities as Christians; also negates complete similarities; distinguishes differences of American Christians and Nigerian Christians, establishing herself as the expert of Nigerian Christianity.
516	Sanjo	Something we wear in Nigeria		
517	Sanjo	Which is white, white, white		
518	Sanjo	Some we put like this and they are (*picks up cloth on table*) there, like this	Ruth, Cathy, Makeda look at clothing.	Claiming social position as expert.
519	Teacher	The bead and sequins and	Students still looking at cloth; teacher and Sanjo looking at each other.	Confirms Sanjo's information and adds information to it.
520	Sanjo	Yeah		Claiming social position as expert.
521	Makeda	How do ya'll		Bids for floor, positioning Sanjo as the expert.
522	Sanjo	Look look good		Sanjo holds floor continuing with previous topic.
523	Makeda	How do ya'll		Second bid for floor.
524	Sanjo	White, white everything	Teacher nods; students looking at Sanjo.	Sanjo holds floor continuing with previous topic.
525	Teacher	U-hum		Confirming.
526	Makeda	Why do ya'll	Students maintaining leaning-in posture.	Third bid for floor with a different question;

(*continued on next page*)

TABLE 4.4 *(continued)*

Line No.	Speaker	Transcript	Group Nonverbal Behavior	Social Interaction and Commentary
527	Makeda	How'd, I mean		Holding the floor by rephrasing the question; positioning Sanjo as the expert.
528	Makeda	How do you all become a Christian in Nigeria	Sanjo and Makeda look at each other.	
529	Sanjo	Nigeria		Confirmation
530	Ruth	Like here we have to be baptized	Ruth and Sanjo look at each other; other students look in Sanjo's direction.	Taking the floor to expand on Makeda's question.
531	Sanjo	Yeah		Claiming social position as expert.
532	Ruth	Ya'll have to be baptized		Initiating interaction for clarification; establishing similarity between American Christians and Nigerian Christians.
533	Sanjo	Yeah		Claiming social position as expert.
534	Ruth	Cool		Gives social status to Sanjo and invokes "teenage" social register for assigning value.
535	Makeda	Are ya dunked in the water		Takes floor; establishing Sanjo as the expert.
536	Makeda	Not dunked in the water but	Students giggle; Karen leans back, looks at Cathy; others looking around at each other	Students establish their positions as experts of American Christianity.
537	Makeda	Dipped in the water		Clarification.

538	Sanjo	Not that deep, like this		
539	Sanjo	They would put someone	Ruth, Cathy leaning in; Karen sitting back; teacher standing, leaning in.	Negates Makeda's added information; adds information as the expert.
540	Sanjo	[*Puts one hand behind her head and the other hand pinches her nose and then leans forward*]		
541	Makeda	We'd go back		
542	Sanjo	I'm goin' to show them a picture		Makeda positions herself as expert.
543	Karen	Yeah, we go back	Teacher looks off camera; Sanjo mimes taking a photograph.	Initiates topic, positioning herself as authority in the group.
544	Makeda	We go the reverse way		Confirming similarity; positioning themselves as experts.
545	Ruth	We go, we go	Karen leans back in chair, holding nose.	
546	Ruth	(*Tips backwards*)	Ruth stands up and leans back.	

that history. The question to ask about such an interpretation is not whether it is right or wrong but whether it is grounded in the event itself and how such an interpretation stands against other interpretations. To some extent, one can claim that an interpretation of the event as silencing the history of European colonialism is grounded in the event. After all, the curriculum, the materials, and the assignments are all selected by officials and educators associated with the school. They had choices that would have allowed them to highlight European colonialism, but they made other choices. The teacher was aware of the history of European colonialism but chose not to mediate the interaction between the students and the curriculum and library materials available. Furthermore, nowhere in the prescribed social studies curriculum across kindergarten through high school is there explicit discussion of European colonialism in Africa or the various liberation movements to resist and overthrow that colonialism. Thus, one cannot make the claim that later on in their schooling the students would address European colonialism in Africa, and thus from this perspective the silence is notable.

However, it is also the case that the interpretation is not grounded in the event. The knowledge that is being built is aligned to contesting the characterization of life in Africa given by the library books (what might be called *official* knowledge) and to building alternative knowledge based on alternative authority (i.e., Sanjo as a bearer of authoritative knowledge). If this is what the classroom language and literacy event is about, does it really make sense to argue for an interpretation based primarily on what is not in the face-to-face interactions of the teacher and students? The answer may depend on one's goal and on whether one is conducting a discourse analysis as part of a broader project exploring power relations or whether one is exploring power relations as part of a broader agenda of understanding a particular classroom or community and the language and literacy events that occur there. Of course, it can also be both, and both interpretations, despite their contradictory nature, can be valid.

DISCOURSE ANALYSIS ACROSS EVENTS: A COMPARATIVE PERSPECTIVE

Before we compare the two lessons discussed in this chapter, we need to address two methodological questions about the creation of a comparative perspective. First, on what basis would two events be selected for comparison? Second, what is the basis for the selection of the dimensions on which a comparison might be made? We need to approach these questions from two different stances. The first is from within the events and settings (an *emic* stance), and the second is from outside of them (an *etic* stance). This matrix is presented graphically in Table 4.5.

The issues displayed in Table 4.5 make clear that any comparison should be a principled and systematic decision, not a matter of convenience or happenstance. Indeed, we argue that it is never the case that a comparison is merely a matter of convenience or happenstance. What appear to be convenience and happenstance is more likely the manifestation of a default interpretive framework, perhaps one that is so close to the researcher that he or she is unable to see it as deriving from a particular ideological position. In other words, comparisons are always intentional and ideological acts. What is being compared, and how, is part of an interpretive act, an ideological formation. Other comparisons could have been chosen with different interpretive results. Why is this particular pair of cases being compared? How is it that this particular pair of cases is present for comparison? Why were the particular dimensions of comparison chosen? Why is this par-

TABLE 4.5

Selecting Events for Comparison

Location	Selection of the Events for Comparison	Selection of the Dimensions of Comparison
Inside the event/ setting (emic stance)	Box 1 Participants explicitly or implicitly name and connect the events and compare them. Events are related through the structure of a social institution and are comparable given that institutional structure.	Box 2 Participants explicitly or implicitly name and use particular dimensions to describe a comparison of events. Dimensions for comparison are grounded in the social institution.
Outside the event/ setting (etic stance)	Box 3 Selection based on a discipline-based theoretical model. Selection based on *a priori* questions and issues. or Selection based on methodological procedures and guidelines. or Selection based on availability of data.	Box 4 Selection based on a discipline-based theoretical model. Selection based on *a priori* questions and issues. or Selection based on methodological procedures and guidelines.

ticular comparison being made at that time and in that situation? Who and what are privileged by this particular comparison? Articulating the basis of the comparison provides the researcher and others with a visible interpretive framework and opens up the possibility for alternative comparisons.

The two lessons we compare in this section were selected because they appeared to us to represent different formulations of how literacy is implicated in power relations and, more specifically, how literacy events may be implicated in transforming power relations. In both classrooms, students had to address written texts associated with academic knowledge (a poem and library books), and those written texts became props for examining knowledge and power relations. We anticipated that a comparative perspective would reveal variations in how teachers and students might use written language to transform extant power relations among people in an event and between people and the social institutions in which they live.

In reference to Table 4.5, the comparative perspective we take here is an etic one, and the dimensions of comparison are etic ones (see Boxes 3 and 4 in Table 4.5). Neither the choice of lessons nor the dimensions of comparison are derived from within the lessons. Although both lessons are conducted within curricular frameworks provided by the same school system, they stem from different disciplines (language arts and social studies). The teachers were unaware of each other, and in discussing their lessons compared them with lessons that are more "traditional"[12] (i.e., those that are didactic and oriented toward the acquisition of authoritative scholastic knowledge). Thus, we are not claiming, and would have no basis on which to claim, that our comparison is an emic one. But we must also acknowledge that the etic perspective we have chosen to pursue through our comparison of the lessons is only one of many different perspectives that could have been pursued. For example, researchers interested in classroom education and social identity in regard to African American students might have also selected these two lessons for comparison but have chosen a different set of dimensions for comparison than we did. In brief, comparative perspectives can vary even in the comparison of the same two events.

A Comparative Perspective on the Uses of Reading in the 7th-Grade Language Arts Lesson and the 6th-Grade Social Studies Lesson

In this section we examine the uses of reading across the two lessons and within two events (one from each classroom) with specific concern for how reading is used with regard to power relations. To create a comparative framework for the uses of reading across the two lessons, we began by placing next to each other the phases of the two lessons (see Fig. 4.7). In Fig. 4.7, we have grouped phases (designated by letters) that are contiguous and that appear to be similar with regard to instructional content or involve complementary phases, such as the silent reading of a poem followed by discussion of that poem.

As one can see in Fig. 4.7, the lessons do not match each other in terms of lesson phases or groups of phases. With the exception of the first and last phases of each lesson (A and H), the phases themselves are different (with regard to turn-taking protocols and with regard to what is happening) and,

---

[12]We made this inference the basis of our interviews with the teachers.

	Seventh Grade Language Arts Lesson	Sixth Grade Social Studies Lesson	
A	1. Introduction of task – pass out poem	1. Organizing for task at table	A
B	2. Read poem in groups silently	2. Questioning Sanjo	
C	3. Teacher asks questions about poem	3. Sanjo demonstrating Clothing	I
	4. Teacher reads poem to the classs	4.Interrogating the book	J
D	5. Discussion in groups about who the main character is	5. With teacher discussion of clothing	K
	6. Teacher directs responses about who the main characters are	6. Writing information on index cards from the library books	L
E	7. Discussion about whether the main character is Black	7. Questioning Sanjo	
	8. Discussion about language, education and opportunity	8. Sanjo demonstrating clothing	
	9. Teacher directed discussion of code switching with voting	9. Teacher and students questioning Sanjo about clothing and family	M
	10. Discussion of definitions	10. Students questioning Sanjo about religion, animals, language, schooling, food	
	11. Maria's story	11. Repulsing intrusion of boys	N
F	12. Interrogation of Andre	12. Continuation of phase 10	M
	13.Maria's story continues	13. Students and Sanjo interact with teacher, summarize information	O
G	14. Discussion of talking Black and talking white	14. Sanjo rejects Makeda's request to demonstrate a folk dance	P
H	15. Coda	15. Students and Sanjo compare being Christian	Q
	16. Leaving	16. Ending	
		17. Filling out evaluation form	H
		18. Leaving	

FIG. 4.7   Side-by-side comparison of lesson phases and uses of reading.

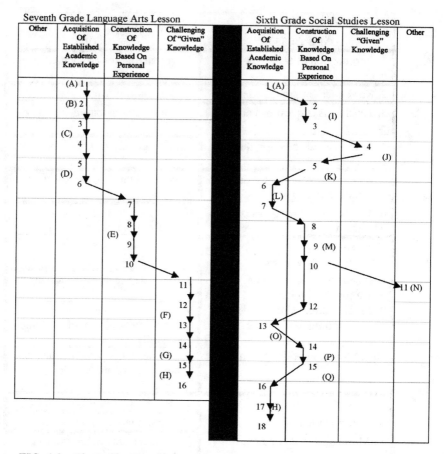

FIG. 4.8   Flow of lesson phases across instructional themes of acquisition of established academic knowledge, construction of knowledge based on personal experience, challenging "given" knowledge, and other.

as Fig. 4.8 shows, the sequencing of the phases is different; that is, although in each lesson the phases flow across the themes of (a) acquisition of established academic knowledge, (b) construction of knowledge based on personal experience, and (c) the challenging of "given"[13] knowledge, the way they flow across these three themes differs.

A general description of the uses of written language in each lesson on a phase-by-phase basis is provided in Fig. 4.9. Because the description is at

---

[13]By *given* we are referring both to authoritative academic knowledge that is taken as a "given" in schools and in a discipline as well as to the process of "giving" that knowledge to students, and we are referring to "folk" knowledge that is taken as a "given" as common knowledge.

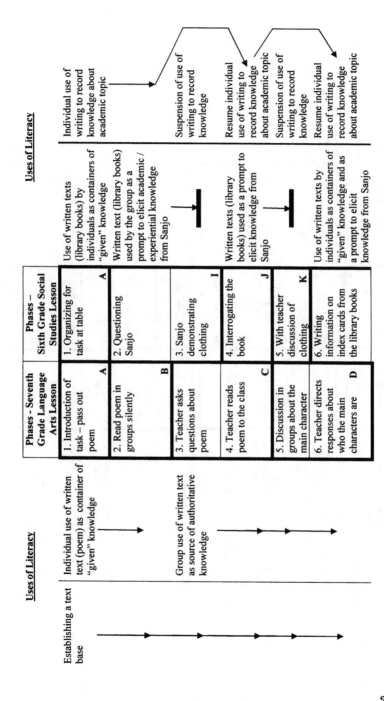

FIG. 4.9   Uses of written language across lesson phases.

Uses of Literacy (left)

Establishing a text base

Individual use of written text (poem) as container of "given" knowledge

Group use of written text as source of authoritative knowledge

Phases – Seventh Grade Language Arts Lesson

1. Introduction of task – pass out poem **A**

2. Read poem in groups silently **B**

3. Teacher asks questions about poem

4. Teacher reads poem to the class **C**

5. Discussion in groups about the main character

6. Teacher directs responses about who the main characters are **D**

Phases – Sixth Grade Social Studies Lesson

1. Organizing for task at table **A**

2. Questioning Sanjo

3. Sanjo demonstrating clothing **I**

4. Interrogating the book **J**

5. With teacher discussion of clothing **K**

6. Writing information on index cards from the library books

Uses of Literacy (right, top)

Use of written texts (library books) by individuals as containers of "given" knowledge

Written text (library books) used by the group as a prompt to elicit academic / experiential knowledge from Sanjo

Written texts (library books) used as a prompt to elicit knowledge from Sanjo

Use of written texts by individuals as containers of "given" knowledge and as a prompt to elicit knowledge from Sanjo

Uses of Literacy (far right)

Individual use of writing to record knowledge about academic topic

Suspension of use of writing to record knowledge

Resume individual use of writing to record knowledge about academic topic

Suspension of use of writing to record knowledge

Resume individual use of writing to record knowledge about academic topic

223

Uses of Literacy (right)

- Individual use of writing to record knowledge about academic topic
- Suspension of use of writing to record knowledge
- Use of writing to reflect

Uses of Literacy (upper)

- Written texts (library books) used as a prompt to elicit knowledge from Sanjo

Phases – Seventh Grade Language Arts Lesson	Phases – Sixth Grade Social Studies Lesson
	7. Questioning Sanjo L
7. Discussion about whether the main character is Black	8. Sanjo demonstrating clothing
8. Discussion about language, education and opportunity	9. Teacher and students questioning Sanjo about clothing and family
9. Teacher directed discussion of code switching with voting	10. Students questioning Sanjo about religion, animals, language, schooling, food M
10. Discussion of definitions E	11. Rejecting intrusion of boys N
11. Maria's story	12. Continuation of phase 10 M
12. Interrogation of Andre	13. Students and Sanjo interact with teacher, summarize information O
13. Maria's story continues F	14. Sanjo rejects request to enact a folk dance P
14. Discussion of Black and talking white G	15. Students and Sanjo compare being Christian Q
15. Coda	16. Ending
	17. Filling out evaluation form
16. Leaving H	18. Leaving H

Uses of Literacy (lower left)

- Public use of written text as evidence for spoken argument
- Use of dialogue from the written text to support arguments about race
- Use of dialogue from the written text to prompt discussion about language, education and opportunity for African-Americans
- Use of the written text as a prompt and a prop for interrogating "given" knowledge about language variation
- Use of dialogue from the written text as illustration of a type of talk - Ebonics
- Use of dialogue from the written text as illustration of a type of talk - Ebonics

FIG. 4.9 *(continued)*

the phase level, it is necessarily broad and inexact, making no differentiation in the uses of literacy among students and making invisible uses of literacy that are either momentary or that involve subtle uses. Nonetheless, as Fig. 4.9 shows, in general the uses of written language in the two lessons differ. In the 7th-grade language arts lesson, the uses of literacy flow from the establishment of a common text base (the analysis of a written text to establish who is in the written text and what happens in it), to the use of the written text as data (on the language that people use), to the use of the written text as a prompt and a prop for interrogating "given" knowledge about language variation. In the 6th-grade social studies lesson, the uses of literacy flow from the use of a written text as a source of authoritative "given" knowledge and the use of writing as a way to record that knowledge, to the use of a written text as a prompt to interrogate "given" knowledge and then as a prompt to elicit authoritative knowledge based on Sanjo's personal experience. The students move in and out of the use of writing to record what gets constructed as authoritative knowledge within their group.

Given the differences in the flow of the lessons, one would not expect the uses of reading to be the same across the two lessons. Also, even if there were surface-level similarities between the uses of reading in one phase in the 7th-grade lesson and the uses of reading in a phase in the 6th-grade lesson, one would need to exercise great care in making any statement about the significance of the similarities or their comparability. A more fruitful approach, in our opinion, and the approach we take in this section, is to explore the variation in how people use literacy to accomplish social relationships and knowledge construction (we focus here on power relations as a part of social relationships and as a part of knowledge construction) and, in so doing, how people transform literacy practices. That is, as Street (1993b) pointed out, people adopt and adapt literacy practices to suit their own needs and agendas and in so doing transform what literacy is.

Earlier in this chapter, we emphasized identification of an entry point as an important part of conducting discourse analysis of a classroom language and literacy event. The same is true for a comparative discourse analysis with the exception that identification of the entry point minimally involves the identification of two events (one from each of the lessons being compared). We used the analyses provided by Figs. 4.7, 4.8, and 4.9 to assist in the identification of entry points. Given our goal—exploring variation in how people use literacy to accomplish social relationships and knowledge construction with an emphasis on power relations—we wanted to examine those phases of the lessons where uses of written language appear likely to be involved in transforming power relations through changes in social relationships and knowledge construction. Thus, in the 7th-grade language arts lesson, based on Fig. 4.9, Phases 9 and 10 would appear to be locations where written language is implicated in challenging "given" knowledge. We might have selected Phases 11, 12, and 13 because they most obviously involve challenges to social relationships (the association of language with racial identity); however, written language is only indirectly implicated in those phases. In the 6th-grade social studies lesson, as shown in Fig. 4.9, whenever the students and the teacher explore Sanjo's clothing and family life in Nigeria they suspend the use of writing to record information and abandon the use of the library books. Although it might be argued that the exploration of Sanjo's clothing and family life in Nigeria is information that is pertinent to the instructional task, as indicated by the students' use of writing to record information for their report (as shown in Fig. 4.9), manifestly there is a separation between the official instructional task and the interaction with Sanjo with regard to clothing and family life.[14] Among the lesson phases that involve the direct use of written language, Phases 2 and 4 involve direct challenges to the written texts (the library books). Phase 4 leads directly to a discussion of Sanjo's clothing and what we earlier identified as a paradigm shift in the lesson, suggesting that something in Phase 4 provided an opportunity for the paradigm shift that occurred in Phase 5. In sum, Phases 9 and 10 in the 7th-grade English lesson, and Phases 4 and 5 in the 6th-grade social studies lesson, appear to provide fruitful entry points. Of course, these are not the only potential entry points. As we have stated throughout this chapter, as an analysis evolves the findings may suggest other and perhaps more fruitful entry points. The purpose of our discussion of entry points was merely to make visible the decision-making process behind our selection of entry points.

A Comparative Microanalysis of Literacy, Power, and Social Relationships in Events From the 7th-Grade Language Arts Classroom and the 6th-Grade Social Studies Classroom

During the first part of the 7th-grade language arts lesson, the teacher and students establish a shared *text world* or *situation model* based on the poem they are studying—who is in the poem, what is happening in the poem, and what the setting is. The teacher has added information beyond what is explicitly mentioned in the poem (that the events in the poem occur in 1865) and scaffolds the students' inferencing about what the situation might be based on the date. Then, in Phase 9, the teacher asks the following:

22	Ms. Wilson:	Now.
23		Over a period of time
24		1865 all the way to 1997
25		there are still people who use terms and phrases

---

[14]The manifest separation of the exploration of Sanjo's clothing and family life from the instructional task does not mean that the students were not learning about family life in Nigeria/Africa. The separation concerns only the accomplishment and display of the instructional task.

26		*de, fo', folks*
27		that are similar to what we read in the poem
28	Theresa:	Yea but ...
29	Ms. Wilson:	Is that by choice
30	Theresa:	Choice
31	Ms. Wilson:	Or is that because *quote unquote* a lack of knowledge

The teacher's questions moves the discussion beyond the establishment of a situation model and provokes students to think about the derivation of language variation. What occurs subsequently is that two students give opposing responses, each with their own explanation. Neither response is grounded in personal experience. Later the teacher emphasizes making an argument based on personal experience. We want to look carefully at lines 22 through 31, because the teacher uses written language (the poem) to make a shift in social relationships between herself and the students and between themselves and "given" knowledge.

Lines 23, 24, 25, 26, and 27 explicitly connect the dialogue in the poem (African American language) to the language that many people in the classroom, and in the students' lives, speak. Each line contains a reference to both the time of the poem and the current time:

23		Over a period of time (the beginning of the period and the end of the period)
24		1865 all the way to 1997 (1865 and 1997)
25		there are still people who use terms and phrases (still)
26		*de, fo', folks* (language behavior from the poem and from contemporary speech)
27		that are similar to what we read in the poem (similar, poem)

This establishes what might be considered a thematic chain (see Halliday, 1985). This thematic chain becomes the context for considering the question that follows (lines 29 and 31).

| 29 | | Is that by choice |
| 31 | | Or is that because *quote unquote* a lack of knowledge |

Lines 23 through 27 and lines 29 and 31 are linked by "that" in lines 29 and 31 and by the use of "lack of knowledge," which is a repetition of an earlier discussion of the situation model invoked by the poem.

The question that follows, "[29] Is that by choice [31] Or is that because *quote unquote* a lack of knowledge," requires the students to use their understandings of language. The rest of the lesson can be viewed as an exploration of what constitutes an appropriate knowledge base for answering the question in lines 29 and 31, what constitutes a knowledge base for understanding language. Thus, the space that is opened up by lines 23 through 31 provides an opportunity for the teacher and the students to explore, reflect on, and transform the power relations embedded in different understandings of language variation; that is, to the extent that a particular language ideology frames how people/students understand their own and others' language use, that language ideology exerts power by privileging particular understandings of language and the people who use language in particular ways. Opening up a space for critically examining language ideologies transforms power relations by undercutting the invisibility of a "given" language ideology.

In brief, in this lesson the teacher opened up a space for critical reflection on language ideologies by asserting a linkage between the dialogue in a written text and the way that people in the students' lives use language. More simply stated, the teacher insisted on a text-to-life connection and thereby provided the validity for using students' own personal experiences and understandings of language. Given the shift in the instructional conversation that occurs within lines 23 through 31, one might characterize what occurs as a paradigm shift (cf. Baynham, 2000).

Earlier, we described a paradigm shift in the 6th-grade social studies lesson, which occurs in Phase 4. As we described earlier, Sanjo is questioning the validity of the information found in the library books on the library table. The teacher enters the group, and Makeda reports to her about the clothing that Sanjo brought to the class. Both Karen and the teacher comment on the clothing, describing the clothing as "cool," "beautiful," and "soft," transforming the instructional conversation from being about the recording of information on notecards from authoritative sources (such as library books) to being about the establishment of affective social relationships between Sanjo and the other students.

The paradigm shift occurs around lines 147 through 172 (in Transcript 4.3). Sanjo has already challenged the information in the library books and shown the students how to wear the clothing she brought with her. The teacher then enters the group.

147	Teacher:	[enters] So
148		Sanjo are the
149		are the clothes that are pictured here in the book
150		do do you think they are pretty accurate to what you really wear
151	Sanjo:	Not this
152		not this type
153	Teacher:	not this style

154	Sanjo:	Yeah
155		they asked for this in the picture
156	Makeda:	This is stuff she told us
157		this is the shirt this is the skirt
158		and this is the little head thing
159	Teacher:	Yeah
160	Makeda:	And this is the little dress thing
161	Teacher:	Ooooh
162		That's beautiful
163		that's soft too
164	Sanjo:	Yeah
165	Sanjo:	They use cotton to make it
166	Teacher:	Did did um did you make this
167		or did someone in your family make it
168	Sanjo:	My grandmother
169	Makeda:	Your grandmother made it
170	Teacher:	Does she sew a lot with you
171	Sanjo:	Yeah
172	Teacher:	That's pretty neat.

The first move that the teacher makes is to open a space for Sanjo to challenge the legitimacy of the information in the library books (lines 149–150). She does so by asking a question and by linking the book to Sanjo's life (a text-to-life connection). Both the form of the teacher's utterance (question), the text-to-life connection, and the positioning of the student as an evaluator of the text-to-life connection are similar to what occurred in the 7th-grade language arts lesson. Part of what is different across the two lessons is that in the 7th-grade classroom the teacher and students had already established a shared situation model based on the written text (the poem), whereas in the 6th-grade lesson it is the situation model that is in question. That is, as the students construct a situation model of family life in Africa, the information they are gathering from the authoritative written texts (the library books) is being challenged, changing the situation model being constructed.

After the 6th-grade teacher opens up a space for Sanjo (and, by implication, the other students in the group as well) to challenge the information in the written text, Makeda then occupies the conversational space, talking for Sanjo about the clothing Sanjo had brought. The teacher then makes two moves in lines 161 through 163 and 166 through 167. In lines 161 through 163, the teacher opens up a space for affective aspects and expressions, creating a paradigm shift in the instructional conversation. The conversation is no longer solely focused on recording information about family life in Africa but is now about the expression of affective reactions and relationships.

The cloth is "beautiful" (line 162) and "soft" (line 163), and evokes the reaction of "Ooooo" (line 161).

One way to characterize the findings of the comparison is that there appear to be three ways of reading manifest in the lessons: (a) teacher and students decode a written text to create a shared and authoritative situation model (as occurs in the 7th-grade language arts classroom prior to Phase 9); (b) teacher and students challenge and interrogate the information in a written text as part of their construction of a situation model (as occurs in the 6th-grade social studies classroom); and (c) although teachers and students may begin with the reading of a written text and with the construction of a situation model, doing so is only a starting point or a platform for exploring issues in their worlds beyond the written text. The teacher and students in the 7th-grade language arts lesson used the poem as a platform for exploring the relationships of language, race, and education. The teacher and the students in the 6th-grade social studies lesson used the library books as a starting point for constructing a different set of social relationships among the students and Sanjo and for understanding Sanjo (and life in Africa) as something familiar, beautiful, loving, and "cool." In each lesson, the teacher and students moved beyond the written text, although they did so in different ways.

So, what can be claimed about reading and power relations based on our comparative analysis of the two lessons? First, although reading was involved in each lesson, we note that the disciplinary contexts of the lesson, the settings, the classroom organization, and the flow of the lessons differed. Second, each lesson began with *reading* defined as the decoding of authoritative written text for information. Such a definition involves a particular set of power relations with regard to knowledge and to the situation models of "worlds" assumed by the written texts and the individuals who produce them. It is also a model of reading valorized by official school policy, given how reading and academic knowledge are tested. Thus, a shift from the official school model of reading to a model of reading as a prompt and as a prop for the interrogation of authoritative information based on personal experience—for storytelling, for the construction of new sets of social relationships, and for the conversational exploration of issues in the students' lives—involves new sets of power relations. The students are required to evaluate the information in the written texts, to examine their social relationships with each other, to examine their assumptions about "given" knowledge, and to examine how the interpret and evaluate their own experiences. In both lessons they are able to do so because the teacher opened up a conversational space for the students by linking the written text to their lives and by extending the conversation beyond the boundaries of the text world invoked by the written text. In each case, the teacher and students adopted an extant model of school literacy and then adapted that model to accommodate agendas beyond those associated with the extant school model of reading.

The dynamics we have discussed with regard to reading and power relations are not the only dynamics in the lessons related to power relations. A full explication of the interpersonal and institutional dynamics in power relations in the lessons is beyond the scope of this section. We have merely illustrated one way in which a comparative discourse analysis of power relations in classroom language and literacy events might be approached.

CONCLUDING COMMENTS

Part of what is at stake in classroom language and literacy events, and in schooling more broadly considered, is not just the power relations related to knowledge but also the model of power at play. More simply stated, are "doing literacy" and "doing learning" organized around the model of power as product, power as process, power as caring relations, or some combination of these models? We further argue that implicit in every classroom language and literacy event (indeed, every social event) is the promulgation of a model of power. In sum, educational researchers interested in understanding power relations therefore need to excavate both the power relations in the event(s) being examined as well as the model of power implied.

Microethnographic discourse analysis provides one means of doing this. It involves a constant movement, back and forth, between data and theorizing, between interrogation of the research endeavor, theoretical constructs, and assumptions, and the fashioning of the data one has gathered. Power relations permeate the research endeavor no less so than they do classroom language and literacy events.

In this chapter we have illustrated one way to work back and forth among theories in the field theories in the event; and close, careful microethnographic analysis of the social interactions of teachers and students with each other. Included in that back-and-forth movement was the use of comparative analysis both within and across data sets. We illustrated how different descriptions of power relations could be made at various levels of a classroom language and literacy event, not such that a description at one level is correct and the other wrong but that all of these descriptions exist as potential resources for teachers and students as they continue to work out how to build their lives both within and beyond the classroom.

Given the illustrations and discussion in this chapter, as well as careful and nuanced discussions of power and education by social and cultural theorists as diverse as hooks (1994), de Certeau (1984, 1997), Street (1995, 1996, 1998), and Noddings (1984, 1992, 1993), among others, we believe it is fair to say that it is no longer sufficient to simply characterize and caricature people, teachers, and students as powerful or powerless, as dependent variables subject to the mediate circumstances of some ethereal macro-level social force or as independent factors whose efforts are simply the result of autonomous developmental and cognitive processes. Neither is it sufficient to simply characterize literacy learning simply as an empowering process or a disempowering process. People, teachers and students, and their uses of language are caught up in complex webs of power relations that they construct, reconstruct, transform, resist, adapt, adopt, maintain, destabilize, and defenestrate, and they do so within and across particular events, constructing the relationships among those events. They do not do so in a social or political vacuum, but neither is the social and political context within which they conduct their face-to-face interactions deterministic. And although it is certainly the case that power relations permeate every event, including every classroom language and literacy event, it is also the case that the analysis of classroom language and literacy events is not wholly defined by the single dimension of power.

Chapter 5

Locating Microethnographic Discourse Analysis Studies of Classroom Language and Literacy Events and the Research Imagination

In this final chapter we focus attention on the relationship of micro-ethnographic discourse analysis studies of classroom language and literacy events to other types of research and lines of inquiry. As we noted in the Introduction and in chapter 1, the discussion throughout this book builds on discussions within what is called the *New Literacy Studies*. In brief, the New Literacy Studies involve an approach to research that foregrounds anthropological and sociolinguistic methods and that closely attends to issues of cultural, political, and economic ideology. There are different emphases within the New Literacy Studies. One line of inquiry concerns the relationship of literacy practices and the new capitalism and its implications for defining work, learning, and identity (Gee, Hull, & Lankshear, 1996; Jones, 2000; Lankshear, Gee, Knobel, & Searle, 1997). Another is concerned with how literacy practices constitute learning practices both inside and outside of classrooms (Gee, 1994, 2003; Knobel, 1999; Luke, 1988; 1995; Ormerod & Ivanic, 2000). Street (1984, 1992, 1993a, 1993b, 1997, 2003) has focused attention on the cultural and political dynamics and diversity of literacy practices, the relationship of literacy practices and nationalism, how literacy practices are related to power relations, and how people adopt and adapt the literacy practices in their lives as part of the borders between their lives and the imposition of the state and dominant social and political institutions. Both the New Literacy Studies and microethnographic discourse analysis approaches to the study of classroom language and literacy events share what Street (1984, 1995b) has labeled an *ideological model* of literacy. Literacy is not a thing in and of itself, a set of autonomous cognitive and linguistic skills, but a set of social and cultural practices embedded in and a part of broader, ongoing, and evolving social, cultural, and political processes. But relationships among research perspectives are not so easily given or assumed. We need to ask: Is there meaningfulness in catgorizing both the New Literacy Studies and microethnographic discourse analysis studies of classroom language and literacy events as ideological approaches to the study of literacy? What would give such a categorization meaningfulness?

In our view, relationships among research perspectives are constructed, not given. In this chapter we focus attention on how relationships among research perspectives are constructed. In brief, one cannot assume a relationship; rather, the key questions to ask are: "Who is building what kind of a relationship among research perspectives? For what purposes? With whom? When? Where? And with what consequences, for whom?"

These questions have importance not just for microethnographic discourse analysis studies but for research studies and research perspectives in general. Thus, much of the discussion in this chapter is not specific to microethnographic discourse analysis studies. In our view, the relationship of research studies and perspectives is not simply one of gathering increased data, knowledge, and perspective but one associated with fashioning the research imagination. By *research imagination*, we are referring to ways of imagining the world and the people in it.

We begin by addressing the concept of multiple research perspectives, focusing our attention on the process involved in the relationship between research studies and perspectives. We label that process *locating*. Then we discuss the concept of the "research imagination" created by the juxtaposition of research studies and perspectives.

LOCATING DISCOURSE ANALYSIS STUDIES OF CLASSROOM LANGUAGE AND LITERACY EVENTS AMONG MULTIPLE PERSPECTIVES

Researchers are fond of comparing the use of multiple research approaches to the situation of several blind people each attempting to describe an elephant. One stands by the trunk and bases her description on what she infers from the shape of the trunk, another does the same standing by the side, another by the tail, and so on. None provides the complete picture, only collectively can they fully describe the elephant. Although the analogy may apply in some cases, with regard to characterizing the relationship of microethnographic discourse analysis studies of classroom literacy events to other research approaches, we reject that analogy. As we see it, some researchers believe that you can study an elephant as it is standing still. Others argue that the elephant must be dissected to be studied, some contend that it must be studied as part of its natural environment, and still others argue that we can understand the elephant only in its relationship to human beings and the uses to which human beings put elephants. And there are a few researchers who argue that we cannot study the elephant at all, only the concept of "elephant-ness." In brief, the differences among approaches to research on classroom language and literacy events are not simple matters of perspective but are as complex and contested as any set of human relationships. And although one might claim that each approach has something to offer and thus all are to be valued, such a compromise is neither principled nor warranted. Different people and different agendas are privileged by some approaches rather than others. Furthermore, it is likely that the elephant would find some approaches less attractive than others, some helpful, and some threatening and destructive.

In our view, the relationships among research perspectives are not given, nor can they be assumed; rather, they are constructed, argued, and negotiated—and this is so even when such processes are not acknowledged. Acknowledged or unacknowledged, we refer to this process as *locating*, juxtaposing a study, series of studies, or line of inquiry with other studies and lines of inquiry.[1]

In chapter 1 we tried to locate our approach to the microethnographic discourse analysis of classroom language and literacy events in five different places. First, we explicitly named the location of our approach within the intellectual movements that have grown out of the Linguistic Turn in the social sciences. Second, we described our approach as evolving out of a series of disciplinary and interdisciplinary lines of inquiry in the humanities and social sciences, and we explicitly named them. They included the New Literacy Studies, sociolinguistic ethnography, humanistic linguistics, anthropological studies of narrative and poetics, ethnomethodology, critical discourse analysis, and related educational studies. Third, we located our approach by citing specific scholars and researchers including literary theorists (Bakhtin, Volosinov, Benjamin, Williams, Morrison, Said), social theorists (Dubois, DeCerteau, Gergen), anthropologists (Street, Geertz, Gumperz, Hymes), linguists (Barton, Gee, Halliday), and educational researchers (Bloome, Green, Egan-Robertson), among others. Fourth, we highlighted and foregrounded two key issues currently being discussed in

---

[1]We use *locating* to refer to intellectual locations, rather than physical ones. For example, a classroom is a physical and material location. Although students and teachers might occupy the same geographic location, their intellectual location(s) might be different. Therefore, a classroom has multiple locations. Intellectual locations are not inside people's heads but rather are social and historical spaces. Furthermore, by naming and acknowledging intellectual location(s), there are opportunities to make visible locations and spaces that might otherwise not be made visible. That is, the concepts of "locating" and "locations" provide another way to articulate issues of privilege, invisibility, and marginalization.

the social sciences and humanities: (a) personhood and (b) events. By doing this we located our approach to the microethnographic discourse analysis of classroom language and literacy events within particular debates in the field and eschewed others. We also distinguished our approach to theorizing events and practices from that often associated with the New Literacy Studies. And fifth, even in chapter 1, the purpose of which was to present the intellectual foundations of our approach, we devoted considerable space to the detailed microethnographic discourse analysis of a classroom event. Doing so is not just an illustration of a theoretical or methodological principle but, given the way we structured those uses of microethnographic discourse analysis, we were locating our approach among approaches to research that foreground a dialectic between theory and method; that is, whose logics of inquiry require a constant recursive analysis of both theory and method as they are being used.

But it is not just in chapter 1 where we worked to locate microethnographic discourse analysis studies. Chapter 2 can be viewed as locating microethnographic discourse analysis studies within the broader scholarship on cultural studies of the classroom, chapter 3 as locating microethnographic discourse analysis studies within current discussions of the construction of social identity, and chapter 4 as locating microethnographic discourse analysis studies within discussions of power relationships. In each chapter we sought to show the contribution of microethnographic discourse analysis studies to the broader discussion and to show how such studies might redefine the broader discussion. Throughout the chapters we continuously raised questions about knowing—what could be known from the perspective of microethnographic discourse analysis studies and what knowledge assumed by a field of study might be called into question. Thus, perhaps less explicitly than with other locations, we were working to locate microethnographic discourse analysis studies of classroom language and literacy events within the broader philosophical debate about what counts as knowledge.

Perhaps it is more accurate to describe what we did in chapter 1 and elsewhere in this book not as locating microethnographic discourse analysis studies but rather an *attempt* to locate the approach. One cannot simply and unilaterally claim a location for a study or line of inquiry. Similar to our discussion of intertextuality earlier in this book, four interactional moves must occur before a location (an intertextual connection) can be said to have been made (cf. Bloome & Egan-Robertson, 1993).

1. *A location must be proposed*

A proposal for locating a research study, perspective, or line of inquiry can be made by a single person, a group, or a social institution. For example, a researcher might suggest that an underlying methodological principle is the same across two or more research perspectives, by explicitly stating that both microethnographic discourse analysis and research conducted within the New Literacy Studies pay close attention to the language people use. Proposals also can be indirect. For example, a social institution[2] might propose that books reporting microethnographic discourse analysis of classroom language and literacy events and books explicitly labeled the New Literacy Studies should be categorized under the same catalog number, or that because the school of education already has a faculty member associated with microethnographic discourse analysis, there is no need to hire another faculty member associated with the New Literacy Studies, as both individuals are viewed as holding similar perspectives.

Notice that locations are proposed at multiple levels: methodology, theoretical foundations, purpose, people involved, techniques, procedures, genre, content, function, situation of use, history, and so on. A proposal for a location can suggest a direct connection between two research perspectives (a microethnographic approach to discourse analysis is directly related to the New Literacy Studies) because they are both categorically related (both approaches fall under the broader category of qualitative research approaches) or a connection based on history (both research perspectives share historical roots in cultural anthropology).

One type of proposal for a location can be labeled an *interdiscoursive* one (cf. Fairclough, 1992). A proposal is made to use the language (or discourse) of one social institution within another—for example, to use the discourse of business in education or the discourse of education in the family. Proposals for interdiscoursivity can also be made with regard to research perspectives; for example, a proposal can be made to use the discourse of experimental psychology research to format and discuss other research perspectives. A faculty member might ask about the "reliability," "replicability," and "quantification of traits" of a microethnographic discourse analysis study. Of course, such a question has no impact unless there is uptake; that is, unless someone acknowledges and recognizes the proposed juxtaposition connection, none is constructed. Thus,

2. *A proposal for an intertextual connection must be acknowledged.*
3. *A proposal for an intertextual connection must be recognized.*

---

[2]Social institutions do not act on their own but are animated by people, yet it is often difficult to identify exactly who the acting people are. For example, at a university a series of committees may have deliberated a policy, had it reviewed by numerous administrators, voted on by a faculty, and then reported in a policy document presented to students. Alternatively, the organizational structure and policies of a social institution, such as a university, may predate any of its members. Their actions are guided by the organizational structure and policies, influencing what they are able to conceive and do. It is in these senses that we can say that a social institution has *acted*.

The acknowledgment and recognition of an locating proposal often occur together, but they are not the same. An *acknowledgment* occurs when an interlocutor acknowledges that a location is being proposed. However, it may be that there is no uptake on the content of the proposal. Simply put, just because someone acknowledges a proposal for a location does not mean that he or she understands the nature of the juxtaposition. For example, consider a proposal made by a doctoral student to a faculty member for a juxtaposition between microethnographic approaches to the analysis of classroom language and literacy events and the New Literacy Studies. Suppose the faculty member is unfamiliar with the New Literacy Studies. The faculty member can acknowledge that a location is being proposed for the doctoral student's microethnographic discourse analysis study but might not recognize the location, cannot make sense of it, and therefore cannot respond to the student in a manner that provides public recognition. Unless the student and the faculty member work to repair the lack of recognition, no interactionally validated location can be made.

Recognition can be full or partial. Full recognition occurs when the interlocutor publicly signals recognition of the various dimensions proposed for a location. Perhaps a location is being proposed at multiple levels: method, techniques, theoretical foundations, audience, situation, and function. A full recognition involves signaling recognition at all of those levels. A partial recognition signals recognition of only a subset of the dimensions.

4. *A location must have social consequence.*

Regardless of whether a location has been proposed, acknowledged, and recognized, if the juxtaposition of locations does not have a consequence for social relationships or social action, then by definition no location has been constructed. The social consequence can be subtle, or it can occur long after the processes of proposing, acknowledging, and recognizing. However, if the process of socially constructing a location for a research study, a research perspective, or line of inquiry is phatic, then it is better labeled a phatic exercise and not a location.

For example, consider a classroom discussion in a university course. The professor has asked the students to brainstorm potential connections between microethnographic approaches to the discourse analysis of classroom language and literacy events and the New Literacy Studies. The students do so, and they discuss each potential connection. But the teacher and the students are only going through the motions—they are engaging in procedural display (cf. Bloome, Puro, & Theodorou, 1987), putting on a performance that looks like a university class but not engaging the content in a substantive manner. Assuming that there are no social consequences for what they have done later or in other settings, what they have done in class is better described as a phatic enterprise or a procedural display and not as the locating of microethnographic approaches within the New Literacy Studies.

The four moves just listed are useful in analyzing the building of relationships among research perspectives. Questions can be asked about what locations are being proposed, at what levels, by whom, to whom, and for what purposes; these can be followed by questions about uptake that provide acknowledgment and recognition. If recognition is signaled, is it full or partial recognition? Finally, questions need to be asked about the social consequences of the location. In sum, the questions to ask about the relationships among research perspectives are "Who is building what kind of a relationship? For what purpose? When? Where? With what consequences, for whom?"

An Assimilationist Approach to Building Relationships Among Research Perspectives

For heuristic purposes, we can distinguish between two broad approaches to building a relationship among research perspectives: (a) an assimilationist approach and (b) a dialogic approach. An assimilationist approach involves adapting ideas and constructs from one research approach and incorporating them into another. When this occurs, the ideas from the other research perspective are transformed (adapted) so that they are consistent with the research perspective into which they are being assimilated. For example, recent research on cognitive processes involved in reading has attended to social and cultural processes. However, it is often the case that when social and cultural processes are incorporated into cognitive studies of reading they are defined as mediating factors; that is, social and cultural processes become aspects of cognitive processing. For convenience, we have labeled this approach to building relationships among research perspectives an *assimilationist* approach.

There are several contexts within which an assimilationist approach may be taken. Researchers operating within a particular perspective may be seeking ways to address a weakness or problem that they cannot otherwise satisfactorily address. Ideas and concepts from other perspectives, redefined, may provide those researchers with a way to address weaknesses or problems. In such a case, assimilating ideas and concepts from another perspective can make for stronger studies. However, there are other contexts as well. It may be that a research perspective has taken on a hegemonic nature. McDermott and Hood (1982) argued that such is the case with psychological research in education. They warned researchers interested in pursuing anthropologically based ethnographic research in educational settings to be wary about the hegemony of psychology research. Anthropological constructs, they cautioned, might be redefined in psychological terms, thus losing both their historical connection to anthropology and their connection to an underlying system of theoretical constructs. For example, reconsider the earlier illustration of interdiscoursivity in locating a microethnographic discourse analysis perspective within experimental psychology. A faculty member asks questions derived from an experimental psychology research perspective about a microethnographic discourse analysis approach. If the microethnographic discourse analysis approach has to justify its worthiness in terms of those questions, then it has been redefined within the discourse of experimental psychology. The power driving such a hegemonic assimilationist approach can be institutional (e.g., the faculty member asking the questions sits on a promotion-and-tenure committee), governmental (e.g., the questions are asked by a member of a government research grant proposal review committee), or other. The pertinent issue is not the assimilationist nature of the locating process but the power behind and in such a locating process and the social consequences that derive from it.

A Dialogic Approach to Building Relationships Among Research Perspectives

A second approach to building a relationship among research perspectives can be labeled a *dialogic* approach. Such an approach begins with the assumption that approaches to research are embodied by people; that is, research does not exist separate from what people—researchers—do. Researchers here refers both to people who formally define themselves as researchers (and who earn a living from engagement in research) and to those who engage in research defined less formally and less systematically.

To build a relationship among perspectives, researchers must engage each other and others in dialogue. We do not mean *dialogue* in a metaphorical sense—we mean it literally. People talk with each other, listen to each other, argue with each other, and mutually decide whether a dialogue is possible and, if it is, how far the usefulness of that dialogue extends for each interlocutor. Such a dialogue may involve researchers who use different approaches, or it may involve researchers and educators, students, parents, or others. To talk about relationships among approaches to research is, therefore, to talk about relationships among people, and such relationships include the full range of complexities involved in any set of relationships among people.

Describing the building of relationships among research perspectives as a dialogic process has as a corollary that the process is also a rhetorical one. We are not using *rhetorical* in the negative sense of that word, which often is associated with manipulation, insincerity, or subterfuge; neither, do we use the term in the sense of one person or side convincing another. Rather, we use rhetorical here to refer to a process in which an argument is mutually constructed and is persuasive to all of the parties involved in the dialogue. Naming it a rhetorical process makes clear the argumentative nature of the relationship and that the argument must be persuasive with respect to a *specific purpose at a specific time and place*.

The notion of a "specific purpose" is key. We assume that interest in building a relationship between or among perspectives is initiated in order to accomplish some specific task or purpose or to address an identified problem. The task, purpose, or problem can be theoretical, methodological, or practical; it can be long term or short term. Regardless, the task, purpose, or problem provides a context for evaluating whether the constructed relationship is useful. Of course, what constitutes the task, purpose, or problem may vary across perspectives. Indeed, negotiating just what is the task, purpose, or problem is part of the process of building a relationship among perspectives. We assume that a dialogic relationship among research perspectives cannot exist in a hegemonic context. The context of dialogue for building relationships among research perspectives can only be one that allows for discussion of the relationship among underlying theory–method connections across research perspectives. Gee and Green (1998) provided an illustrative case. They examined how research perspectives from sociolinguistic analysis, critical discourse analysis, and interactional analysis on the one hand might be brought together with ethnographic research on the other hand. They insisted that the relationship needed to be built at the level of a "logic of inquiry"; that is, they examined the underlying theory–method connections within and across the various research perspectives and sought to understand how those logics might be brought together to address the problem of the contextualized and grounded analysis of people's linguistic interactions. Their approach was neither *additive* (use all the methods associated with all the research perspectives) nor *synthetic* (merge different methods together), but *syncretic*, creating a new logics of inquiry (related to and built on the logics of inquiry associated with the various research perspectives).

Complementary, Parallel, Antagonistic, and Null Set Relationships Among Research Perspectives

Different perspectives may provide complementary, parallel, antagonistic, or null set definitions of the task, purpose, or problem. *Complementary relationships* refer to the use of multiple methodologies where there is compatibility with regard to the underlying theoretical assumptions about language, people, and knowledge. *Parallel relationships* refer to the use of multiple methodologies where the compatibility of underlying theoretical assumptions is finessed. For example, a methodology for the analysis of cognitive processes is used to describe what occurs during a classroom event, and a methodology for the analysis of social relationships is used to describe that same event (see Green & Harker, 1988, for illustrations). The methodologies provide parallel analyses, but there might be no theoreti-

cally driven argument about the complementary nature of the two perspectives. *Null set relationships* refer to relationships among research
perspectives that appear on the surface to have some connections to one
other but on deeper inspection are understood to be not at all about the
same thing. For example, ophthalmological research on the eyesight of
schoolchildren and microethnographic studies of classroom language and
literacy events might appear to be methodologically related because they
both concern reading (after all, most reading instruction in classrooms is
premised on the assumption that the students have adequate eyesight),
but a closer look at the methodologies of such studies reveals that they are
not about the same thing (which is not to suggest that the studies have no
value, only that the research perspectives and agendas are unrelated). *Antagonistic relationships* refer to mutually exclusive theoretical constructs
across research perspectives. Antagonistic relationships among research
methodologies are frequently overlooked in efforts to build a comprehen-
sive picture of classroom language and literacy events, or one set or the
other is dropped out of consideration altogether. Yet antagonistic relationships among methodologies can provide important insights about the
cultural and political nature of research itself on classroom language and
literacy events. Also, acknowledgment of antagonistic relationships
among methodologies should provide researchers with a sense of caution
in projecting their findings and insights broadly, with the understanding
that it is not just their findings they are promulgating but their definitions
of language, being human, and knowledge.

Recognizing the nature of the relationships among the definitions is
important to building a relationship among perspectives. Such recognition sets boundaries on expectations for what might reasonably be accomplished.

In our view, it is rarely the case that a study has a single location. Rather,
the process of locating a study is ongoing, constantly being negotiated and
renegotiated, such that it is perhaps more accurate to consider multiple locations rather than a single location and to view any location as temporary.
To the extent to which a study gains some of its meaningfulness and significance from its location, its meaningfulness and significance will change as
its locations change. Consequently, no study has a determinate meaning.

RESEARCH IMAGINATION

We view the process of locating as part of the way that the research imagination is fashioned. The phrase *research imagination* may seem a bit of an
oxymoron to individuals who view research as a factual presentation di-
vorced from creative processes. "Research" and "imagination" would
seem to be incompatible concepts. However, as we have argued throughout this book, any research effort is a fashioning, a way of looking at the

world that simultaneously frames the world while enabling one to learn about it. The imagination associated with research is different than the imagination associated with literary works such as poetry and novels (see Atkinson, 1990; Bazerman, 1997) or that associated with journalism (see McDermott, Gospodinoff, & Aron, 1978). Although the research imagination creates a narrative no less than literary works or journalism does, the warrants for constituting the actions, actors, objects, scenes, and their relationships differ. The narratives that are told differ, the circumstances of their telling differ, the audiences to whom they are told differ, and the uses of the narratives differ (for a discussion of these issues, see Bloome, 2003b, and Toolan, 1988).

We derived the phrase *research imagination* from the title of Paul Atkinson's (1990) book, *The Ethnographic Imagination,* in which he addresses the complexity of writing ethnography. Atkinson asks questions about how ethnographers create *vraisemblance*, a sense that what they are writing about is accurate. He asks questions about the metaphors used, the conception of audience, and how writers establish authority for representation. Given that no representation is ever complete or void of the influence of the author's background, context of writing, or of the audience, Atkinson asks how the representation is a fashioning of what occurs in the field, of the people and events investigated.

Although an ethnographic report is a fashioning (and, in a similar manner, so is any bit of research, regardless of its epistemological assumptions), this does not in and of itself make it false or ungrounded. Rather, to label it a *fashioning* is to acknowledge that the process of writing an ethnographic study (or any study, for that matter) is a complex human process, caught up in all the complexities of human relationships in addition to the complexities of language.

Research imagination, then, refers both to the process of fashioning research and to an ongoing conversation about how researchers imagine the "other," themselves, and the world in which we all live. This is no less true of researchers who call themselves empiricists than of those who call themselves phenominologists, or of those who label their research as experimental, naturalistic, quantitative, qualitative, clinical, ethnographic, or microethnographic.

Research imagination is neither a romantic notion nor necessarily a benevolent one. Although using other terminology, Said (1979) pointed out that it was the research imagination that prepared the ground for the European colonialization of the Middle East and northern Africa. Similarly, it was the research imagination that prepared the ground for acts of brutality against people labeled insane, mentally ill, criminal, or otherwise non-normative (cf. Foucault, 1965, 1980). Alternatively, the research imagination can create opportunities for action that allow marginalized individuals to improve the conditions of their lives. For example, ethnographic studies of cultural processes in learning created a research imagination that has led to culturally responsive pedagogies (e.g., Gay & Banks, 2000; Ladson-Billings, 1992, 1994; Lee, 1993, 1997; Lipka & Mohatt, 1998) and community-oriented pedagogies (e.g., Egan-Robertson & Bloome, 1998; Kutz, 1997; Luke, O'Brien, & Comber, 1994; Walsh, 1991). Of course, as an abstract concept the research imagination is neither benevolent nor malevolent; rather, it is in the fashioning and the use of the research imagination that claims, arguments, and contestations can be made about whether a research imagination is benevolent.

What, then, might be said about the research imagination being fashioned in this book, through our discussion of microethnographic discourse analysis studies of classroom language and literacy events? First, we must acknowledge that the research imagination is never fashioned within a single book but rather exists in the dialogue or interplay between and among people. So, in large part, the answer to this question is that it depends on how various concepts and arguments within the book are taken up, by whom, where, to accomplish what, and how. Second, proposed throughout this book are conceptions of people, knowledge, culture, language, literacy, and classroom life that are in motion and indeterminate. They are located not in a fixed set of ideas but are seen as inherently indeterminate—and not just within the research domain but as indeterminate and evolving within the everyday lives of people in classrooms (and elsewhere). We have argued that people act on the situations in which they find themselves, that they are acted upon, and that they react as well, and they do so using the broad range of available tools and resources, including those that are given and those they create. We have also argued that people are historical by definition and that the research enterprise be viewed as a "peopled" one, subject to the same types of questions and conceptions as the study of any set of social events. In brief, we have argued that the research imagination is an imagination not only of the other, of the studied, but also of the research community and of researchers.

Appendix

Transcription Key

↑   = rising intonation at end of utterance

XXXX   = undecipherable

Stress

| = short pause
| | | = long pause

⌐   = interrupted by the next line
L

⌐ Line 1   = overlap
L Line 2

Vowel+   = elongated vowel

*   = voice, pitch or style change

Words   = boundaries of a voice, pitch or style change

Nonverbal behavior or transcriber comments for clarification purpose

Student   = unidentified student speaking

Students   = many students speaking at once

References

Allen, G. (2000). *Intertextuality*. New York: Routledge.

Atkinson, P. (1990). *The ethnographic imagination: Textual constructions of reality*. London: Routledge.

Au, K. (1980). Participation structures in a reading lesson with Hawaiian children. *Anthropology and Education Quarterly, 11*, 91–115.

Austin, J. (1962). *How to do things with words*. Oxford, England: Clarendon.

Baker, C. (1993). Literacy practices and social relations in classroom reading events. In C. Baker & A. Luke (Eds.), *The critical sociology of reading pedagogy* (pp. 141–160). Amsterdam: John Benjamins.

Bakhtin, M. (1981). Discourse in the novel. In M. Holquist (Ed.). (C. Emerson & M. Holquist, Trans.), *The dialogic imagination* (pp. 259–422). Austin: University of Texas Press. (Original work published 1935)

Bakhtin, M. (1986). The problem of speech genres. In C. Emerson & M. Holquist (Eds.). (V. W. McGee, Trans.), *Speech genres and other late essays* (60–102). Austin: University of Texas Press. (Original work published 1953)

Balibar, E. (1990). In D. T. Goldberg (Ed.), *Anatomy of racism* (pp. 283–294). Minneapolis: University of Minnesota Press.

Barrett, S. R., Stockholm, S., & Burke, J. (2001) The idea of power and the power of ideas: A review essay. *American Anthropologist, 103*, 2, 468–480.

Barton, D., & Hamilton, M. (1998). *Local literacies: Reading and writing in one community*. London: Routledge.

Barton, D., Hamilton, M., & Ivanic, R. (Eds.). (2000). *Situated literacies: Reading and writing in context*. London: Routledge.

Bauman, R. (1986). *Story, performance and event*. Cambridge, England: Cambridge University Press.

Bauman, R., & Briggs, C. (1990). Poetics and performance as critical perspectives on language and social life. *Annual Review of Anthropology, 19*, 59–88.

Bauman, R., & Sherzer, J. (Eds.). (1974). *Explorations in the ethnography of speaking*. Cambridge, England: Cambridge University Press.

Baynham, M. (1995). *Literacy practices: Investigating literacy in social contexts*. London: Longman.

Baynham, M. (2000). Narrative as evidence in literacy research. *Linguistics and Education, 11,* 99–118.

Bazerman, C. (1997). Reporting the experiment: The changing account of scientific doings in the philosophical transactions of the Royal Society, 1665–1800. In R. A. Harris (Ed.), *Landmark essays on rhetoric of science: Case studies* (pp. 169–186). Mahwah, NJ: Hermagoras.

Beaugrande, R de. (1997). The story of discourse analysis. In T. A. van Dijk (Ed.), *Discourse as structure and process.* (pp. 35–62). Thousand Oaks, CA: Sage.

Becker, A. (1988). Language in particular: A lecture. In D. Tannen (Ed.), *Linguistics in context* (pp. 17–35). Norwood, NJ: Ablex.

Benjamin, W. (1969). *Illuminations.* New York: Schocken.

Bercaw, L., & Bloome, D. (1998, April). Beyond the pedagogization of classroom discourse: The structure of talk in one third space event. Paper presented at annual meeting of the American Educational Research Association, San Diego, CA.

Birdwhistell, R. (1977). Some discussion of ethnography, theory, and method. In J. Brockman (Ed.), *About Bateson: Essays on Gregory Bateson* (pp. 103–144). New York: Dutton.

Bloome, D. (1985). Reading as a social process. *Language Arts, 62,* 134–142.

Bloome, D. (1989). Beyond access. In D. Bloome (Ed.), *Literacy and classrooms* (pp. 53–106). Norwood, NJ: Ablex.

Bloome, D. (1993). Necessary indeterminacy: Issues in the microethnographic study of reading as a social process. *Journal of Reading Research, 16,* 98–111.

Bloome, D. (1997). This is literacy: Three challenges for teachers of reading and writing. *Australian Journal of Language And Literacy, 20,* 107–115.

Bloome, D. (2003a). Anthropology and research on teaching the English language arts. In J. Flood, J. Jensen, D. Lapp, & J. Squire (Eds.), *Handbook of research in teaching the English language arts* (pp. 53–66). Mahwah, NJ: Lawrence Erlbaum Associates.

Bloome, D. (2003b). Narrative discourse. In A. Graesser, M. Gernsbacher, & S. Goldman (Eds.), *Handbook of discourse processes* (pp. 287–320). Mahwah, NJ: Lawrence Erlbaum Associates.

Bloome, D., & Bailey, F. (1992). From linguistics and education, a direction for the study of language and literacy. In R. Beach, J. Green, M. Kamil, & T. Shanahan (Eds.), *Multiple disciplinary perspectives on language and literacy research* (pp. 181–210). Urbana, IL: NCRE and NCTE.

Bloome, D., & Carter, S. (2001). Lists in reading education reform. *Theory Into Practice, 40,* 150–157.

Bloome, D., Cassidy, C., Chapman, M., & Schaafsma, D. (1988). Debates and training, journeys and economics, disease: Reading instruction and underlying metaphors in *Becoming a Nation of Readers.* In J. Davidson (Ed.), *Counterpoint and beyond: A response to* Becoming a Nation of Readers (pp. 5–16). Urbana, IL: National Council of Teachers of English.

Bloome, D., & Egan-Robertson, A. (1993). The social construction of intertextuality and classroom reading and writing. *Reading Research Quarterly, 28,* 303–333.

Bloome, D., & Katz, L. (2003). Methodologies in research on young children and literacy. In J. Larson, N. Hall, & J. Marsh (Eds.), *Handbook of research in early childhood literacy* (pp. 381–399). London: Sage.

Bloome, D., Katz, L., Solsken, J., Willett, J., & Wilson-Keenan, J. (2000). Interpellations of family/community and classroom literacy practices. *Journal of Educational Research, 93,* 155–164

Bloome, D., Puro, P., & Theodorou, E. (1989). Procedural display and classroom lessons. *Curriculum Inquiry, 19,* 265–291.

Bloome, D., & Solsken, J. (1988, December). Cultural and political agendas of literacy learning: Literacy is a verb. Paper presented at the annual meeting of the American Anthropological Association, Phoenix, AZ.

Bloome, D., & Theodorou, E. (1988). Analyzing student–student and teacher–student discourse. In J. Green & J. Harker (Eds.), *Multiple perspective analyses of classroom discourse* (pp. 217–248). Norwood, NJ: Ablex.

Brandt, D., & Clinton, K. (2002) Limits of the local: Expanding perspectives on literacy as a social practice. *Journal of Literacy Research, 34*(3), 337–356.

Buber, M. (1976). *I and thou.* New York: Simon & Schuster.

Butler, J. (1990). *Gender trouble.* London: Routledge.

Cairney, T. H. (2002). Bridging home and school literacy. *Early Child Development and Care, 172,* 153–172.

Cairney, T., & Ashton, J. (2002). Three families, multiple discourses: Parental roles, constructions of literacy and diversity of pedagogic practice. *Linguistics and Education, 13,* 303–345.

Carter, S. P. (2001). *The possibilities of silence: African-American female cultural identity and secondary English classrooms.* Unpublished doctoral dissertation, Vanderbilt University.

Cazden, C. (1988). *Classroom discourse: The language of teaching and learning.* Portsmouth, NH: Heinemann.

Cazden, C., John, V., & Hymes, D. (Eds.). (1972). *Functions of language in the classroom.* New York: Teachers College Press.

Champion, T. (1998). "Tell me somethin' good": A description of narrative structures among African-American children. *Linguistics and Education, 9,* 251–286.

Champion, T. (2002). *Understanding storytelling among African American children: A journey from Africa to America.* Mahwah, NJ: Lawrence Erlbaum Associates.

Christian, B., & Bloome, D. (in press). Learning to read is who you are. *Reading and Writing Quarterly.*

Cisneros, S. (1984). *House on Mango street.* Houston, TX: Arte Publico Press

Clifford, J., & Marcus, G. E. (1986). *Writing culture: The poetics and politics of ethnography.* Berkeley: University of California Press.

Collins, J., & Blot, R. (2003). *Literacy and literacies: Texts, power and identity.* New York: Cambridge University Press.

Collins, P. H. (2000). *Black feminist thought: Knowledge, consciousness, and the politics of empowerment.* New York: Routledge.

de Certeau, M. (1984). *The practice of everyday life.* Berkeley: University of California Press.

de Certeau, M. (1997). *Culture in the plural.* Minneapolis: University of Minnesota Press.

Diamondstone, J. (1998). Tactics of resistance in student–student interaction. *Linguistics and Education, 10,* 107–137.

Dore, R. (1976). *The diploma disease: Education, qualification, and development.* Berkeley: University of California Press.

Dorr-Bremme, D. (1990). Contextualization cues in the classroom: Discourse regulation and social control functions. *Language in Society, 19,* 379–402.

DuBois, J. W. (1991). Transcription design principles for spoken discourse research. *Pragmatics, 1,* 71–106.

Dubois, W. E. B. (1969). *The souls of Black folk.* New York: Signet.

Duranti, A. (1997). *Linguistic anthropology.* New York: Cambridge University Press.

Duranti, A., & Goodwin, C. (Eds.). (1992). *Rethinking context: Language as an interactive phenomenon.* Cambridge, England: Cambridge University Press.

Eagleton, T. (1996). *Literary theory: An introduction*. Minneapolis: University of Minnesota Press. (Original work published 1983)

Edwards, J. A. (2001). The transcription of discourse. In D. Schiffrin, D. Tannen, & H. Hamilton (Eds.), *The handbook of discourse analysis* (pp. 321–348). Malden, MA: Blackwell.

Edwards, J. A, & Lampert, M. D. (1993). (Eds.). *Talking data: Transcription and coding of spoken data*. Hillsdale, NJ: Lawrence Erlbaum Associates.

Eemeron, F. H., Grootendorst, R., Jackson, S., & Jacobs, S. (1997). Argumentation. In T. van Dijk, (Ed.), *Discourse as structure and process* (pp. 208–229). Thousand Oaks, CA: Sage.

Egan-Robertson, A. (1994). *Literacy practices, personhood, and student researchers of their own communities*. Unpublished doctoral dissertation, University of Massachusetts.

Egan-Robertson, A. (1998a). Learning about culture, language, and power: Understanding relationships among personhood, literacy practices, and intertextuality. *Journal of Literacy Research, 30*, 449–487.

Egan-Robertson, A. (1998b). Learning About Culture, Language, and Power: Understanding Relationships Between Personhood, Literacy Practices, and Intertextuality. *Report*, National Research Center on English Learning and Achievement: 55.

Egan-Robertson, A., & Bloome, D. (Eds.). (1998). *Students as researchers of culture and language in their own communities*. Cresskill, NJ: Hampton.

Ellen, R. (Ed.). (1984). *Ethnographic research: A guide to general conduct*. New York: Academic.

Eliot, T. S. (1975). Tradition and individual talent. In F. Kermode (Ed.), *Selected prose of T. S. Eliot*. (pp. 37–44). London: Faber and Faber.

Erickson, F., & Shultz, J. (1977). When is a context? *Newsletter of the Laboratory for Comparative Human Cognition, 1,* 5–12.

Essed, P., & Goldberg, D. T. (Eds.). (2002). *Race critical theories*. Malden, MA: Blackwell.

Fahnestock, J. (1997). Arguing in different forums: The Bering Crossover controversy. In R. A. Harris (Ed.), *Landmark essays on rhetoric of science: Case studies* (pp. 53–68). Mahwah, NJ: Hermagoras.

Fairclough, N. (1989). *Language and power.* London: Longman.

Fairclough, N. (1992). *Discourse and social change*. Cambridge, England: Polity.

Fairclough, N. (1995). *Critical discourse analysis*. London: Longman.

Foster, M. (1997). *Black teachers on teaching*. New York: New Press.

Foucault, M. (1965). *Madness and civilization*. New York: Vintage.

Foucault, M. (1980*). Power/knowledge: Selected interviews and other writings, 1972–1977* (C. Gordon, Ed.). New York: Pantheon.

Freire, P. (1995). *Pedagogy of the oppressed*. New York: Continuum. (Original work published 1970)

Freire, P., & Macedo, D. (1987). Literacy: Reading the word & the world. South Hadley, MA: Bergin & Garvey.

Gay, G. (2000). *Culturally responsive teaching: Theory, research, practice*. New York: Teacher College Press.

Gee, J. P. (1994). *The social mind: Language, ideology, and social practice*. Westport, CT: Greenwood.

Gee, J. P. (1996). *Social linguistics and literacies: Ideology in discourses* (2nd ed.). London: Taylor & Francis.

Gee, J. P. (1999). *An introduction to discourse analysis: Theory and method*. New York: Routledge.

Gee, J. P. (2000). The New Literacy Studies: From "socially situated" to the work of the social. In D. Barton, M. Hamilton, & R. Ivanic (Eds.), *Situated literacies: Reading and writing in context* (pp. 180–196). London: Routledge.

Gee, J. P. (2003). *What video games have to teach us about learning and literacy.* New York: Palgrave Macmillan.

Gee, J. P., & Green, J. (1998). Discourse, analysis, learning, and social practice. In P. D. Pearson (Ed.), *Review of research in education* (pp. 119–169). Washington, DC: American Educational Research Association.

Gee, J. P., Hull, G., & Lankshear, C. (1996). *The new work order: Behind the language of the new capitalism.* Boulder, CO: Westview.

Geertz, C. (1973). *The interpretation of cultures.* New York: Basic Books.

Geertz, C. (1983). *Local knowledge: Further essays in interpretive anthropology.* New York: Basic Books.

Gergen, K. (1999). *An invitation to social construction.* Thousand Oaks, CA: Sage.

Gergen, K. & Davis, K. (Eds.). (1985) *The social construction of the person.* New York: Springer-Verlag.

Giddens, A. (1979). *Central problems in social theory: Action, structure, and contradiction in social analysis.* Berkeley: University of California Press.

Giddens, A. (1984). *The constitution of society: Introduction to the theory of structuration.* Berkeley: University of California Press.

Gilmore, P. (1987). Sulking, stepping, and tracking: The effects of attitude assessment on access to literacy. In D. Bloome (Ed.), *Literacy and schooling* (pp. 98–120). Norwood, NJ: Ablex.

Gitlin, A. (Ed.). (1994). *Power and method: Political activism and educational research.* New York: Routledge.

Goffman, E. (1981). *Forms of talk.* Philadelphia: University of Pennsylvania Press.

Goldberg, D. T. (1990). The social formation of racist discourse. In D. T. Goldberg (Ed.), *Anatomy of racism* (pp. 295–318). Minneapolis: University of Minnesota Press.

Goodenough, W. (1981). *Culture, language, and society.* Menlo Park, CA: Cummings.

Green, J. (1983). Exploring classroom discourse: Linguistic perspectives on teaching–learning processes. *Educational Psychologist, 18,* 180–199.

Green, J., & Bloome, D. (1998). Ethnography and ethnographers of and in education: A situated perspective. In J. Flood, S. Hesth, & D. Lapp (Eds.), *A handbook for literacy educators: Research on teaching the communicative and visual arts* (181–202). New York: Macmillan.

Green, J., & Harker, J. (Eds.). (1988). *Multiple perspective analysis of classroom discourse.* Norwood, NJ: Ablex.

Green, J., & Smith, D. (1983). Teaching and learning: A linguistic perspective. *The Elementary School Journal, 83,* 352–391.

Green, J., & Wallat, C. (1981). Mapping instructional conversations. In J. Green & C. Wallat (Eds.), *Ethnography and language in educational settings* (pp. 161–195). Norwood, NJ: Ablex.

Gumperz, J. J. (1986). *Discourse strategies.* New York: Cambridge University Press.

Gumperz, J. J., & Herasimchuk, E. (1973). The conversational analysis of social meaning: A study of classroom interaction. In R. Shuy (Ed.), *Georgetown University Round Table on Languages and Linguistics, 1972. Sociolinguistics: Current trends and prospects* (pp. 1–21). Washington, DC: Georgetown University Press.

Gumperz, J. J., & Hymes, D. (Eds.). (1972). *Directions in sociolinguistics: The ethnography of communication.* New York: Holt, Rinehart & Winston.

Hall, S. (1990). Cultural identity and diaspora. In J. Rutherford (Ed.), *Identity, community, culture, difference* (pp. 222–237). London: Lawrence & Wishart.

Hall, S. (1996). Introduction. In S. Hall & P. du Gay (Eds.), *Questions of cultural identity* (pp. 1–17). Thousand Oaks, CA: Sage.

Hall, S., & Gay, P. (Eds.). (1996). *Questions of cultural identity.* Thousand Oaks, CA: Sage.

Halliday, M. A. K. (1978). *Language as social semiotic*. London: Edward Arnold.
Halliday, M. A. K. (1985). *An introduction to functional grammar*. London: Edward Arnold.
Halliday, M. A. K., & Hasan, R. (1985). *Language, text, and context*. Geelong, Victoria, Australia: Deakin University Press.
Halliday, M. A. K., & Martin, J. R. (1993). *Writing science: Literacy and discursive power*. Pittsburgh, PA: University of Pittsburgh Press.
Hanks, W. (2000). *Intertexts: Writings on language, utterance, and context*. Lanham, MD: Rowan & Littlefield.
Heap, J. (1980). What counts as reading: Limits to certainty in assessment. *Curriculum Inquiry, 10*, 265–292.
Heap, J. (1985). Discourse in the production of classroom knowledge: Reading lessons. *Curriculum Inquiry, 15*, 245–279.
Heap, J. (1988). On task in classroom discourse. *Linguistics and Education, 1*, 177–198.
Heath, S. (1982). What no bedtime story means: Narrative skills at home and at school. *Language in Society, 11*, 49–76.
Heath, S. (1983). *Ways with words*. New York: Cambridge University Press.
Heras, A. I. (1993). The construction of understanding in a sixth grade bilingual classroom. *Linguistics and Education, 5*, 275–300.
hooks, b. (1981). *Ain't I a woman: Black women and feminism*. Boston: South End.
hooks, b. (1990). *Yearning: Race, gender, and cultural politics*. Boston: South End.
hooks, b. (1994). *Teaching to transgress: Education as the practice of freedom*. New York: Routledge.
hooks, b. (2000). *Feminism is for everybody: Passionate politics*. Boston: South End.
hooks, b., & Manning, M. (Eds.). (2000). *Feminist theory: From margin to center*. Boston: South End.
Hymes, D. (1974). *The foundations of sociolinguistics: Sociolinguistic ethnography*. Philadelphia: University of Pennsylvania Press.
Hymes, D. (1996). *Ethnography, linguistics, narrative inequality: Toward an understanding of voice*. London: Taylor & Francis.
Ivanic, R. (1998). *Writing and identity: The discoursal construction of identity in academic writing*. Amsterdam: John Benjamins.
Janeway, E. (1980). *Powers of the weak*. New York: Knopf.
Jefferson, G. (1978). Sequential aspects of storytelling in conversation. In J. Schenkein (Ed.), *Studies in the organization of conversation* (pp. 219–248). New York: Academic.
Jones, K. (2000). Becoming just another alphanumeric code: Farmers' encounters with the literacy and discourse practices of agricultural bureaucracy at the livestock auction. In D. Barton, M. Hamilton, & R. Ivanic (Eds.), *Situated literacies: Reading and writing in context* (pp. 70–90). London: Routledge.
Kaomea, J. (2003). Reading erasures and making the familiar strange: Defamiliarizing methods for researching formerly colonized and historically oppressed communities. *Educational Researcher, 32*(2), 14–25.
Knobel, M. (1999). *Everyday literacies; Students, discourse and social practice*. New York: Peter Lang.
Kreisberg, S. (1992). *Transforming power: Domination, empowerment, and education*. Albany: State University of New York Press.
Kress, G. (1996). Representational resources and the production of subjectivity: Questions for the theoretical development of critical discourse analysis in a multicultural society. In C. R. Caldas-Coulthard & M. Coulthard (Eds.), *Texts and practices: Readings in critical discourse analysis* (pp. 15–31). London: Routledge.

Kulick, D., & Stroud, C. (1993). Conceptions and uses of literacy in a Papua, New Guinean village. In B. Street (Ed.), *Cross-cultural approaches to literacy*. Cambridge, UK: Cambridge University Press.

Kutz, E. (1997). *Language and literacy: Studying discourse in communities and classrooms*. Portsmouth, NH: Boynton/Cook Heinemann.

Labov, W. (1972). *Sociolinguistic patterns*. Philadelphia: University of Pennsylvania Press.

Ladson-Billings, G. (1992). Reading between the lines and beyond the pages: A culturally-relevant approach to literacy teaching. *Theory Into Practice, 31*, 312–320.

Ladson-Billings, G. (1994). *Dreamkeepers*. San Diego, CA: Jossey-Bass.

Lankshear, C., Gee, J. P., Knobel, M., & Searle, C. (1997). *Changing literacies*. London: Taylor & Francis.

Lee, C. (1993). *Signifying as a scaffold for literary interpretation: The pedagogical implications of an African American discourse genre*. Urbana, IL: National Council of Teachers of English.

Lee, C. (1997). Bridging home and school literacies: Models for culturally responsive teaching, a case for African-American English. In J. Flood, S. Heath, & D. Lapp (Eds.), *Handbook of research on teaching literacy through the communicative and visual arts* (pp. 334–345). New York: Simon & Schuster/Macmillan.

Lemke, J. (1990). *Talking science: Language, learning, and values*. Norwood: Ablex.

Lemke, J. (1995). *Textual politics: Discourses and social dynamics*. London: Taylor & Francis.

Lewis, C. (2001). *Literacy practices as social acts: Power, status, and cultural norms in the classroom*. Mahwah, NJ: Lawrence Erlbaum Associates.

Lin, L. (1993). Language of and in the classroom: Constructing the patterns of social life. *Linguistics and Education, 5*, 367–410.

Lipka, J., & Mohatt, G. (1998). *Transforming the culture of schools: Yup'ik Eskimo examples*. Mahwah, NJ: Lawrence Erlbaum Associates.

Lips, H. (1991). *Women, men and power*. Mountain View, CA: Mayfield.

Luke, A. (1988). The non-neutrality of literacy instruction: A critical introduction. *Australian Journal of Reading, 11*, 79–83.

Luke, A., O'Brien, J., & Comber, B. (1994). Making community texts objects of study. *Australian Journal of Language and Literacy, 17*, 139–149.

Macbeth, D. (2003). Hugh Mehan's "Learning Lessons" Reconsidered: On the differences between the naturalistic and critical analysis of classroom discourse. *American Educational Research Journal, 40*(1), 239–280

Marshall, H. (Ed.). (1992). *Redefining student learning: Roots of educational change*. Norwood, NJ: Ablex.

Marx, A. W. (1998). *Making race and nation: A comparison of the United States, South Africa, and Brazil*. Cambridge, England: Cambridge University Press.

McDermott, R. P., Gospodinoff, K., & Aron, J. (1978). Criteria for an ethnographically adequate description of concerted activities and their contexts. *Semiotics, 24*, 246–275.

McDermott, R., & Hood, L. (1982). Institutional psychology and the ethnography of schooling. In P. Gilmore & A. Glatthorn (Eds.), *Children in and out of school* (pp. 232–249). Washington, DC: Center for Applied Linguistics.

Mehan, H. (1979). *Learning lessons*. Cambridge, MA: Harvard University Press.

Mehan, H. (1980). The competent student. *Anthropology and Education Quarterly, 11*, 131–152.

Michaels, S. (1981). "Sharing time": Children's narrative styles and differential access to literacy. *Language in Society, 10*, 423–442.

Michaels, S. (1986). Narrative presentations: An oral preparation for literacy with first graders. In J. Cook-Gumperz (Ed.), *The social construction of literacy* (pp. 95–116). Cambridge, England: Cambridge University Press.

Miller, P., Nemoiani, A., & Dejong, J. (1986). Early reading at home: Its practice and meanings in a working class community. In B. Schieffelin & P. Gilmore (Eds.), *The acquisition of literacy: Ethnographic perspectives* (pp. 3–15). Norwood, NJ: Ablex.

Mishler, E. (1991). Representing discourse: The rhetoric of transcription. *Journal of Narrative and Life History, 1,* 255–280.

Mitchell, C., & Weber, S. (1999). *Reinventing ourselves as teachers: Beyond nostalgia.* Philadelphia, PA: Falmer Press.

Mitchell, J. C. (1984). Typicality and the case study. In R. Ellen (Ed.), *Ethnographic research: A guide to general conduct* (pp. 238–241). New York: Academic.

Morris, J. E. (1998, April). *Female students and the construction of knowledge in the "Third Space": Theoretical implications for multicultural education.* Paper presented at the annual conference of the American Educational Research Association, San Diego.

Morris, J. E. (2003). What does Africa have to do with being African American? A microethnography of identity in an urban middle school classroom. *Anthropology and Education Quarterly, 34.*

Morrison, T. (1994). *Nobel lecture in literature, 1993.* New York: Knopf.

Muldrow, R., & Katz, L. (1998, April). The teacher's roles and identities as a participant in the "third space." Paper presented at annual meeting of the American Educational Research Association, San Diego.

Noddings, N. (1984). *Caring: A feminist approach to caring and moral ethics.* Berkeley: University of California Press.

Noddings, N. (1989). *Women and evil.* Berkeley: University of California Press.

Noddings, N. (1992). *The challenge to care in schools: An alternative approach to education.* New York: Teachers College Press.

Noddings, N. (1993). *Educating for the intelligent: Belief or unbelief.* New York: Teachers College Press.

Ochs, E. (1979). Transcription as theory. In E. Ochs & B. B. Schieffelin (Eds.), *Developmental pragmatics* (pp. 43–72). New York: Academic.

O'Connor, M. C., & Michaels, S. (1993). Aligning academic task and participation status through revoicing: Analysis of a classroom discourse strategy. *Anthropology and Education Quarterly, 24,* 318–335.

Ormerod, F., & Ivanic, R. (2000). Texts in practices: Interpreting the physical characteristics of children's project work. In D. Barton, M. Hamilton, & R. Ivanic (Eds.), *Situated literacies: Reading and writing in context* (pp. 91–107). London: Routledge.

Outlaw, L. (1990). Toward a critical theory of "race." In D. T. Goldberg (Ed.), *Anatomy of racism* (pp. 58–82). Minneapolis: University of Minnesota Press.

Patterson, A. (1992, October). Individualism in English: From personal growth to discursive construction. *English Education,* 131–146.

Phillips, S. (1972). Participant structures and communicative competence: Warm Springs children in classroom and community. In C. Cazden, V. John, & D. Hymes (Eds.), *Functions of language in the classroom* (pp. 370–394). New York: Teachers College Press.

Radtke, L. H., & Stam, H. J. (Eds.). (1994). *Power/gender: Social relations in theory and practice.* Thousand Oaks, CA: Sage

Ramage, J. D., Bean, J. C., & Johnson, J. (2001). *Writing arguments: A rhetoric with readings* (5th edition). Boston: Allyn & Bacon.

Reisigl, M., & Wodak, R. (2001). *Discourse and discrimination: Rhetorics of racism and anti-semitism.* London: Routledge.

Robinson, J. L. (1987). Literacy in society: Readers and writers in the worlds of discourse. In D. Bloome (Ed.), *Literacy and schooling* (pp. 327–353). Norwood, NJ: Ablex.

Rorty, R. (1992). *The linguistic turn: Essays in philosophical method.* Chicago: University of Chicago Press.

Rymes, B. (2001). *Conversational borderlands: Language and identity in an alternative urban high school.* New York: Teachers College Press.

Sacks, H., Schegloff, E., & Jefferson, G. (1974). A simplist systematics for the organization of turn taking in conversation. *Language, 50,* 696–735.

Said, E. (1979). *Orientalism.* New York: Vintage.

Said, E. (1985). Orientalism reconsidered. In F. Barker, P. Hulme, M. Iversen, & D. Loxley (Eds.), *Europe and its others: Proceedings of the Essex Conference on the Sociology of Literature* (Vol. 1, pp. 14–27). Colchester, England: University of Essex.

Schutz, A. (2004). Rethinking domination and resistance: Challenging postmodernism. *Educational Researcher, 33*(1), 15–23.

Scollon, R., & Scollon, S. (1981). *Narrative/literacy and face in interethnic communication.* Norwood, NJ: Ablex.

Sheridan, D., Street, B., & Bloome, D. (2000). *Writing ourselves: Literacy practices and the Mass-Observation Project.* Cresskill, NJ: Hampton.

Shultz, J., Florio, J., & Erickson, F. (1982). Where's the floor? Aspects of the cultural organization of social relationships in communication at home and in school. In P. Gilmore & A. Glatthorn (Eds.), *Children in and out of school* (pp. 88–123). Washington, DC: Center for Applied Linguistics.

Shweder, R. A., & Miller, J. G. (1985). The social construction of the person: How is it possible? In K. Gergen & K. Davis, (Eds.), *The social construction of the person.* (pp. 41–69). New York: Springer Verlag.

Smith, D. (1989). *The everyday world as problematic: A feminist sociology.* Boston: Northeastern University Press.

Smith, D. (1990). *Conceptual practices of power: A feminist sociology of knowledge.* Boston: Northeastern University Press.

Stavans, I. (2001). *On borrowed words: A memoir of language.* New York: Viking.

Street, B. (1984). *Literacy in theory and practice.* New York: Cambridge University Press.

Street, B. (1992). Literacy and nationalism. *History of European Ideas, 16,* 225–228.

Street, B. (1993a). Culture is a verb. In D. Graddol (Ed.), *Language and culture* (pp. 23–48). Clevedon, England: Multilingual Matters/British Association of Applied Linguists.

Street, B. (1993b). Introduction. In B. Street (Ed.), *Cross-cultural approaches to literacy* (pp. 1–21). Cambridge, England: Cambridge University Press.

Street, B. (1995a). Academic literacies. In D. Baker, C. Fox, & J. Clay (Eds.), *Challenging ways of knowing in maths, science and English* (pp. 101–134). Brighton, England: Falmer.

Street, B. (1995b). *Social literacies: Critical approaches to literacy in development, ethnography and education.* London: Longman.

Street, B. (1996). Literacy and power: Open letter. *Australian Journal of Adult Literacy Research and Practice, 6,* 7–16.

Street, B. (1997). The implications of the New Literacy Studies for literacy education. *English in Education, 31,* 26–39.

Street, B. (1998). New literacies in theory and practice: What are the implications for language in education? *Linguistics and Education, 10,* 1–34.

Street, B. (2003). What's "new" in new literacy studies? Critical approaches to literacy in theory and practice. *Current Issues in Comparative Education, 5*(2).

Street, B., & Street, J. (1991). The schooling of literacy. In D. Barton & R. Ivanic (Eds.) *Writing in the community* (pp. 143–166). London: Sage.

Takaki, R. (1994). *A different mirror.* Boston: Little, Brown.

Tannen, D. (1989). *Talking voices: Repetition, dialogue, and imagery in conversational discourse.* Cambridge, England: Cambridge University Press.

Toolan, M. (1988). *Narrative: A critical linguistic introduction.* London: Routledge.

Toulmin, S. (1958). *Uses of argument.* New York: Cambridge University Press.

Twymon, S. (1990). *Early reading and writing instruction in the homes and school of three five-year old children from Black working-class families.* Unpublished doctoral dissertation, University of Michigan.

Tyler, S. A. (1987). *The unspeakable: Discourse, dialogue, and rhetoric in the postmodern world.* Madison: University of Wisconsin Press.

van Dijk, T. (1996). Discourse, power, and access. In C. R. Caldas-Coulthard & M. Coulthard (Eds.), *Texts and practices: Readings in critical discourse analysis* (pp. 84–104). London: Routledge.

Van Leeuwen, T. (1996). The representation of social actors. In C. R. Caldas-Coulthard & M. Coulthard (Eds.), *Texts and practices: Readings in critical discourse analysis* (pp. 32–70). New York: Routledge.

Volosinov, V. N. (1973). *Marxism and the philosophy of language* (L. Matejka & I. R. Titunik, Trans.). Cambridge, MA: Harvard University Press. (Original work published 1929)

Volosinov, V. N. (1973). *Marxism and the philosophy of language.* (L. Matejka & I. R. Titunik, Trans.). New York: Seminar Press.

Waddell, C. (1997). The role of pathos in the decision-making process: A study in the rhetoric of science policy. In R. A. Harris (Ed.), *Landmark essays on rhetoric of science: Case studies* (pp. 127–150). Mahwah, NJ: Hermagoras.

Walkerdine, V. (1990). *Schoolgirl fictions.* London: Verso.

Walkerdine, V. (1997). *Daddy's girl: Young girls and popular culture.* London: Macmillan.

Walsh, C. (Ed.). (1991). *Literacy as praxis.* Norwood, NJ: Ablex.

Watson, K., & Young, B. (2003). Discourse for learning in the classroom. In S. Murphy & C. Dudley-Marling (Eds.), *Literacy through language arts: Teaching and learning in context* (pp. 39–49). Urbana, IL: National Council of Teachers of English.

Weedon, C. (1996). *Feminist practice and poststructuralist theory* (2nd ed.). Oxford, England: Blackwell.

Wells, G. (1993). Re-evaluating the IRF sequence: A proposal for the articulation of theories of activity and discourse for the analysis of teaching and learning. *Linguistics and Education, 5,* 1–37.

West, C. (2000, July). A grand tradition of struggle. *English Journal, 39*(4) 39–44.

White, N. (2002). Discourses of power: An analysis of homework events. *Linguistics and Education, 13,* 89–136.

Williams, R. (1977). *Marxism and literature.* Oxford, England: Oxford University Press.

Yeats, W. B. (1996). *Among school children.* In R. J. Finneran (Ed.), *The collected poems of W. B. Yeats* (2nd ed., pp. 215–217). New York: Simon & Schuster. (Original work published 1928)

Author Index

Subject Index